Many Buddhas, One Buddha

Many Buddhas, One Buddha

A Study and Translation of *Avadānaśataka* 1–40

Naomi Appleton

equinox

SHEFFIELD UK BRISTOL CT

Published by Equinox Publishing Ltd.

UK: Office 415, The Workstation, 15 Paternoster Row, Sheffield, South Yorkshire S1 2BX
USA: ISD, 70 Enterprise Drive, Bristol, CT 06010

www.equinoxpub.com

First published 2020

British Library Cataloguing-in-Publication Data
A catalogue record for this book is available from the British Library.

ISBN: 978 1 78179 896 6 (hardback)
978 1 78179 897 3 (paperback)
978 1 78179 898 0 (ePDF)

Library of Congress Cataloging-in-Publishing Data
Names: Appleton, Naomi, 1982- author, translator.
Title: Many buddhas, one Buddha : a study and translation of Avadānaśataka 1-40 / Naomi Appleton.
Other titles: Tripiṭaka. Sūtrapiṭaka. Avadāna. Avadānaśataka. Selections. English.
Description: Sheffield, South Yorkshire ; Bristol, CT : Equinox Publishing Ltd, 2020. | Includes bibliographical references and index. | Summary: "Many Buddhas, One Buddha introduces a significant section of the important early Indian Buddhist text known as the Avadānaśataka, or "One Hundred Stories", and explores some of its perspectives on buddhahood. This text, composed in Sanskrit and dating to perhaps the third to fifth centuries of the Common Era, is affiliated with the Sarvāstivāda or Mūlasarvāstivāda, and thus provides important evidence of the ideas and literatures of lost non-Mahāyāna schools of Indian Buddhism. The text is a rich literary composition, in mixed prose and verse, and includes some elaborate devotional passages that illuminate early Indian perspectives on the Buddha and on the role of avadāna texts. The book introduces the first four chapters of the Avadānaśataka through key themes of these stories, such as predictions and vows, preparations for buddhahood, the relationship between Śākyamuni and other buddhas, and the relationship between full buddhahood and pratyekabuddhahood. The study of these stories closes with an argument about the structural design of the text, and what this tells us about attitudes towards different forms of awakening. The second part of the book then presents a full English translation of stories 1-40"-- Provided by publisher.
Identifiers: LCCN 2019022546 (print) | LCCN 2019022547 (ebook) | ISBN 9781781798966 (hardback) | ISBN 9781781798973 (paperback) | ISBN 9781781798980 (ebook)
Subjects: LCSH: Gautama Buddha. | Tripiṭaka. Sūtrapiṭaka. Avadāna. Avadānaśataka--Criticism, interpretation, etc. | Tripiṭaka. Sūtrapiṭaka. Avadāna. Avadānaśataka--Criticism, Textual. | Buddhism--India--History. | Enlightenment (Buddhism) | Buddhas. | Buddhist literature, Sanskrit--Translations into English.
Classification: LCC BQ1557 .A67 2020 (print) | LCC BQ1557 (ebook) | DDC 294.3/823--dc23
LC record available at https://lccn.loc.gov/2019022546
LC ebook record available at https://lccn.loc.gov/2019022547

Typeset by Witchwood Production House Ltd, Sheffield

Contents

Preface vii

Part A: Study 1

Crossing the flood of rebirth 2
The *Avadānaśataka* 5
Many *buddhas* 10
Śākyamuni's past lives 21
Independent buddhahood 29
Miracles, offerings, aspirations and predictions 37
And then the Buddha smiled 41
Structure of the *Avadānaśataka* 45
Many *buddhas*, many Buddhisms 52
One Buddha, many lessons 54
Part A Notes 55

Part B: Translation 63

Note on the translation 64
First Decade (stories 1–10) 66
Second Decade (stories 11–20) 97
Third Decade (stories 21–30) 143
Fourth Decade (stories 31–40) 167
Part B Notes 216

Glossary 223
Bibliography 235
Index 239

Preface

I first began work on the *Avadānaśataka* in 2012 as part of my interest in how *jātaka* stories feature in a variety of Buddhist textual contexts. I translated chapters 2 and 4, and shared my — then draft — translations in the open-access journal *Asian Literature and Translation* (in 2013 and 2014 respectively). My reflections on what these two decades tell us about the *jātaka* genre formed a paper at the 2014 IABS Congress in Vienna, and this paper was revised and published in the *Journal of the International Association of Buddhist Studies* in 2015. I had intended to step away from the text at that point, but it was too late: I was totally hooked on what I found to be a wonderfully intriguing collection of stories, and one that had not — I felt — received the attention it deserved.

It was therefore at that Vienna conference that Karen Muldoon-Hules and I hit upon the idea of bringing together a group of colleagues to produce a full translation and further study of the *Avadānaśataka*: Justin Fifield, David Fiordalis and Andy Rotman agreed to join us. I volunteered to tackle the third chapter, on *pratyekabuddhas*, and soon found myself delving into their intriguing characterization across other texts as well, resulting in an article on *paccekabuddhas* and their relationship with the Buddha and Bodhisatta in Pāli *jātaka* stories (for the Lance Cousins memorial volume *Buddhist Path, Buddhist Teachings* [Equinox, 2019]) and another on *pratyekabuddhas* as verbal and non-verbal teachers (for *In Dialogue with Classical Indian Traditions: Encounter, Transformation and*

Interpretation, edited by Brian Black and Chakravarthi Ram-Prasad [Routledge, 2019]).

Meanwhile, conversations — virtual and in person — with the other translators gradually refined my rendering of the text's long formulaic passages. Reading Andy Rotman's careful translation of the *Divyāvadāna*, which shares many features with the *Avadānaśataka*, further advanced my understanding of the text. My translation and study of chapter 3 also had a knock-on effect on how I viewed chapters 2 and 4, both in terms of their translation and their role within the overall collection.

By the 2017 IABS Congress in Toronto we — team *Avadānaśataka* — had a full-draft English translation, which I read with glee on the flight over. We held a fantastic panel in which we shared our reflections on aspects of the text. However, we also met and faced up to the enormous task of trying to reconcile our various translation styles into a readable and consistent overall translation. Perhaps I was naïve to ever think that possible; certainly, as the conversations continued by email and phone over subsequent months, it became clear that a full unified translation was not on the cards. Nonetheless, our other aim of prompting further work on a neglected text had certainly borne fruit, and all of our translations were enhanced by reading each other's renderings. In addition, a long café conversation with Karen in Toronto in 2017 was particularly helpful in reaching agreed translations of formulae, many of which are retained in this volume.

And so I here present my translation — but also in many ways *our* translation — of the first four chapters of the *Avadānaśataka*, introduced through a discussion of what emerges as the key linchpin for this portion of the text, namely the relationship between Śākyamuni Buddha and other awakened beings. Other portions of the text are still being worked on by other members of the team and I hope they will also appear in print in the future. I outline the reasons for considering chapters 1–4 to be a distinct textual unit on pages 7–9.

Although Justin Fifield had originally taken responsibility for translating the first chapter — indeed, this formed a part of his master's thesis *Faith, Miracles and Conversion in the Avadānaśataka: A Translation and Analysis of the First Decade of Stories* (University of Texas at Austin, 2008) — he has been kind enough to let me adopt 'his' decade, which was a necessary move for the completeness of the volume. As I set about producing my own translation of that chapter I found that it provided further evidence against the judiciousness of a team translation, for I differed from his rendering far more often than we coincided. Sometimes the differences were in understanding, but more often they reflected word and phrase choices; often my choices were dictated by the decisions I had already reached about how best to render the formulaic passages. That said, I have also benefitted greatly from referring to his translation, as well as from his dissertation more broadly. As with so many texts, I believe that readers will benefit from having alternative translations available, to enrich their understanding.

In addition to all the other members of the team of translators, I am grateful to several other colleagues, including the audiences at various conference and seminar presentations, for their comments on the materials that come together in this book. Brian Black read an early draft for one of our many regional meet-ups and offered insightful feedback. Chris Clark also offered helpful comments on the introduction. John Strong, who revealed himself to be the reader for the press, gave much encouragement but also some very necessary corrections and suggestions, which have strengthened the resulting book significantly. My wonderful partner, Anas, provided the title one evening as I was struggling to find a phrase that encapsulated the book's argument.

For many of the technical terms my translation follows the careful renderings made by Andy Rotman in his two-volume translation of the *Divyāvadāna* (Wisdom, 2008, 2017); my Glossary is also dependent on his in many ways. I am grateful to Andy for being so relaxed about this, due to his commitment to the idea of scholarship as a team effort, an idea to which I also passionately subscribe.

A scholar who expressed continual support for our work on the *Avadānaśataka* was the late Steven Collins. Indeed, Steve sat through the entire Vienna IABS panel, in the front row, and offered countless pertinent remarks. His many publications and, in more recent years, our email correspondence, greatly enriched my own thinking about Buddhist narrative, and his untimely death in 2018 was a great loss both personally and to the field. I would therefore like to dedicate this book to his memory.

PART A
Study

Crossing the flood of rebirth

In the twenty-seventh tale of the *Avadānaśataka* (AvŚ), Śākyamuni Buddha and his monks are travelling on foot when they reach a river they wish to cross. The Buddha asks the ferrymen if they can assist, but they demand a fee — a fee that the Buddha and his monks cannot pay, since they have renounced all but the most basic of possessions. The Buddha responds:

> I have also been a ferryman. I carried across Nanda, who had fallen in the river of passion; Aṅgulimāla, who had fallen in the foaming sea of hatred; the proud young Mānastabdha, who had fallen into the ocean of pride; and Urubilva-Kāśyapa, who had fallen into the flood of delusion. And I never asked for a ferry-fee![1]

One of the ferrymen then agrees to take him across, but as the monks are boarding the ferry the Buddha disappears from the near shore and reappears on the other side. This miracle precedes a sermon, and this prompts the attainment of the fruits of stream-entry by the ferryman; in other words, he is now on the path to becoming an awakened disciple himself. A second ferryman is so awestruck that he makes a grand almsgiving, and is then predicted to become a future *pratyekabuddha* (or 'solitary *buddha*') called Saṃsārottaraṇa, 'Traverser of the Realm of Rebirth'.

To a reader of Indian Buddhist texts the imagery here is all very familiar. The Buddha helps his followers to cross the waters of delusion, hatred, pride and passion — in other words, the waters of *saṃsāra*, the cycle of rebirth — to the further shore of awakening. He, however, needs no such assistance. Here lies an important difference between the two main forms of awakening (*bodhi*) included in early Indian Buddhist sources: the awakening of a full and complete *buddha* (*samyaksambodhi*), and the awakening of a 'hearer' or disciple (*śrāvakabodhi*), also known as becoming an *arhat* or 'worthy one'. Full and complete *buddha*s, often simply referred to as *buddha*s, discover the truth themselves without a teacher, found a community of followers and teach them the path to awakening. These followers, if they sincerely practise a *buddha*'s teachings, may go on to become *arhats*. The Buddha, that is to say the most recent *buddha* and founder of the present Buddhist community, known as Śākyamuni Buddha, is a full and complete *buddha*. Thanks to his guidance even the most challenging of his followers – such as Nanda, who was obsessed with his wife even after entering the monastic life, and Aṅgulimāla, a reformed serial killer[2] – were helped across the flood of rebirth to the further shore of *nirvāṇa*. (Readers will note that, for clarity, I use 'the Buddha' to denote Śākyamuni Buddha and '*buddha*' to refer to the category.)

There is a third type of awakening mentioned in this story as well: *pratyekabodhi*, or the awakening of a 'solitary *buddha*' or perhaps 'independent *buddha*'. This type of awakening is only available during the long times between Buddhisms, when arhatship is impossible. Like full *buddhas*, *pratyekabuddhas* realize the truth themselves, without the teachings of a full *buddha* or access to the Buddhist monastic path; unlike full *buddhas*, *pratyekabuddhas* do not found a Buddhist community, though they can – according to some sources – teach a small number of other advanced beings and help them towards either immediate *pratyekabodhi* or another form of awakening in a future lifetime.[3]

These interim awakened beings, though included in the threefold typology of awakening that is found throughout early Indian Buddhism, are viewed with some ambivalence, and this is perhaps implicit in the story. The ferryman who is predicted to become a *pratyekabuddha* helps others cross the water, yet only in mundane terms: when he becomes a *pratyekabuddha* he will have crossed himself, but will not take others with him, much as he refused to transport the Buddha and his monks. Although there is no explicit comment on this in the story, one cannot help wondering if the relationship between the Buddha and the ferryman is supposed to engage the audience in reflecting on the limitations of *pratyekabodhi* and to reinforce the Buddha's superiority as one who helps others across rather than simply helping himself.

All three types of awakening are included in the tales of the *Avadānaśataka*, or 'One Hundred Stories', though not always within a single story as here. The acknowledgement of the validity of all three paths to awakening demonstrates that this text is not part of the Mahāyāna movement, which held that only full and complete awakening (*samyaksambodhi*), achieved through the path of the *bodhisattva*, was ultimately valid. This is a text about many types of advanced beings, from *buddha*s and *pratyekabuddha*s of the past and future, to women and men who have achieved awakening as *arhat*s, to those whose merit has led them to a heavenly rebirth. The text also contains ten cautionary tales of how meanness leads to rebirth as a hungry ghost.[4] But throughout all these disparate tales, Śākyamuni Buddha remains central, as revealer of the past and future, as well as participant in the deeds and fruits of other awakening beings. Thanks to him, many others can cross the flood of rebirth.

This book introduces some of the rich narratives that explore Śākyamuni Buddha's centrality through a translation of stories 1–40 of the *Avadānaśataka*. The questions that guide the introduction to this translation are twofold: (1) How did the Buddhist community that composed this text understand the relationship between the founder of their tradition — the 'historical' Buddha Śākyamuni — and other forms of awakened beings? (2) How did they understand the place of Śākyamuni Buddha in relation to the wider category of full and complete buddhahood, and in relation to the long lineage of past *buddhas* believed from the earliest days to have preceded him? These questions were fundamental to the debates and divergences that rocked the Buddhist tradition in the centuries following their founder's death. They are also questions that are fundamental to the stories told about the Buddha and *buddhas* in early Buddhist literature, and they are particular concerns of the *Avadānaśataka*.

The Avadānaśataka

The *Avadānaśataka* is a collection of 100 stories in Sanskrit prose and verse. According to the latest research by Demoto, it was composed probably in the fourth or fifth century CE, perhaps by members of the Sarvāstivāda school, and revised by the Mūlasarvāstivāda up to the seventh century.[5]

The Sarvāstivāda school was an important branch of Buddhist monasticism from around the second century BCE to the seventh century CE, and was particularly influential in the northwest, where it contributed to the early transmission of Buddhism through Central Asia to China.[6] The name refers to the teaching (*vāda*) that 'everything exists' (*sarvam asti*), which in turn relates to the position that all phenomena (*dharmas*) exist in the past, present and future. As such, the Sarvāstivāda school in part identifies itself through reference to a particular understanding of how actions in the past are able to affect the present, and how actions of the present affect the future. The school remains famous for its *Abhidharma* literature, which systematically addresses the constituents of experience, and which greatly influenced the development of wider Buddhist philosophical traditions. The *Avadānaśataka*, if indeed it does originate within this school, presents an alternative to such systematic philosophical literature, by offering a carefully curated series of stories about how the past, present and future relate to one another in the lives of significant individuals.

The Mūlasarvāstivāda, whose relationship to the Sarvāstivāda is still little understood, is best known for its copious *vinaya*, or collection of monastic regulatory texts, which is still in use in Tibetan lineages.[7] The *Mūlasarvāstivāda Vinaya* contains a wealth of narrative material, and much of it has overlap with the *Avadānaśataka* as well as other *avadāna* collections such as the *Divyāvadāna*.[8] Whatever the exact history of its interaction with these two Buddhist schools, it is clear that the *Avadānaśataka* gives us a glimpse into an early form of Buddhist narrative which allies with neither the Mahāyāna movement nor the other major form of Buddhism now extant, namely the Theravāda.

The *Avadānaśataka* bears the marks of being a conscious literary composition, divided as it is into ten chapters of ten stories each; these are consequently often referred to as decades. Though not made explicit in the text itself, a further subdivision into three sections is also possible: stories 1–40 concern forms of buddhahood and pratyekabuddhahood; stories 41–60 concern good and bad rebirth possibilities; and stories 61–100 concern *arhat*s or awakened disciples of the Buddha.

It is the first subsection, namely stories 1–40, that forms the focus of this book, though some discussion of the wider textual structure and contents will also feature. The first ten of these stories tell of ten people who are predicted to future buddhahood by Śākyamuni Buddha. The second decade contains stories of Śākyamuni Buddha's own past-life encounters with ten *buddha*s of the distant past. The third offers ten tales of *pratyekabuddha*s: eight concern people predicted by Śākyamuni Buddha to become *pratyekabuddha*s in the future, while the remaining two concern past *pratyekabuddha*s and their karmic backstories in the time of past *buddha*s. In the fourth chapter we return to stories of Śākyamuni Buddha's past lives, this time in times of no past *buddha*s.

As such, these four chapters all address buddhahood, whether the relationship between Śākyamuni Buddha and other *buddha*s, his own qualifications for buddhahood, or his ability to predict future *buddha*s. The third decade is at first sight an outlier, since it addresses not full and complete buddhahood but pratyekabuddhahood, though each of the *pratyekabuddha*s has an important past-life encounter with the Buddha (or, in two cases, a past *buddha*). As noted above, the *Avadānaśataka* deals with all three types of awakening, with stories 61–100 containing stories of *arhat*s of different backgrounds. These stories tend to present the past lives of the *arhat*s-to-be in times of past *buddha*s (or their *stūpa*s), adding further to the network of interactions between different awakened beings that is set up in the first four chapters of the text.

Table 1 **The ten chapters of the *Avadānaśataka***

Decade	Stories	Theme
First	1–10	Śākyamuni predicts others to future buddhahood
Second	11–20	Śākyamuni's past-life encounters with *buddhas* of the past
Third	21–30	*pratyekabuddhas*
Fourth	31–40	Śākyamuni's past lives, with no past *buddhas*
Fifth	41–50	*pretas* (hungry ghosts)
Sixth	51–60	*devas* (gods)
Seventh	61–70	members of Śākyan clan who become *arhats*
Eighth	71–80	female *arhats*
Ninth	81–90	male *arhats*
Tenth	91–100	*arhats* with bad karma, plus *Aśokāvadāna*

Although a full assessment of the *Avadānaśataka* would of course include all three forms of awakening, there are good reasons to consider chapters 1–4 as a unit in their own right. One important reason is the fact that these four chapters are separated from those about arhatship by two other chapters of a rather different nature: chapter 5 tells of *preta*s or hungry ghosts, and the acts of demerit that led to their unfortunate rebirth, while chapter 6 contains stories of the attainment of the *deva* realm, or heavenly rebirth. The structure of the text therefore leads us naturally to consider the first four chapters together, separately from the stories of the other type of awakening.

Another reason for considering stories 1–40 as a unit is the way in which they are framed by stories 1 and 40: The first story opens with news of the Buddha's recent awakening, and the effects of this news on a generous brahmin who has hitherto been a supporter of 'heretics' (*tīrthikas*); his conversion to support of the Buddha is the first of many in the text. Story 40 brings the time period of the frame narrative to the end of the Buddha's life, as it tells of his conversion of his last personal disciple, and of his *parinirvāṇa*. While there is no clear chronology of the frame narratives between those two stories, they do appear to function as bookends.

Another good reason to consider these stories together is that the tales of full buddhahood and pratyekabuddhahood are interweaved with one another rather than being presented in a sequence. While chapters 1, 2 and 4 all concern full buddhahood, *pratyekabuddhas* appear in chapter 3. Other patterns emerge: chapters 1 and 3 are dominated by stories of Śākyamuni Buddha predicting others to future attainments of awakening, while chapters 2 and 4 concern his own past lives. We could take the position that the ordering of these chapters was accidental or unthinking, yet the text as a whole bears many hallmarks of a carefully constructed composition. We might therefore prefer to assume a deliberate placing of the chapters, and explore what purpose is served by the resulting order. We will return to the question of what motivates the structure of the *Avadānaśataka* towards the end of this study.

Although these four chapters do stand apart as a subsection of the *Avadānaśataka*, they also contain features that are characteristic of the text as a whole. The *Avadānaśataka* is characterized by three things in particular:

1. The use of many — and sometimes lengthy — formulaic passages.[9]

2. A structure that places acts in one time period as having results in another: in other words, a focus on karmicly significant deeds, which is generally characteristic of the *avadāna* genre as a whole. Broadly speaking, one can divide the stories into those in which a 'past' deed has results in the narrative 'present' of Śākyamuni Buddha, and those in which a 'present' deed in relation to Śākyamuni Buddha has predicted results in a 'future' time.[10]

3. The presence of Śākyamuni Buddha as narrator of the past or predictor of the future, for the purpose of teaching his audience.

The third of these characteristics has perhaps been least commonly noted, yet it relates very closely to the second. Time revolves around Śākyamuni and his narrative present, and every story begins and ends in his presence. Deeds either take place in relation to him, or have fruits that manifest in relation to him, and everything is explained by him. He is thus central in temporal terms, and his ability to see both the past and the future is also crucial to the framing of the stories. In addition to being a revealer of the past and predictor of the future, Śākyamuni is also a miracle-worker, and — perhaps most importantly — a teacher. Almost every story (the exceptions are discussed below) ends with the Buddha exhorting his audience to learn something specific from the story, such as to live in reliance on him, honour the three types of awakened being, work to overcome meanness, or appreciate that good deeds result in good fruits and bad deeds in bad fruits.

This closing formulaic exhortation is one example of the many formulaic passages that pepper the text, and it helpfully demonstrates both the benefits of fixedness and the possibilities brought by flexibility. While several formulae repeat, the exact same lesson is not present in every story. The formula has not been chosen at random or unthinkingly, but to suit the story and the lesson it contains. In the four decades under discussion here, the lesson is often to revere and honour the Buddha, and to live in reliance on him. The Buddha, that is to say Śākyamuni Buddha, is at the heart of this text.

Many *buddhas*

Let us begin at the beginning, with the first two chapters of the text. The first ten stories of the *Avadānaśataka* set up the Buddha, that is to say Śākyamuni Buddha, as someone who identifies future *buddhas*. The second ten show Śākyamuni's own past-life encounters with past *buddhas*. As such, both decades are concerned with the multiplicity of *buddhas* that have existed — and will exist — throughout the ages; in line with non-Mahāyāna understandings, such *buddhas* can only exist one at a time, but stretch infinitely into the past and future. Furthermore, they concern the relationship between the *buddha* of our present Buddhism, Śākyamuni, and his 'type' — the full and complete *buddha*.

The narratives of the first chapter are all based on the same basic pattern. In each of the stories, an individual has an impressive encounter with Śākyamuni Buddha (usually involving a miraculous display of some sort) and makes a vow to achieve future buddhahood. In all except AvŚ 3, which simply states that the person made a fervent aspiration (*praṇidhāna*) to unsurpassed complete awakening, the vow is formulaic in nature:

> By this root of virtue, the arising of this thought and this properly given gift, may I become a *buddha* in this dark world that is leaderless and without a guide. May I carry across those beings who have not crossed over, liberate those who are not liberated, console those in need of consolation, bring to complete *nirvāṇa* those who have not entered complete *nirvāṇa*.[11]

The Buddha then smiles, and a long formulaic passage (on which more below) details how rays of light emerge from the smile, travel through the cosmos, and re-enter the Buddha's *uṣṇīṣa*, or the protuberance on the top of his head. Prompted by his attendant Ānanda, the Buddha then predicts that this person will indeed achieve buddhahood, in a formula that echoes the aspiration:

> Through this root of virtue, the arising of this thought, and this properly given gift, after three incalculable aeons he[12] will attain awakening, and having fulfilled the six perfections that are pervaded with great compassion he will become a full and perfect *buddha* named X, with the ten powers, four confidences, three special applications of mindfulness and great compassion. This is the gift of one who has a faithful thought towards me.[13]

These two passages, with their echoes of one another, reinforce the qualities required for buddhahood, namely great roots of virtue or merit (*kuśalamūla*), a sincere intention (*citta*) or fervent aspiration (*praṇidhāna*), and a properly given gift (*deyadharmaparityāga*). This is enough to earn a prediction to future buddhahood, but the attainment itself also requires the fulfilment of the six perfections and great compassion. The mention of such challenging qualities reminds the audience that achieving buddhahood is not so simple as it might look at first glance.

In addition to showing what is required for a prediction to — and the eventual attainment of — buddhahood, the stories of this decade also tell us some important things about Śākyamuni Buddha. Most obviously, they show his impressive ability to predict someone to future buddhahood, in a process that also involves suffusing the cosmos with rays of coloured light. They also show his ability to prompt people into making fervent aspirations, often through the performance of miracles; for a summary of the miraculous occurrences in this chapter, see Table 2. That these stories are supposed to prompt us to be in awe of Śākyamuni Buddha is reinforced by the formulaic ending to the first story. Here, as in most of the *Avadānaśataka* stories, the Buddha ends his teaching with an exhortation to his audience, and in this case it is the following:

> In this way, monks, you should train: 'We will honour, revere, respect and worship the teacher. And having honoured, revered, respected and worshipped the teacher, we will live in reliance on him.' In this way, monks, you should train.[14]

Table 2 **Summary of the stories of chapter 1**

Story	**Aspirant and offering**	**Miracle**	**Predicted to become a *buddha* called:**
1. Pūrṇabhadra	Rich brahmin householder, Pūrṇa, offers food to Buddha.	Buddha makes his monks invisible and fills their bowls.	Pūrṇabhadra (Completely Good[15])
2. Yaśomatī	Yaśomatī, daughter of a general, offers food and flowers to the Buddha.	Flowers become a jewelled pavilion above Buddha's head.	Ratnamati (Bejewelled)
3. Lazybones (*Kusīda*)	Lazy boy Nanda, after conversion makes money at sea then makes offering to Buddha and his monks.	Buddha emits magical rays of light, and gives boy a staff that produces vision of jewels when hit.	Atibalavīryaparākrama (Hero of Very Powerful Vigour)
4. The Caravan Leader (*Sārthavāha*)	Trader who succeeds in voyage thanks to his devotion to Buddha, then makes too small an offering on return, but later a larger one.	1. Smoke of offered incense becomes like a thundercloud 2. Jewels become like a parasol or pavilion over Buddha's head	Ratnottama (Supreme Jewel)
5. Soma [missing][16]			
6. Vaḍika	Boy Vaḍika is cured from bodily and mental pain by Buddha, then makes an offering.	Buddha cures the boy, including with help from Śakra.	Śākyamuni
7. Lotus (*Padma*)	Gardener offers lotus to Buddha.	Lotus becomes like a cartwheel over Buddha's head.	Padmottama (Supreme Lotus)

Table 2 (continued)

Story	**Aspirant and offering**	**Miracle**	**Predicted to become a *buddha* called:**
8. Pañcāla	Two warring kings, of northern and southern Pañcāla, subdued by the Buddha. One becomes *arhat*, the other makes offering and aspiration.	Buddha creates illusory army.	Vijaya (Victor)
9. Incense (*Dhūpa*)	Follower of Pūraṇa realizes the Buddha is superior.	Disciple of Buddha uses Act of Truth to show superiority of Buddha.	Acala (Unshakeable)
10. The King (*Rāja*)	Merchant assists King Prasenajit and is rewarded with temporary kingship, during which time he makes offerings to the Buddha.	None.	Abhayaprada (Giving Safety)

Oddly, although almost every other story in the text ends with some sort of formulaic exhortation to train or learn from the story, tales 2–10 omit this.[17] However, one assumes its presence is to be implied, and certainly the stories convey a strong sense of the Buddha's impressive power as visionary, wonder-worker and teacher, worthy of such an exhortation.

While all the stories run according to this general set formula, there are variations particularly in the ways in which miracles and offerings relate to one another. For example, in AvŚ 1, 2 and 7 a person makes an offering spontaneously, or after having heard about or seen the Buddha. The object that is offered is then the basis of some miraculous vision — for example, the offering floats above the Buddha's head — and this further prompts the donor to aspire to buddhahood. In AvŚ 3, however, the miraculous vision — a staff that produces images of jewels when hit — leads to the lazy boy going off to make his fortune, and only later does he then make an offering to the Buddha and an aspiration to buddhahood. Likewise in AvŚ 6, the miracle — the curing of a boy's incurable illness — precedes the offering, while in AvŚ 8 a miraculous vision causes the humbling of two warring kings, one of whom then makes an offering and aspiration.

In AvŚ 4 the order of events is different again, in a way that emphasizes the instability of a person's intention: in order to ensure the success of his voyage, a trader declares he will give half his gains to the Buddha, but when he returns — with much wealth — he regrets this promise. In an amusing twist that is echoed by contemporary tax-avoidance tactics, he sells his goods to his wife for two small coins, buys some incense and offers *that* to the Buddha. After the Buddha makes the incense smoke rise up into thunderclouds, the trader is overawed, regrets his decision once again, and invites the Buddha for a meal. He offers jewels to the Buddha, and these become like a pavilion or jewelled parasol above the Buddha's head. This second miraculous occurrence then prompts his aspiration to future buddhahood. This story, with its two sequences of offering-plus-miracle, and its swithering donor, demonstrates the full flexibility of the motif.

The final two stories present further variations, particularly in relation to the role of the miracle. In AvŚ 9, the Buddha himself is not involved in converting the follower of the rival teacher Pūraṇa. Rather, it is left to an unnamed disciple to do this by using an Act of Truth — in this case, a powerful statement about the Buddha's supremacy — to make some offerings fly through the air to him. (As we will discuss further below, Acts of Truth are a useful cause of miracles for beings other than the Buddha, for the truth is powerful enough to bend the laws of nature.[18]) While the miracle is thus present in some sense, the usual gift is not, and this is reflected in the absence of any reference to a gift in the Buddha's later prediction.[19] Meanwhile, in AvŚ 10 it is the miracle that is missing: a faithful layman remains stable in his support of the Buddha, and his offerings are followed by the standard aspiration and prediction, without any intervening miracle.

Thus, in this decade we have several possible orders for events, most of which include the key elements of gift, miracle, aspiration and prediction:

gift — miracle — aspiration — prediction
miracle — gift — aspiration — prediction
small gift — miracle — large gift — miracle — aspiration
— prediction
gift — aspiration — prediction
miracle — aspiration - prediction

In addition, the type of miracle and the agency behind them varies. Those stories that emphasize the miracle before the offering tend to portray the Buddha's deliberate interventions: he sets out to cure a boy, or incite a lazy child to action, or subdue some warring kings. When the offering itself is subject to some impressive transformation, the events seem more spontaneous, although AvŚ 2 notes that such feats are 'not possible through careful training or hard work or as the result of previous actions, but only by *buddhas* through their *buddha*-power, and by gods through their god-power',[20] underlining the Buddha's continued agency. Even when it is not the Buddha who performs the miracle, the miracle still reflects the Buddha's power. Thus, AvŚ 9 shows us how an unnamed disciple of the Buddha can also work wonders, but this is possible only through a powerful statement of truth about the Buddha's greatness. We will return to the relationship between miracles, aspirations and predictions later.

Another focus of this chapter seems to be the role of miracles in converting new followers. Thus, for example, the first person to be predicted to future buddhahood is a brahmin who initially invites hundreds of thousands of 'heretics' (called both *tīrthika* and *pāṣaṇḍika*) for an almsgiving or sacrifice, before hearing about the magnificent Buddha and inviting him instead. In AvŚ 3, a lazy child fails even to look up at eight visiting non-Buddhist ascetics, including Pūraṇa, though he later leaps to his feet to greet the Buddha. Likewise, homage to non-Buddhists in AvŚ 6 has no effect on the child's illness, which the Buddha alone can cure, and we meet a follower of Pūraṇa again in AvŚ 9, in which he loses a competition with a follower of the Buddha. Meanwhile, in AvŚ 7 it is a follower of Nārāyaṇa (in other words, the deity better known as Viṣṇu) who is outdone by Anāthapiṇḍada, prominent follower of the Buddha. While 'heretics' also feature elsewhere in the text, they are particularly concentrated here, as if we are being invited to see how incredibly powerfully the Buddha was able to convert supporters following his awakening, news of which frames the opening of the text.[21]

The focus on Śākyamuni that is clearly established in the first chapter continues in the second. Here we again encounter many characters with a claim to buddhahood, but in this case they are *buddhas* of the past rather than of the future. In each story, Śākyamuni Buddha tells of his own past life encounter with a past *buddha*. As in the first decade, the events in the past are repeated with small variations: Śākyamuni Buddha-to-be is a high-ranking human (eight times a king, once a brahmin, once a caravan leader) who performs some act of service for a *buddha* of the past. These events are summarized in Table 3.

In addition to the stories of the past, however, the stories of this decade have — sometimes quite lengthy — frame stories in the 'present' time of Śākyamuni Buddha. Each story of the past, we are told, is recounted to explain a present act of service or pleasant situation that Śākyamuni experiences. Thus his past serenading of a past *buddha* leads to being honoured by musicians in his final life (in AvŚ 17), and his past offering of valuable cloth to a past *buddha* leads to being offered the same by King Bimbisāra in the 'present' (in AvŚ 19). This structure often means that any miraculous occurrence caused by a past *buddha* is balanced by one caused by Śākyamuni, so for example in AvŚ 14 the robe of a past *buddha* cures an epidemic, and so too Śākyamuni cures an epidemic. The *buddhas* of the past are certainly not able to outdo the Buddha of our present.

Śākyamuni Buddha's position is reinforced by the role of another character who features in half of the stories in this decade: the king of the gods Śakra, also known as Indra, and a deity familiar across other early Indian religious groups as well as Buddhism.[22] Śakra has already appeared once in the first decade: he is summoned by the Buddha in AvŚ 6 to bring medicinal herbs from Gandhamādana Mountain to cure a sick boy. The motif there involves the Buddha having a 'worldly thought' (*laukika citta*): in other words, a thought that is readable by the gods, about how great it would be if Śakra would come. This motif really takes off in chapter 2, where we see how obligingly the king of the gods offers support to the Buddha: in AvŚ 12 he brings costly sandalwood and oversees the construction of a palace, while in AvŚ 13 he sends rain to save merchants lost in desert; in both cases, he is prompted by a 'worldly thought'. It is only Śākyamuni who seems to have a direct line to the king of the gods: when Śakra sends rain again later in AvŚ 13, during a past-time narrated by Śākyamuni, it is because a king (Śākyamuni in a past life) bathes the past *buddha* Candana during a famine. Hence, the rain is out of respect for the past *buddha*, but it is not commanded by him, having been orchestrated by the king. Śakra does also offer honour unprompted, however, when in AvŚ 16 he performs the quinquennial festival and prompts great faith in other beings, while in AvŚ 20 he helps a householder provide for the Buddha, at the request of the senior monk Mahāmaudgalyāyana.

Table 3 **Summary of the stories of chapter 2**

Story	**Frame**	**Buddha-to-be was:**
11. The Sailors (*Nāvikā*)	Buddha honoured by sailors.	caravan leader who ferried past *buddha* across river and made resolve to buddhahood.
12. The Post (*Stambha*)	Buddha honoured by Śakra with sandalwood post and palace.	king who provided for past *buddha* for rainy season retreat.
13. The Bath (*Snātra*)	Buddha makes Śakra rain for desert-stranded merchants.	king who provided for past *buddha* for rainy season; during drought king bathed past *buddha*, causing Śakra to send rain.
14. The Plague (*Īti*)	Buddha cures epidemic through loving-kindness; brahmins and householders become faithful.	king who provided for past *buddha* for rainy season; during epidemic the past *buddha's* robe was paraded through the city to cure everyone.
15. The Miracle (*Prātihārya*)	Buddha takes on the form of Śakra and descends into sacrificial arena to convert brahmins.	king who wished to provide for past *buddha* in his faithless land so had magnificent monastery built; past *buddha* performed miracle and converted everyone.
16. The Quinquennial Festival (*Pañcavārṣika*)	At time when support of Buddha and his monks is forbidden, Śakra and the gods perform a festival to honour him and thereby persuade the king (Ajātaśatru) to retract his decree.	king who provided for past *buddha* for rainy season and thereby cured an epidemic, then performed the festival.

Table 3 (continued)

Story	Frame	Buddha-to-be was:
17. The Eulogy (*Stuti*)	Buddha, with help of Pañcaśikha, outperforms the finest musician in the land, and he becomes an *arhat*. Musicians entertain Buddha and his monks, Buddha smiles and predicts their pratyekabuddhahood.	king who, along with female musicians, saw past *buddha* in fire meditation, became faithful and awoke him from meditation with music; resolved to buddhahood.
18. The Boon (*Varada*)	Condemned criminal takes refuge in Buddha and is allowed (by King Prasenajit) to ordain; becomes an *arhat*.	brahmin well-versed in *Vedas*, who offered past *buddha* his seat and praised him in 100 *padas*, then resolved to buddhahood.
19. The Cloth of Kāśi (*Kāśikavastra*)	Buddha and monks greatly honoured by Bimbisāra and the citizens, with food, drink and *kāśi* cloth.	king who offered past *buddha* food and a very valuable cloth, then after his *parinirvāṇa* built a *stūpa*.
20. Divine food (*Divyabhojana*)	Wealthy householder, with help of Śakra and other gods, makes grand offering to Buddha and disciples, then resolves to buddhahood; Buddha smiles and predicts such.	king who supported past *buddha* for rainy season, and made jewelled image of him.

It is in AvŚ 15 that we get the strongest sense of the Buddha's superiority over the gods, and also by implication his superiority over the brahmins who hold the gods supreme. In this story a group of brahmins are performing a ritual and entreating the god Śakra — whom they refer to as 'Lover of Ahalyā' in a reference to Vedic and Brahmanical lore — to appear. Using his amazing *buddha*-vision the Buddha sees this, and also sees that the brahmins have planted virtuous roots in the past and thus are ripe for conversion. He takes on the form of Śakra and begins to descend into the sacrificial arena. News of this spreads fast and, after a vast crowd has assembled to see the god, the Buddha takes on his proper form and gives them all a powerfully transformative *dharma* teaching. If we were not already convinced of whose presence we should be pursuing, this story certainly leaves us in no doubt.

Given the clear focus on the supremacy of the Buddha, we might expect this chapter to also demonstrate his qualification for buddhahood through the stories of his past encounters with *buddhas*. After all, the stories place Śākyamuni in a lineage of past *buddhas*, in parallel to other collections such as the Pāli *Buddhavaṃsa*, or sections of the *Mahāvastu*, or a Gandhāran *Many Buddhas Sūtra* from the first century BCE.[23] In each of these texts the Buddha encounters a series of past *buddhas* and renews his aspiration to future buddhahood at their feet, receiving a prediction in return. However, it is intriguing to note that in the *Avadānaśataka* stories the Bodhisattva (as we assume him to be, though the term is notably absent from this chapter of the text[24]) only makes an aspiration in three of the stories (AvŚ 11, 17, 18), and he never receives a prediction. In addition, no indication is given that the ten past *buddhas* are in any chronological order, and the names do not have easy parallels in other lists of past *buddhas*.[25] This could be explained by the idea that the past *buddhas* in this chapter may have been understood as early, before the formal path to buddhahood began for Śākyamuni. However, such an interpretation is not indicated by the text, which seems less intent on establishing the Buddha as part of an auspicious lineage and more interested in establishing the unique and independent achievement of our narrator, Śākyamuni Buddha. Unlike the future *buddhas* of chapter 1, Śākyamuni-to-be does not require confirmation of his future buddhahood.

Chapters 1 and 2 of the *Avadānaśataka*, therefore, share a focus on placing Śākyamuni in relation to the general 'type' of *samyaksambuddha*: he is established as the identifier – and perhaps even creator – of future *buddhas*, and as one who has served many *buddhas* of the past, but without needing their confirmation of his destiny. Chapter 2 also resonates with another decade of the text, however: namely, the fourth, which also recounts stories of Śākyamuni's past lives, although this time without the presence of any past *buddhas*. It will therefore make sense to skip over the third chapter for the moment, and explore what is going on in chapter 4.

Śākyamuni's past lives

Both the second and fourth decades contain stories of the Buddha's past lives, but they are rather different types of story. While the second decade echoes texts like the *Buddhavaṃsa*, the fourth decade matches up more closely to what we might think of as 'classical' *jātakas*, such as those in the *Jātakatthavaṇṇanā* or *Jātakamālā*, in which the Bodhisattva carries out various deeds in past times when no *buddhas* exist.[26] The tales are summarized in Table 4.

Two things are immediately striking about these stories: Firstly, the deeds done by the Buddha in his past lives are often extreme in their virtue, and contrast strikingly with the types of virtuous deeds he carried out in chapter 2, which usually involved simply feeding a past *buddha* and his monks or making an offering. Here the Bodhisattva instead demonstrates great compassion and self-sacrifice, or loving-kindness and patience, and then instructs his monks to emulate the same, albeit in a more generalized and attainable manner. The second striking thing is the absence of *buddhas*

Table 4 **Summary of the stories of chapter 4**

Story	**Frame**	**Buddha-to-be was:**	**In this way, monks, you should train:**
31. Padmaka	Monks troubled by illness, but Buddha remains well.	king who jumped off his terrace with a resolve to become a *rohita* fish in order to cure his citizens; resolved to help them also when he becomes Buddha.	We will cultivate compassion towards all beings.
32. The Morsel (*Kavaḍa*)	Buddha gives teaching on merits of giving, and monks are impressed by this.	king who shared his storehouses during a famine and even gave his last mouthful of food to a brahmin (= Śakra) so impressing him enough to bring rain.	We will give gifts and make merit.
33. Dharmapāla	Buddha maintains friendly thoughts towards Devadatta despite his murderous attempts.	prince whose mother demanded to drink his blood, yet he maintained friendly thoughts towards his parents and the executioners.	We will cultivate friendly thoughts towards all beings.
34. Śibi	A monk is unable to thread his needle and cries out, 'Who desires merit?' Buddha replies that he does.	King Śibi, giver of great gifts; gave blood to insects, eye to vulture and brahmin (= Śakra); Śakra declared he will soon be a Buddha.	We will give gifts and make merit.
35. Surūpa	Buddha's teaching inspires the fourfold assembly to respect towards the *dharma*.	king who willingly sacrificed his son and wife to a *yakṣa* (= Śakra) in order to hear a verse of *dharma*; Śakra declared he will soon be a Buddha.	We will revere the *dharma*.

Table 4 (continued)

Story	Frame	Buddha-to-be was:	In this way, monks, you should train:
36. Maitrakanyaka	Buddha teaches proper reverence for one's parents.	merchant's son, who went to sea against his mother's wishes, kicking her first; visited heavenly places (for supporting his mother) then a hell with a rotating wheel in his head (for abusing his mother) from which he was freed when he declared he wanted nobody else to have to endure it.	We will honour our mother and father.
37. The Hare (*Śaśa*)	Buddha struggles to make a monk separate from his relations and enter the forest, but eventually succeeds, and he becomes an *arhat*.	hare who was devoted to his friend a hermit; persuaded the hermit to stay in the forest despite lack of food by offering himself into the fire as a meal; saved by the hermit, made act of truth persuading Śakra to send rain, then made a resolve to buddhahood.	We will dwell as good friends, not as evil friends.
38. The Dharma-seeker (*Dharmagaveṣī*)	Buddha sweeps the Jeta Grove while Anāthapiṇḍada is away, and speaks in praise of cleaning. Later persuades Anāthapiṇḍada to come and hear the *dharma*, because the *dharma* deserves respect.	prince-become-king who desired the *dharma* and offered to enter a fire pit in exchange for a verse of *dharma* from a *yakṣa* (= Śakra).	We will revere the *dharma*.

Table 4 (continued)

Story	Frame	Buddha-to-be was:	In this way, monks, you should train:
39. Anāthapiṇḍada	Buddha prevented by a brahmin from crossing a line in the sand until Anāthapiṇḍada discharges a debt on the Buddha's behalf.	prince who gave surety for a friend's gambling debt (friend = Anāthapiṇḍada) but never paid.	One should strive to avoid taking what is not given.
40. Subhadra	Subhadra becomes the last personal disciple of the Buddha and attains *parinirvāṇa* before him.	leader of herd of deer, who sacrificed himself to ensure the escape of his herd, even returning to save a stray young deer (= Subhadra); resolved that in future he would save them from *saṃsāra*. [embedded story: Subhadra = deity who helped Kāśyapa Buddha's nephew Aśoka return to his uncle's presence in time to receive a teaching and attain arhatship, and enter *parinirvāṇa* before the Buddha; deity resolved to do so too in time of future Buddha]	We will dwell as good friends, not as evil friends.

during these stories, which seems to prompt the extremity of the Bodhisattva's virtue. The difficulties of being in a time without Buddhism are particularly emphasized by AvŚ 35 and 38, in which the Bodhisattva demonstrates his willingness to go to extreme lengths to hear a single verse of the *dharma*;[27] at the end of the story the monks are exhorted to revere the *dharma*.

The distinction between these different types of positive deed resonates with a pattern identified by Reiko Ohnuma in her exploration of gift-of-the-body *jātakas*. She argues that stories of the Bodhisattva's bodily sacrifice are only necessary in times of no Buddhism, and that this is what lies behind the generic distinction between *jātaka*s, which she suggests are primarily about the Bodhisattva's acquisition of the perfections required for buddhahood, and *avadāna*s, which she sees as being characterized by devotional acts (2007: 41). As she argues (2007: 43):

> By means of the *jātaka*s, the bodhisattva is lauded and exalted for the magnificent lengths he went to during his previous lives – but by means of the *avadānas*, ordinary Buddhists receive the message that such magnificent acts are now unnecessary, thanks to the presence of Buddhism in the world as a powerful field of merit.

I would be cautious about forming any single understanding of what defines a *jātaka* or *avadāna*, since the genres seem to vary greatly between different texts composed in different times and places. Nonetheless, Ohnuma's observation is clearly pertinent for the *Avadānaśataka*: in the stories of the second chapter, the closing teaching is to honour and live in reliance on the teacher (the Buddha). In other words, the lessons are all, in Ohnuma's terms, 'devotional', and the past-life deeds also involve offerings to an awakened being. In chapter 4, by contrast, both the closing lesson and the demonstrated deeds are independent of Buddhist figures and institutions; only a vague and not specifically Buddhist *dharma* features, along with general Buddhist ethical principles. As a result of the absence of Buddhism, the Buddha's deeds cannot be simple devotional interactions but must instead take on a different character.

A neat illustration of this shift in emphasis is found in the shifting role of the king of the gods, Śakra. As we saw, in chapter 2 (and, to a lesser extent, chapter 1), Śakra appears as a supporter of the Buddha, often summoned by a 'worldly thought', and ready to do his bidding. In chapter 4, however, he takes on a different role: that of tester of the Bodhisattva.[28] Thus, in AvŚ 32, he takes on disguise as a brahmin and asks for the last morsel of food that is possessed by a king (Śākyamuni-to-be) during a famine. In AvŚ 34, the famous story of King Śibi, he asks for an even more impossible gift: the generous king's eyes. In AvŚ 35 and 36, Śakra takes disguise as a *yakṣa* and offers the Bodhisattva a verse of the *dharma* in return for a yet more impossible gift: the life of a dear family member or indeed of himself. In every case, of course, the Bodhisattva does not even hesitate, and more than passes Śakra's test, leading to extensive praise. Only in AvŚ 29 does Śakra appear as a simple supporter of the Buddha, when he joins a number of exalted beings in offering to pay the Buddha's debt, while in AvŚ 37 he sends rain after seeing the powerful self-sacrifice of the Bodhisattva-hare. Thus, the different roles played by Śakra in these two types of story map clearly onto Ohnuma's distinction between the devotional focus of *avadāna*s and the role of *jātaka*s in celebrating the virtues of the Buddha-to-be.

There are some limitations to the applicability of Ohnuma's categories, however. The first is that there is no concern with the 'perfections' (*pāramitā*) required for buddhahood here; indeed, the general association between the *jātaka* genre and the perfections has been overplayed in both Buddhist and scholarly assessments of early *jātaka* sources.[29] In chapter 4 of the *Avadānaśataka* the perfections are only mentioned in passing once, in a list given by a monk in the frame story to AvŚ 34 (discussed below), and nowhere do we meet any suggestion that the past-life stories are meant to illustrate Śākyamuni's acquisition of the qualities required for buddhahood.[30] In addition, none of the stories is called by the term *jātaka*,[31] and the Buddha-to-be is only referred to as Bodhisattva in four of the stories (AvŚ 31, 36, 37, 38). There is also little emphasis on any other aspect of his preparation for buddhahood: only in AvŚ 37 do we see the Bodhisattva aspire to future buddhahood, while AvŚ 31 and 40 show him aspiring to help others after he has achieved buddhahood. Twice Śakra declares that the Bodhisattva's virtues suggest he will soon be a Buddha (AvŚ 34, 35).

The stories do not therefore seem particularly concerned with showing the Bodhisattva's readiness for buddhahood, nor with illustrating a path to that attainment. Instead, the relationship between the frame story in the 'present' time of the Buddha and the past-life story is more often one of continuity: the Buddha tells most of these stories to explain how his values have remained the same. He gives gifts now, and gave even more impressive gifts in the past. He valued the *dharma* in the past, and values it now too. This is underscored by a phrase he utters in six of the stories, when the monks express surprise at some impressive experience in the narrative present:

> O monks, what is the marvel in this now, when the Tathāgata has eradicated attachment, hatred and delusion, is free from birth, ageing, sickness, death, grief, lamentation, suffering, melancholy and mental anguish, and is all-knowing, knowledgeable in all ways, master of all that is to be known? In times past, when I was affected by attachment, hatred and delusion and was not free from birth, ageing, sickness, death, grief, lamentation, suffering, melancholy and mental anguish, . . .[32]

In other words, the Buddha draws attention to the fact that he had superior virtue even in a past time when he was less accomplished. Why, then, would his monks be surprised at his 'present' virtues?

The surprise of the monks in several of these stories is forgivable, however, for some of the values that the Buddha praises or exhibits are unexpected. The monks are sometimes surprised by his extraordinary virtue, such as his ability to cultivate friendly thoughts towards his murderous cousin Devadatta, which frames AvŚ 33. In AvŚ 36 they are surprised that he speaks of the importance of respecting one's parents, which is not always considered a mainstream teaching within a primarily monastic tradition.[33] The Buddha also surprises his monks by remaining interested in merit despite having already achieved buddhahood, and thus having passed beyond mundane concerns. The most striking illustration of this is in AvŚ 34, where we meet a monk who is struggling to thread his needle in order to sew up his robes. He cries out in frustration, hoping for an assistant, 'Who in the world wishes for merit?'[34] To his shock, the Buddha himself replies that he does. But, insists the monk, 'this hand of yours has accumulated generosity, good conduct, forbearance, vigour, meditation and wisdom during three incalculable aeons,'[35] the implication being that the Buddha, having acquired the six perfections here listed, should be beyond the mundane act of helping a monk thread his needle. The Buddha, however, shows himself to be not only concerned for the welfare of his monks, but completely insatiable when it comes to the acquisition of merit.

Another surprising revelation made by the Buddha in this chapter is his chequered past, for there are two stories of his bad deeds and their fruits: in AvŚ 36 the Bodhisattva experiences the karmic results of kicking his mother on the head, though both deeds and fruits are within the past life and so do not taint the Buddha's final-life experience. In AvŚ 39, by contrast, the past-life deed — failure to pay a gambling debt, equated in the story to taking what is not given and hence a breach of the second precept — has results in the Buddha's final life, when he is prevented from crossing a line that his creditor has drawn in the ground. Although the wording of the text makes it possible to see his inability to cross as a *decision*, in order simply to teach the inevitability of the results of deeds, the exact situation is left vague, and the Buddha is left stationary until Anāthapiṇḍada comes to pay the debt.[36] The Buddha's susceptibility to negative karmic fruits even after his achievement of awakening is a matter of some debate within early Buddhist texts.[37] Here, however, it seems simply to be underscoring the Buddha's continued interest in deeds and their fruits, which also motivates his demonstrations of continued virtue.

The focus on merit and demerit links the stories of this decade to those that follow in the remainder of the text, especially the next two chapters on rebirth in the realms of hungry ghosts or gods respectively. Indeed, the general lessons for the Buddha's audience that close the stories of chapter 4 are simple and wide-ranging: honour your parents, cherish the *dharma*, give gifts and make merit, keep good company and value friendship. The Buddha performs no miracles in this chapter, and makes no predictions, but rather comes across as very human and even humble. This, however, is balanced by stories of extreme acts that can scarcely be designed for emulation, such as bodily gift-giving. The two time periods — the 'present' time of the Buddha and the past time without — are thus particularly strongly contrasted in these stories. The Buddha's heroism in the past is matched with humility in the present. He may have jumped into a fire for the sake of a verse of teaching, but he will still help you thread your needle, or sweep his own hermitage. That much at least we can hope to emulate.

Independent buddhahood

The third decade of the *Avadānaśataka*, nestled between the two chapters of Śākyamuni's past-life stories, is concerned with *pratyekabuddhas*. The term *pratyekabuddha* is usually translated as 'solitary *buddha*' or 'lone *buddha*',[38] though I tend to prefer 'independent *buddha*', since in the wider literature they are rarely in fact solitary. Such figures are said to attain awakening without access to teachings, like a full and perfect *buddha* (*samyaksambuddha*), but unlike a full *buddha* they do not go on to found communities of followers.[39] The place of *pratyekabuddhas* in the threefold typology of awakening, somehow sitting between *samyaksambuddhas* and *arhats*, presumably affects their inclusion in the *Avadānaśataka*, alongside stories of other types of awakening. This rationale for their inclusion is reinforced by the closing teaching that the Buddha gives his monks in eight of the ten *pratyekabuddha* stories: namely, to 'pay homage to *buddhas*, *pratyekabuddhas* and *śrāvakas*'; in the remaining two stories he closes by telling them to 'revere the teacher' (in other words, himself).

In eight of the stories in this decade, someone (or, in one story, a group) encounters Śākyamuni Buddha, and he predicts them to future pratyekabuddhahood in a long formulaic passage involving his magical beaming smile (on which more below). Prompted by Ānanda, the Buddha explains, with reference to the same three criteria found in chapter 1's predictions to full buddhahood: a root of virtue, a properly given gift, and the arising of a thought or intention will lead the person to become a *pratyekabuddha*. Often there is also an interim prediction that they will avoid negative rebirths for a number of aeons.

In half of the stories the prediction follows some sort of aspiration, referred to in AvŚ 25, 26, 28 and 30 through the statement that the person 'developed an intention' (*cetanāṃ puṣṇāti*). In AvŚ 28, 29 and 30 this intention is spelled out, as the person states their wish to achieve *pratyekāṃ bodhiṃ*, but only in AvŚ 29 is this referred to as a *praṇidhāna*, or 'fervent aspiration', the term used throughout chapter 1 and elsewhere in the text for a karmicly potent vow. In the remaining stories there is no aspiration, and the prediction simply follows an act of merit, such as the offering of a lotus, a golden disc or food. As such, the stories fit a broader pattern already identifiable within the text, in which a gift leads to receipt of a prediction to some future-life attainment. In particular, they echo the stories of chapter 1, yet they tend to downplay the role of a vow or aspiration, which is so obviously considered necessary in the stories of prediction to full buddhahood in that earlier decade. For further discussion of the relationship between aspiration, prediction and offering, see below.

Another intriguing feature of this series of predictions is worth noting. In only one of the ten stories does the person predicted to *pratyekabodhi* respond, and that is in AvŚ 24, where the aspirant is given a prediction by the past *buddha* Vipaśyin, causing him great delight. In none of the stories in which Śākyamuni Buddha makes a prediction — even those with an explicit aspiration — do we see the aspirant respond to their prediction. Indeed, we have no sense that they have even heard it. Instead, the *pratyekabuddha*-to-be recedes into the background, as the text moves on to praise the Buddha's impressive vision and magical qualities. This is the same as in chapter 1, where Śākyamuni predicts the future attainment of full buddhahood, but only in AvŚ 1 does the recipient of the prediction respond, in this case by increasing his support for the Buddha and his community.[40]

Because the *Avadānaśataka* stories in which individuals are predicted to future *pratyekabodhi* stop at the point of prediction, we do not see *how* this attainment comes about, nor what transformation occurs as a result of the attainment. As such, two important aspects familiar from other narratives about *pratyekabuddha*s are absent: (1) characters coming to terms with impermanence and the dangers of worldly life, and thereby attaining *pratyekabodhi*; (2) *pratyekabuddha*s who are powerful fields of merit (or demerit) and teachers who often teach through the performance of miracles. These two absences are worthy of further discussion, since they are present as echoes, and shed light on the rationale of the *Avadānaśataka*.

To begin with the second aspect, it is clear already that in these particular stories it is Śākyamuni Buddha who is the powerful field of merit, not *pratyekabuddha*s. It is also Śākyamuni Buddha who performs miracles that inspire faith. Six of the stories involve the Buddha performing miracles that humble or awe the *pratyekabuddha*s-to-be. These miraculous displays often involve the offering made to the Buddha, so for example one motif found in AvŚ 22 and 24 (as well as in AvŚ 7) is that a person throws a lotus over the Buddha (in 24 it is Vipaśyin Buddha), and it stays in the air above his head, grows to the size of a cartwheel, and follows the Buddha wherever he goes. In AvŚ 28, a gift of sandal leads to the whole city being suffused with the scent of it, and in AvŚ 30 not only is a group of revellers spontaneously made sober but their gift of blue lotuses creates a parasol or pavilion above the Buddha's head and suffuses the city with blue

Table 5 **Summary of the stories of chapter 3**

Story	**Summary**	**Miracle?**	**Aspiration?**	**Smile and prediction?**
21. Candana	Ruined *stūpa* explained: prince born of lotus, lotuses spring up at his feet. Seeing that they fade he becomes a *pratyekabuddha*. Past life: renouncer in time of Kāśyapa.	*Pratyekabuddha* displays miracles	No	No
22. The Lotus (*Padma*)	Little boy throws lotus at Buddha	Lotus floats above Buddha	No	Yes
23. The Disc (*Cakra*)	Woman promises golden disc to Nārāyaṇa if husband returns safe, but gives to Buddha instead.	No (but woman over-awed by Buddha's appearance)	No	Yes
24. Daśaśiras	Ruined *stūpa* explained: prince born of lotus, renounces and attains *pratyekabodhi*. Past life: offered lotus to Vipaśyin Buddha; seeing wife in pain of childbirth vowed to never be born from a woman again.	*Pratyekabuddha* displays miracles. Sub-story: lotus floats above Vipaśyin Buddha.	Sub-story: to never be born from a woman.	Sub-story: prediction from Vipaśyin Buddha.
25. Sūkṣmatva	Rich merchant becomes dissatisfied with wealth and makes big offering of food to Buddha and monks.	Teaching	Intention	Yes
26. Śītaprabha	Rich merchant becomes dissatisfied with wealth and makes big offering of food to Buddha and monks.	Teaching	Intention	Yes

Table 5 (continued)

Story	Summary	Miracle?	Aspiration?	Smile and prediction?
27. The Sailors (*Nāvikā*)	One boatman offers to transport Buddha and monks for free, and miracle causes him to attain stream-entry. Another is overawed and gives alms.	Buddha reaches further shore without a boat.	No	Yes (of second boatman)
28. Gandhamādana	Girl grinding sandal-paste sees Buddha and makes offering.	City filled with scent of sandal.	Yes	Yes
29. Nirmala	Gardener gives tooth-cleaning stick to Buddha.	Stick becomes full-grown tree.	Yes	Yes
30. Valgusvarā	Drunken revellers encounter the Buddha and give offerings.	Everyone immediately sober. Blue light/canopy.	Yes	Yes

light like sapphires. In AvŚ 29, a gifted tooth-cleaning stick, when discarded by the Buddha after use, turns into a fully grown banyan tree, complete with fruits and flowers, under which the Buddha then gives a sermon.

As in chapter 1, miracles not only result from offerings but also prompt them: In AvŚ 27, which opened this introduction, the Buddha crosses a river without a boat, shocking a ferryman into a great gift of alms. On other occasions the miracle takes the form of a sermon,[41] as in AvŚ 25 and 26, where it is a *dharma* teaching that leads to the humbling of the *pratyekabuddha*-to-be and the generation of an intention to achieve awakening. The audience is thus left with a profound appreciation of the power of the Buddha, and the amazing field of merit that he represents.[42] In combination with his illuminating smile and his ability to make predictions, we are left in no doubt of the Buddha's centrality, and his superiority to the beings with whom he is interacting. This is all rather similar to the first chapter of the text, in which Śākyamuni's miracle-working and ability to predict future *buddhas* is foregrounded over and above the future attainment itself.

Only the two stories of past *pratyekabuddhas* (21 and 24) break this pattern, since both of these *pratyekabuddhas* performed 'various miracles' (*vicitrāni prātihāryāni*) before disappearing through the sky. Equally vague mentions of miraculous displays are also found when *pratyekabuddhas* appear as fields of merit elsewhere in the text, so these two stories tap into a wider trope. These two same stories also offer rare opportunities to see how *pratyekabodhi* itself is achieved, an aspect entirely absent from the remaining eight stories.

In AvŚ 24, all we hear about the cause of *pratyekabodhi* is that the individual – a prince – felt that his father committed blameable acts, and so he asked to renounce, and was granted permission to do so. His subsequent attainment is overshadowed by the story of how, in a past life, he had made an offering to Vipaśyin Buddha and received a prediction. In that same past life he made a fervent aspiration (*praṇidhāna*) not to be born of a woman, after hearing his wife's screams during childbirth; this explains his birth from a lotus during his final lifetime. We do not learn much from this story about how *pratyekabodhi* is achieved, nor what might prompt the pursuit of it.

We find a richer narrative of the attainment in AvŚ 21, the other story of a past *pratyekabuddha*. He too is born from a lotus (though we are not told why) and adopted by the king. Wherever the boy goes, lotuses spring up beneath his feet. One day there is a festival in the city, and the citizens ask that the prince be allowed to join them, so that he can decorate the city with lotuses. He does so, but, as soon as the sun touches the lotuses, they wither. He realizes that this is just like the body. Right there he achieves the thirty-seven factors of awakening and becomes a *pratyekabuddha*. Gods come to give him monastic robes, and he then flies up into the sky and performs miracles. This story has much in common with *pratyekabuddha* narratives elsewhere in early Buddhist literature, where *prayekabuddha*s are often associated with signs of impermanence or of the need for solitude or renunciation.[43] Their awakening is direct and experiential, resulting from a shocking encounter, for example with a withered leaf, or a deep reflection on the dissatisfactory nature of worldly life. The fact that this story contains these wider resonances may explain its inclusion despite its failure to match the standard model of the chapter: namely, the formulaic prediction to future *pratyekabodhi* by the Buddha Śākyamuni.

The power of impermanence is also touched upon, though in a lesser way, in AvŚ 25 and 26, which are almost identical to one another. In both stories, a wealthy man realizes that his extensive possessions are of no comfort, that wealth is impermanent and changeable, as insubstantial as the moon reflected in water. He decides to give his wealth away, and invites the Buddha and his monks to receive alms. Having heard a sermon he becomes faithful and develops a firm intention. He is then predicted to future pratyekabuddhahood. Thus, although impermanence is important to the plot, it prompts almsgiving and the resulting aspiration and prediction, rather than the attainment of *pratyekabodhi* itself. Once again, the intervention of Śākyamuni is made central.

There is one final piece of evidence in the *Avadānaśataka* to suggest that the association of *pratyekabuddhas* with solitude, impermanence and renunciation may have been known but deliberately effaced. In AvŚ 28, the merit-making donor who receives a prediction to *pratyekabodhi* is a girl who grinds sandal-paste and then makes an offering of the sandal-paste and her bracelets. This story echoes a famous trope that is found in several Pāli *jātaka* tales and the *paccekabuddha* stories of the *Sutta Nipāta* commentary, as well as in an early Jain story of a *pratyekabuddha*. The trope concerns the image of two bracelets jangling noisily on the arm of a woman pounding sandal, prompting a man to reflect that solitude is better, like a silent single bracelet. The motif is particularly associated with the famous lineage of renouncing kings of Mithilā, who are said in both Jain and Buddhist traditions to be ideal kings who become ideal renouncers and, in most narratives, *pratyekabuddhas*.[44] I would suggest that AvŚ 28 preserves a slightly scrambled version of that motif, or perhaps a conscious allusion to it. The motif has, however, lost its association with being a prompt for renunciation, because the *pratyekabuddha* stories of this chapter of the *Avadānaśataka* are not interested in that theme.[45]

Although it seems evident that there is a lack of concern with the actual cause of the attainment of *pratyekabodhi* in these stories, perhaps this is not quite correct. Instead, what the text seems to be emphasizing is that the *cause* of the attainment is the powerful encounter with the Buddha (or, in the two cases of past *pratyekabuddhas*, a past *buddha*). As the Buddha explains in this formulaic passage from AvŚ 22, which is repeated with some variation in all eight stories of predicted future *pratyekabodhi*:

> This boy, Ānanda, through this root of virtue and the arising of this thought, and through this properly given gift, will not fall into misfortune for fifteen aeons. Having experienced the happiness of heavenly and human births, he will become a *pratyekabuddha* called Padmottara. This is the gift of one who has a faithful thought towards me.[46]

Thus the predictions given to *pratyekabuddhas*-to-be in the *Avadānaśataka* do not explain exactly how the person will eventually attain awakening, only that they will, and that this will be as a result of their act of merit, their aspiration and their gift; indeed, the three criteria are identical to those noted in the first chapter's stories of prediction to full buddhahood. In contrast to the first chapter, the predictions to pratyekabuddhahood omit the proximate criteria for full buddhahood, namely the six perfections and great compassion, and likewise omit the description of what means to be a full *buddha*, complete with the ten powers, four confidences and so on. The immediate cause and the attainment itself are not important: what matters is the powerful encounter with the Buddha that leads to his confirmation of the attainment.

As we can see, the *Avadānaśataka* shows little interest in the aspects that characterize stories of *pratyekabuddhas* elsewhere, such as their immediate and experiential awakening as a result of a vision or sign, or their career of solitary wandering. Instead, the stories are mainly concerned to present the relationship between the *pratyekabuddhas* and the Buddha, through the focus on humbling miracles, predictions and devotional interactions. In this, of course, they fit a broader pattern in the text. Now that we have explored each chapter in turn, it is worth making some general remarks about the ways in which miracles, aspirations and predictions function in these stories.

Miracles, offerings, aspirations and predictions

As should now be very clear, despite the different types of story contained in each of the four chapters under discussion, the stories share an important focus on miracles, offerings, aspirations and predictions, though not necessarily all at once. The different ways in which these elements feature in each of the decades is, I would argue, key to understanding the rationale of the text and its component parts, and will occupy our discussion for the remainder of this study.

Before we begin, I should outline what has thus far been implicit: namely, what I mean by the terms under discussion. I do not wish to provide a systematic study of the different terms for – and resonances of – these key features either within the *Avadānaśataka* or more broadly in early Buddhist literature, though such a project would certainly be worthwhile. My purpose in discussing these features, as will become clear, is to form an argument about the focus of these forty stories and their relationship to one another. Nonetheless, some brief definitions are in order.

By 'miracle' I mean an impressive display that is beyond the normal scope of human action, and which has the power to humble or convert – usually expressed by the statement that the audience attained faith (*prasāda*); some but not all of these displays are explicitly called *prātihārya*.[47] In these stories, miracles are generally performed by a *buddha*, most often Śākyamuni Buddha, and range from making people invisible to suffusing the whole cosmos with light to giving a powerful *dharma* teaching. While *pratyekabuddha*s and *arhat*s are also capable of miraculous displays, these are only rarely mentioned, and not narrated in any detail. The agency of the Buddha is not always prominent, with some miraculous occurrences seeming to happen naturally as a result of his power: for example, the many cases in which an offering flies over the Buddha's head and expands, transforms or suffuses a large space with light or fragrance. When non-awakened beings do something powerful that overcomes the normal laws of nature, this is said to be as a result of a powerful statement of truth, such as in the case of a disciple of the Buddha in AvŚ 9, and the Bodhisattva's miracles in AvŚ 31 and 37.

By 'offerings' I refer to any gift or act of service performed, usually for a *buddha*. It is these offerings – whether of food or flowers or a verse of praise – that tend to characterize an encounter with a *buddha*, either prompted by his awesome appearance or a humbling miracle. By 'aspirations' I refer to both formal *praṇidhāna* declarations — which I translate, following Rotman, as 'fervent aspirations', though others have called them 'vows' — and more general statements of intent.

'Predictions' are rather more easily identified, when a character — almost always in our case Śākyamuni Buddha — explains a future attainment. However, they still present some interesting issues, especially for a text that likely emerged within the Sarvāstivāda school, which holds that phenomena (*dharmas*) exist in all three time-modes. It is interesting that the term I have here translated as 'prediction', *vyākaraṇa*, more generally means 'explanation' and is used in relation to past events as well. In theory at least, there is no difference between the Buddha's vision of the past and his vision of the future. Nonetheless, it is notable that references to the future in this text — as in most others within early Buddhism — are vague and general.[48] Future attainments are noted, perhaps with one or two details such as the person's name, but no narrative is given for the future; stories are for the past. What, then, is a 'prediction' in this text? Is it simply confirmation of something by someone who can see the future as if it has already happened (because, in some sense, it already has)? Or does the Buddha actually *change* something through his prediction? This is something that is left open in the stories, though certainly we are led to believe that the encounter with the Buddha transforms the future, even if the subsequent prediction only confirms that this transformation has taken place.

Having briefly explored what we mean by miracles, offerings, aspirations and predictions, let us summarize the roles of these four features within our stories. In chapter 1 an offering and aspiration were presented as essential (with one exception where no gift was given) to the receipt of a prediction to future buddhahood; miracles, usually performed by Śākyamuni, featured in all but one story as a prompt for the necessary aspiration. In chapter 2, Śākyamuni-Buddha-to-be provides support for past *buddhas* in every story, but makes an aspiration only three times and never receives a prediction. Some sort of miracle is performed by past *buddhas* in four of the stories, and by Śākyamuni in four of the frame stories. In chapter 3, an act of service towards (usually) Śākyamuni Buddha results in a prediction to *pratyekabodhi*, sometimes following an aspiration. Śākyamuni causes a miraculous display in five of the stories, and in two more converts people through the miracle of the *dharma*. In an additional story a past *buddha* also performs a miracle to the same effect, and in two a *pratyekabuddha* is said to produce some generic miraculous displays, though these are not described.

In contrast to all three opening decades, chapter 4 is strikingly free from miracles and offerings, and only contains three aspirations and no predictions. Alternatively, we might say that the *nature* of the miracles and offerings is completely different in this decade. Instead of a person offering food or flowers to the Buddha and receiving a prediction in return, the Bodhisattva in these stories offers his last mouthful of food, or his wife, or his own body, either out of a general insistence on generosity or out of a desire for that rarest of things — in times of no Buddhism — namely, a single verse of the *dharma*. The miracles are not in the form of flowers growing to the size of cartwheels, or incense offerings pervading whole cities; rather, they take the form of the extraordinary — might we say miraculous? — commitment that the Bodhisattva demonstrates to Buddhist values. Even in the frame stories, in the time of Śākyamuni, miraculous occurrences are conspicuously absent, and instead the setting is pleasingly mundane: the Buddha sweeps his hermitage, offers to help a monk thread his needle, struggles to enable a novice to separate from his family, maintains friendly thoughts towards his nemesis Devadatta, and is held back on his walk by a line in the sand. He doesn't even manifest his magnificent illuminating smile.

The fourth decade is, therefore, different in several important ways to the other three chapters under consideration. (I might add that this decade also seems to me to be very different to the rest of the *Avadānaśataka*,[49] though I leave other scholars to discuss the role of miracles and offerings in the text more broadly.[50]) Yet it also shares an important feature with chapters 1–3: namely, a clear focus on the person of Śākyamuni Buddha. He, after all, is the recipient of the vast majority of offerings, and the predictor of almost every attainment (the one exception being AvŚ 24, where a past *buddha* predicts someone to *pratyekabodhi*). He is also the one who performs the majority of the miracles, miracles that range from visual displays to pertinent teachings to extraordinary acts of self-sacrifice.

That Śākyamuni lies at the heart of this complex network of offering, miracle, aspiration and prediction is further demonstrated by the trope of the Buddha's smile, which we have mentioned several times already and will now address in detail.

And then the Buddha smiled

In all ten of the opening stories of the *Avadānaśataka*, two of the second chapter (stories 17 and 20) and eight of the *pratyekabuddha* stories, the Buddha predicts someone to future awakening accompanied by a long formulaic passage about his magical smile.[51] This formula, the longest in the whole text by some considerable margin, does not appear after story 30, and so would appear to have special significance in connection to the stories of buddhahood and pratyekabuddhahood that we have been discussing.

The passage details how, when the Buddha smiles, rays of light emanate from him and pervade the hells, where they warm the cold hells and cool the hot hells, and project an image of the Buddha that inspires faith in the hell-beings such that they are immediately reborn in more fortunate circumstances. These rays of light also travel through the heaven realms shouting out 'Impermanent! Suffering! Empty! Not-self!' and inciting the heaven-beings to strive towards awakening. The rays of light then re-enter the Buddha's body, and the place in which they do so indicates what sort of prediction he is about to make.[52]

The various options for prediction, and the relevant body parts into which the rays of light return, are listed as follows:

> If the Blessed One wishes to explain past actions, they disappear into the Blessed One's back; if he wishes to explain future actions, they vanish into his front. If he wishes to predict arising in a hell, they disappear into the soles of his feet, while if he wants to predict arising as an animal, they enter his heel, and if he wants to predict arising as a hungry ghost, they vanish into his big toe, and if he desires to predict arising as a human, they disappear into his knee. If he wishes to predict rule as an armed wheel-turning king [*balacakravartin*], they enter the palm of his left hand, while if he wishes to predict rule as a wheel-turning king [*cakravartin*], they disappear into the palm of his right hand. If he wishes to predict arising as a god, they vanish into his navel. If he wishes to predict awakening as a disciple [*śrāvaka*], they enter his mouth, while if he wants to predict awakening as a *pratyekabuddha*, they vanish into the circle of hair between his eyebrows, and if he wants to predict unsurpassed and perfect full buddhahood, they disappear into his *uṣṇīṣa*.[53]

Despite these many stated options, in the *Avadānaśataka* we only see two of these realized.[54] In all ten stories of the first chapter, the predictions are to full buddhahood, so the rays of light enter the Buddha's *uṣṇīṣa*. In the eight stories of the third chapter in which the formula occurs (22, 23, 25, 26, 27, 28, 29 and 30), the prediction is to pratyekabuddhahood, and so the light enters his *ūrṇā*, or the circle of hair between his eyebrows. Likewise in AvŚ 17 the prediction is to pratyekabuddhahood, while the prediction in AvŚ 20 is to full buddhahood. Thus the smile formula is only used when the Buddha predicts to full buddhahood or pratyekabuddhahood.

There is another limitation to the formula as well: it is always related to Śākyamuni Buddha and a question-and-answer exchange with his close follower Ānanda. Although one assumes that the same smile may (indeed must) be possible for other *buddhas* too, it is notable that, in story 24, in which the past *buddha* Vipaśyin predicts someone to pratyekabuddhahood, this is done without a glorious smile or the rays of magical light that emerge from it, despite this formula featuring heavily in the *pratyekabuddha* chapter overall.

There is another lengthy formulaic passage in the *Avadānaśataka* that also speaks of the Buddha's great vision and compassion, and which is also only ever used in relation to Śākyamuni despite being presented as something true of all *buddhas*. The formula, which appears fourteen times in the text,[55] eight of these in the first four chapters,[56] tells of how there is nothing that *buddhas* do not see and know. Being greatly compassionate and endowed with an impressively long numerical list of qualities, they look around to find those in need of help.[57] The passage often leads to the Buddha intervening in some difficult situation, for example rescuing merchants, or else alerts the Buddha to an opportunity to teach or convert. Even its five appearances in chapter 2, a chapter in which the focus is at first glance on stories of Śākyamuni's past-life encounters with *buddhas* of the past, are in the frame narrative in the time of Śākyamuni's own buddhahood, and refer to his magnificent qualities. Thus, it is not only the smile that is *theoretically* true of all *buddhas*, but *actually* presented in praise of Śākyamuni Buddha.

We might therefore ask: what do these two lengthy formulae achieve in the text? Given that the smile formula in particular is incredibly long and repeated in story after story, there must be some intention behind its inclusion, and I would argue that its presence should prompt us to think about the purpose of the text as a whole. Whether or not the formulae of the *Avadānaśataka* are the result of an oral composition is hard to ascertain, but they would certainly appear to be related to a tradition of oral recitation or performance of the text. For audiences of such an oral presentation of the stories, the formulae might be viewed as something like refrains, building familiarity with key moments of the text, and perhaps even providing opportunities for audience participation.

In particular, the lengthy tour of the cosmos provided in the smile formula prompts us to consider the visual impact of the text's recitation. I would argue that this formula provides a visual meditation for the text's author, reciter and audience. Let us pause to imagine the effects on the audience of the passage, of visualizing the rays of light and their progress through the cosmos, symbolizing the compassionate teaching of the Buddha before re-entering his magnificent body and prompting a prediction to future awakening. This isn't extraneous narrative or textual padding; it is a core part of the experience of the text, and its power increases with every repetition. Indeed, perhaps the audience do not only *visualize* the light of the Buddha permeating the cosmos; perhaps they even *make it so* through the recitation.

Not only does the formula make manifest the Buddha's power in the cosmos, it also represents his supernormal vision. His smile is literally beaming, but it is also a *knowing smile*. As such, Śākyamuni's power to see — and create — future *buddhas* is repeatedly underscored, as is his ability to transcend the human realm. To smile is human, but to have that smile set off such an amazing and transformational series of events is superhuman. That this formula is associated solely with Śākyamuni Buddha emphasizes the centrality of the Buddha as linchpin around which the whole of our Buddhist experience revolves; the same might be said of the function of the related formula detailing the Buddha's ability to see those in need of help, for although the list is of generic *buddha*-qualities they are made manifest in the person of Śākyamuni.

Indeed, both the smile formula and that about the Buddha's ability to know when people are in need of help might be labelled 'devotional', in the sense that they function to praise the Buddha and inspire or strengthen faith in his amazing qualities. Other formulae also share this focus, in particular the passage that opens every single one of the 100 stories, which lists the many beings — wealthy and powerful humans, gods and spirit-deities — who worship the Buddha. Indeed, an encounter with the person of the Buddha, repeatedly said to be 'adorned with the thirty-two marks of a great man and the eighty secondary marks, his body shining, arrayed with light that extended a fathom, radiance in excess of a thousand suns, like a living mountain of jewels, handsome in his entirety',[58] usually results in great faith for the person *within* the story, as might also be expected for an audience outside it.

This latter description of the Buddha's impressive physical form is used not only of Śākyamuni but also other *buddhas*. Likewise, each *buddha* of the past is introduced with a repeated refrain detailing that he is:

> a *tathāgata*, an *arhat*, fully and perfectly awakened, perfected in knowledge and conduct, a well-farer, an unsurpassed knower of the world, a tamer of people who should be tamed, a teacher of gods and humans, a *buddha*, a blessed one[59]

The restriction of repeated lists of virtues to Śākyamuni alone is therefore not universal in the text. Neither can we suggest that formulae are always — or even usually — used to praise exalted beings, for we also find formulaic descriptions of wealthy householders, virtuous kings, pregnancy and child-rearing. Nonetheless, the observation that the two longest repeated passages in the *Avadānaśataka* concern the Buddha's qualities, and are exclusively used for Śākyamuni, does indicate something of the value placed on him by the text. And these forty stories in particular seem to build up a picture of Śākyamuni Buddha as someone decidedly unique.

Structure of the *Avadānaśataka*

The *Avadānaśataka* exhibits a certain logic to its structure. The first story opens with 'the whole world filled with the glory of the Blessed One's recent awakening'[60] while the last begins with the Buddha's death and sets its main events in the time of Aśoka, shifting the time frame of the narrative several hundred years forwards. The last four chapters as a whole concern *arhats* of varying kinds, while the two chapters that precede these concern types of rebirth: as *pretas* (hungry ghosts) in the fifth, and among the *devas* (gods) in the sixth. The first four chapters, as we have seen, address buddhahood and pratyekabuddhahood, forming a unit of their own, and also ending — in story 40 — with the time of the Buddha's *parinirvāṇa*, in this case with a story about the conversion of his last personal disciple, Subhadra. (Curiously, AvŚ 40 also contains a reference to a character called Aśoka, though here this is a disciple and nephew of Kāśyapa Buddha, who is helped by a deity living in an *aśoka* tree who is identified as Subhadra in a past life. Whether or not this is a deliberate echo of story 100 is hard to determine.)

How do these different chapters relate to one another and to the collection as a whole? Once again, viewing Śākyamuni as a central figure helps the composition of the text to make more sense. An important observation is worth underlining in this regard: the *Avadānaśataka* stories are not only about the attainment of awakening or rebirth. Rather, they are also about the karmic networks or meritorious encounters between various types of being through an incredibly long timescale. In the first four decades in particular, we can see a picture building up of how the Buddha relates to other *buddhas* and to *pratyekabuddhas* past and future. It is these relationships, I argue, and the desire for Śākyamuni Buddha to emerge as the linchpin, that determine the placement of the chapters in relation to one another. Taking each decade in turn will help to illuminate this further.

In the first decade, every story involves a person encountering Śākyamuni Buddha, who smiles and predicts them to future buddhahood. The Buddha is, in some sense, the source of their awakening, even though they will become full and complete *buddhas* without a teacher. His predictions begin, in the opening story of the collection, shortly after his own achievement of full buddhahood. All the predictions involve Śākyamuni Buddha's magnificent cosmos-illuminating smile.

This pattern is in some sense reversed in the second decade, where every story involves Śākyamuni-Buddha-to-be (not once called the Bodhisattva) encountering a past *buddha*. However, though he resolves to future buddhahood in three stories, he never receives a prediction. This may be because these stories are understood to be early on in his long multi-life career, before the series of predictions known from other texts, or it may be because receiving a prediction was not seen as a necessary component of his encounters. Either way, instead of receiving a prediction, in two stories (17 and 20) Śākyamuni *makes* a prediction (accompanied by his beaming smile), once to buddhahood and once to pratyekabuddhahood, during the part of the story set in the narrative present of his life and community. Thus, the Buddha is established as part of an auspicious lineage, but without showing dependence on the other *buddhas* for his own achievement of buddhahood. He benefits from the merit of the encounter, but then goes on to independently achieve awakening and predict others to that attainment.

In the third decade, the majority of stories involve someone encountering Śākyamuni Buddha and being predicted to pratyekabuddhahood; thus again the Buddha is shown as in some sense the source of their awakening, even though their type of awakening is achieved without a teacher. The two stories of past *pratyekabuddhas* are similarly framed by stories of their own past-life encounters with past *buddhas*, and in one case this involves the only prediction in these stories *not* to emanate from Śākyamuni: Vipaśyin Buddha predicts future *pratyekabodhi*, though without the beaming smile that we have come to expect from such encounters. None of the *pratyekabuddhas* is fully independent; their attainment is dependent on an encounter with a more accomplished being: namely, a full *buddha*.

In the fourth decade, the majority of stories feature the Bodhisattva exhibiting great virtue in a time without Buddhism. His independence and the strength of his virtue and commitment are demonstrated, as he willingly gives up his life for the sake of a verse of the *dharma*, or exudes kindness towards his parents as they murder him. He is truly extraordinary. I would argue, therefore, that the fourth decade is intended to be the crown of these first four chapters, since here the Buddha and his past-life self are completely independent from other awakened beings. As we have discussed, the acts that he undertakes in this chapter are significantly different to the simple exchanges of chapters 1 through 3, and the focus is on his own deeds; there are no miracles, no conversions and no smiling predictions.

This argument, of course, assumes the fourth decade to be unique in a positive way, rather than an outlier or misfit. However, it is notable that this chapter of the text was excluded from the various verse *avadānamālā* texts that drew on the *Avadānaśataka* several centuries later. The *Kalpadrumāvadānamālā*, for example, after beginning with the *Aśokāvadāna* that forms AvŚ 100, recounts the first stories of each of the decades of the *Avadānaśataka* except the fourth, followed by the second stories of each of the decades except the fourth. The *Ratnāvadānamālā* broadly continues this pattern, taking the third and fourth stories from each decade in turn, but again skipping over the fourth decade of the *Avadānaśataka* altogether.[61] These and similar approaches suggest that, by the time of the *avadānamālās*, the stories of AvŚ 31–40 were considered to be so different that they did not qualify as *avadānas*. Nonetheless, acknowledging their different character, more aligned to 'classical' *jātaka* literature, should not excuse us from trying to understand their place in the *Avadānaśataka*.

Reflecting on the structural rationale on the text is also helpful when considering the inclusion and positioning of the stories about *pratyekabuddhas*. One of the challenges of the category of *pratyekabuddhas* for early Buddhism is that they appear to be quite independent; indeed, I would even go so far as to argue that 'independent *buddha*' is probably a better translation of the term than 'solitary *buddha*' since they are rarely actually solitary. After all, what defines *pratyekabuddhas* is that they realize the truth independently of a teacher, in a time of no Buddhism, like full *buddhas*. They therefore offer a potential challenge to the Buddha, whose realization is otherwise presented as foundational for the Buddhist community.

Thus by presenting *pratyekabuddhas* as dependent on the Buddha (or on past *buddhas*), the *Avadānaśataka* stories find room for this category but neutralize it by showing that only full *buddhas* can be the source of awakening.[62] *Pratyekabuddhas*, we learn, can only achieve what they do because of a past-life devotional interaction with a full *buddha*. Indeed, we only come to know about their future attainment due to the magnificent display of an illuminating smile by Śākyamuni Buddha himself. As such, their chapter of the text is nestled among three other chapters about the better type of buddhahood, and thrown into sharp relief by the magnificent past-life deeds of Śākyamuni Bodhisattva in the fourth chapter. There is only one truly 'independent *buddha*' in this text, and that is Śākyamuni.[63]

It is worth noting that the inferiority of *pratyekabuddhas* is also reinforced elsewhere in the *Avadānaśataka*. Several other stories in the collection concern people's past-life encounters with *pratyekabuddhas* and the karmic merit or demerit they earn as a result of these encounters. In six of the tales in the last decades of the text, the individuals who have such an encounter specify in their resulting aspiration that they wish to have a teacher 'even more distinguished' (*prativiśiṣṭataraṃ*) than the *pratyekabuddha* they have just met. Their aspiration is fulfilled in a later lifetime, when they become followers of the Buddha.[64]

Likewise, Śākyamuni Buddha also features elsewhere in the collection, not least as the teacher of the many *arhats* in stories 61–100. Other *buddhas* also appear, for the *arhats* tend to plant the roots of their attainment in the time of past *buddhas*. For example, all ten of the Śākyans of whom we hear in chapter 7 served the *stūpa* of the past *buddha* Vipaśyin in some way, while many other attainers of arhatship formerly served or followed past *buddhas* including Kāsyapa, Krakucchanda and Kanakamuni.[65] The implication, of course, is that *arhats* achieve awakening in part as a result of encountering *buddhas* in the past, and even entering their monastic communities. In some cases, *arhats* planted their virtuous roots — at least in part — through an encounter with a *pratyekabuddha* (see AvŚ 80, 88, 89, 90, 96, 98 and 99; in AvŚ 94, 96, 98 and 99 the negative consequences of mistreating a *pratyekabuddha* are also explored). However, in all of these cases they are said to have renounced under Kāśyapa Buddha later on as well, suggesting once again a sense of insufficiency in the person of a *pratyekabuddha*. In two cases (AvŚ 81 and 97), we find past lives of *arhats* in which they encounter Śākyamuni Bodhisattva. Indeed, in some stories, particularly those in chapter 9, the *arhats* under discussion have had multiple past lives in the times of different significant figures, sometimes in addition to other karmicly potent past experiences without any 'special' beings present.[66]

This complex web that is built up in the text as a whole, in which different aspirants to different types of awakening have a variety of transformative encounters with one another, is also well demonstrated in story 40, which closes our portion of the text. Here we find Śākyamuni Buddha on his deathbed, converting his last personal disciple Subhadra, who achieves arhatship as a result and, shortly thereafter – and before the Buddha – enters complete *nirvāṇa*. The Buddha explains events through two past-life stories: his own past life as a deer who saved his herd, last of all the young deer now reborn as Subhadra; and Subhadra's past life as a tree-deity who helped a nephew and disciple of Kāśyapa Buddha reach awakening just in time, before the final *nirvāṇa* of Kāśyapa. It is in this story that we finally find mention of Śākyamuni's prediction to future buddhahood by a past *buddha*, but only indirectly: the tree-deity resolves to achieve awakening as the last personal disciple of the person that Kāśyapa Buddha has predicted to future buddhahood as Śākyamuni. What we seem to have here is a transition into later chapters of the text, from the focus on buddhahood that has occupied stories 1–40. To add further complexity to all the layers of interactions here, between *buddhas* and *arhats* and aspiring *arhats* and aspiring *buddhas*, the tree-deity belongs to an *aśoka* tree, and Kāśyapa's nephew is also called Aśoka, perhaps a deliberate echo of story 100, with its tale of the great Buddhist patron the emperor Aśoka.

While this web of encounters is certainly not limited to stories 1–40 – indeed, it is amplified and extended as the text progresses – the construction of this web begins with the chapters under discussion in this book. As such, *buddhas* and *pratyekabuddhas* are set up as powerful fields of merit (and demerit) ready for the stories later in the collection. In addition, Śākyamuni Buddha is established as the revealer and navigator of this vast web, as well as a central actor within it. This status of Śākyamuni as having the same attainment as others yet somehow standing above them is summed up neatly in AvŚ 19, where he enters the town surrounded by his monks, and is described as:

> restrained and surrounded by restrained people, peaceful and surrounded by the peaceful, freed and surrounded by the freed, calmed and surrounded by the calm, tamed and surrounded by the tamed, an *arhat* surrounded by *arhat*s, dispassionate and surrounded by the dispassionate, an agent of faith and surrounded by agents of faith, like a bull among a herd of cattle, like an elephant among a group of young elephants, like a lion among a group of predators, like a goose among a flock of geese, like a *suparṇa* among a flock of birds, like a sage surrounded by a group of students, like a good horse among a herd of horses, like a hero among a group of warriors, like a guide among a band of travellers, like a caravan leader among a caravan of merchants, like a guildsman among a group of city-dwellers, like the ruler of a castle among a group of courtiers, like a wheel-turning monarch surrounded by his thousand sons, like the moon among the collection of stars, like the sun surrounded by its thousand rays, like Dhṛtarāṣṭra among a troop of *gandharvas*, like Virūḍa among a group of *kumbhāṇḍas*, like Virūpākṣa surrounded by a troop of *nāgas*, like Dhanada among a group of *yakṣas*, like Vemacitri surrounded by a group of antigods, like Śakra among the group of thirty gods, like Brahmā surrounded by Brahmā's retinue, like the tranquil ocean, like a watery thundercloud, like a lord of elephants free from rut.[67]

As this passage makes clear, the Buddha's disciples may be equal to him in some sense, yet he still stands apart. We might make the same observation about the position of Śākyamuni in relation to other *buddhas* and to *pratyekabuddhas*: he is the most impressive example of his 'type', a leader and a central figure. To paraphrase George Orwell's famous line from *Animal Farm*, all awakened beings are equal, but some are more equal than others.

Many *buddhas*, many Buddhisms

What are the implications of this perspective on buddhahood for the history of Buddhist thought more broadly? The ways in which different Buddhist communities reconciled their devotion towards the Buddha who founded their community with the existence of other awakened beings – including the wider category of buddhahood – expose many of the key debates and disagreements that led to the divergence into different groups and movements. Most obvious among these developments was of course the Mahāyāna, or 'Great Vehicle', which scholars tend now to agree emerged as a collection of movements across different monastic lineages.[68] Despite the many different expressions of early Mahāyāna thought and practice, a key idea was the rejection of the three paths to awakening. Instead, for the Mahāyāna, the only real form of awakening is full and complete buddhahod (*samyaksambodhi*). As such, the *Avadānaśataka* is clearly not Mahāyāna, since it acknowledges all three paths as valid. Nonetheless, the idea that the other paths are dependent on full buddhahood through a multi-life series of devotional encounters exposes a shared tension over how the Buddha (and full buddhahood more generally) relates to other forms of awakened being.

A similar tension over how the Buddha relates to other awakened beings can also be found in other early Buddhist literature. For example, the *Apadāna* of the Theravāda *Khuddaka Nikāya* explores similar themes to the *Avadānaśataka*, especially through many stories of monks and nuns planting virtuous roots through encounters with past *buddhas*.[69] The commentary to this text also records the idea that *pratyekabuddhas* are able to achieve their particular form of awakening only because of past-life encounters with full *buddhas*. Indeed, this network of encounters with the Buddha at the centre would appear to be a key aspect of other members of the early *avadāna* genre too, such as the *Mahāvastu* and the *Divyāvadāna*. While non-Mahāyāna schools, most notably the Theravāda, accept that arhatship may be the mainstream goal, all early Buddhist groups lauded the Buddha as superior. He was, after all, the realizer of the *dharma*, the founder of the monastic community, and the supreme teacher who helped (and continues to help) countless beings across the flood of rebirth.[70]

While there is general agreement that a full and complete *buddha* is superior to *arhat*s and *pratyekabuddha*s, we see more variety when we look at the ways in which Śākyamuni Buddha in particular is portrayed in relation to past *buddhas*. Here, the *Avadānaśataka* seems to be taking a more unique approach, since it shows little interest in the Buddha's repeated aspirations at the feet of increasingly standardized lists of past *buddha*s, as recalled in other early Buddhist texts of varying affiliations. Neither does it show Śākyamuni to be essentially identical to past *buddha*s, as in, for example, the famous discussion of six past *buddha*s in the *Mahāpadāna Sutta* of the *Dīgha Nikāya*. Instead, the *Avadānaśataka* presents Śākyamuni Buddha as largely independent. He has served past *buddha*s, but this tells us more about his ability to recognize and respect them than it does about his interest in becoming one himself. A range of other people make aspirations and receive predictions at his feet, but Śākyamuni requires no such encounters. As well as being the source of predictions, he is the supreme worker of wonders, and converts and teaches through his amazing powers and presence. Here again we recall the fact that the *Avadānaśataka* emerged in a region and time period that saw the rise in Mahāyāna movements with their multiplicity of *buddha*s and *bodhisattvas*. This collection of narrative shares the general position that buddhahood is supreme, but defends the case for the uniqueness of Śākyamuni Buddha.

One Buddha, many lessons

As I have highlighted in this introduction, if there is one clear result of reading *Avadānaśataka* stories 1–40, it is awe at the magnificence of the Buddha. Yet one of the things that makes him so magnificent, as we are repeatedly reminded in the text, is his amazing teaching ability. As such, it is no surprise to find that, within the buddhological framework of the *Avadānaśataka*, there are multiple teachings, many of them of continuing relevance for the text's audience. We hear stories of people suddenly struck by the impermanence that characterizes existence; of greedy merchants and mean ferrymen; of young girls aspiring to buddhahood; of young boys tortured by the fear of death; of kings determined to support *buddhas*; of men and women overawed by the miracle-working of the Buddha. The tales remind us to be wary of possessions, to value friendship, to focus on helping others rather than ourselves, to keep our promises, to respect our parents, to give gifts and make merit, and above all to honour the teacher — the Buddha — and live in reliance on him.

It is time to enter the rich pastures that make up *Avadānaśataka* 1–40. I can only hope that readers will get as much pleasure and edification from the text as I have.

Part A Notes

1 *aham api bhavanto nāvikaḥ pūrvam āsam mayā hi rāganadīpatito nandas tāritaḥ dveṣārṇavapatito 'ṅgulimālaḥ mānārṇavapatito mānastabdho māṇavaḥ mohārṇavapatita uruvilvakāśyapas tāritaḥ na ca me tarapaṇyaṃ yācitā iti* (AvŚ 27; Speyer 1902: 148).

2 Stories about both of these monks, and the others mentioned in the Buddha's retort, are well known across a variety of Buddhist texts. For a particularly extensive and elegant version of Nanda's story, see Aśvaghosa's *Saundarananda* poem from perhaps the second century CE, translated in Covill 2007.

3 On *pratyekabuddhas* as teachers, see Appleton 2019b. In the *Avadānaśataka* the role of *pratyekabuddhas* is usually to inspire faith and prompt an aspiration on the part of a would-be *arhat*.

4 For a translation and study of this chapter, see Rotman 2020.

5 Dating, as with many early Indian texts, is uncertain, but the case made in Demoto 2006: 209–12, based on revised dates for the translations into Chinese and Tibetan, is convincing. The revisions by the Mūlasarvāstivāda were largely limited to changes to the final story of the text (which does not concern us here) and the insertion of various additional teachings extracted from *āgama* texts. The original attribution to the Sarvāstivāda is harder to determine, and some scholars suggest the *Avadānaśataka* is largely dependent on the *Mūlasarvāstivāda Vinaya* so must have always belonged to that school: see the helpful summary of evidence in Muldoon-Hules 2017, 179–86, and the discussion in Formigatti 2016.

6 We have a fairly substantial set of scriptures thanks to Chinese translations and Central Asian manuscript finds, though the history of the school's many branches, and its relation to other schools, is still the subject of debate. For a thorough exploration of Sarvāstivāda teachings, texts and history, see Willemen, Dessein and Cox 1998.

7 Its name, which means the 'Root Sārvāstivāda', indicates that it may be a subgroup of the Sarvāstivāda that self-identifies as more authentic. However, its separate *vinaya* suggests otherwise. See discussion in Willemen, Dessein and Cox 1998.

8 The relationship between these texts is helpfully summarized in Muldoon Hules 2017: 179–86, while Rotman (2008: 15–30) also addresses the role of *avadānas* for the Mūlasarvāstivāda school, with a particular focus on the *Divyāvadāna*. Panglung (1981) provides an invaluable summary of the stories of the *Mūlasarvāstivāda Vinaya*.

9 These are so prevalent that Feer, in his French translation, removed them all to a numbered appendix. While I too have had to abbreviate the longest formula (that of the Buddha's smile, which appears twenty times) in the translation in this volume, in general I would argue that these

passages are worth preserving in full, as part of the character of the text and a hint at its performative context; see further discussion below. On the possible oral composition of the text, see Collett 2006.

10 As John Strong noted in his 1979 article, it is important not to make too much of this distinction, for two reasons: future predictions are to buddhahood and pratyekabuddhahood, which can only be attainments of the narrative future, since neither can exist in the narrative present of Śākyamuni Buddha; and notions of time in Sarvāstivāda thought tend not to place much emphasis on the distinction between past, present and future (Strong 1979: 228–9). As will become clear during this study, the centrality of Śākyamuni — expressed temporally as well as in other ways — appears nonetheless to be important to the text's rationale.

11 *anenāhaṃ kuśalamūlena cittotpādena deyadharmaparityāgena cāndhe loke anāyake apariṇāyake buddho bhūyāsam atīrṇānāṃ satvānāṃ tārayitā amuktānāṃ mocayitā anāśvastānām āśvāsayitā aparinirvṛtānāṃ parinirvāpayiteti* (AvŚ 1; Speyer 1902: 4 [and also AvŚ 2, 4, 7, 8, 9, 10]). Story 5 is lost from the Sanskrit. In story 6 there is an additional phrase — *yathaivāhaṃ bhagavatā anuttareṇa vaidyarājena cikitsita evam aham apy anāgate 'dhvani* (Speyer 1902: 32), 'just as the Blessed One, unsurpassed king of doctors, healed me, may I too in a future time . . .' — between *deyadharmaparityāgena* and the remainder of the formula. This formula also appears in story 20, when Śākyamuni Buddha encounters another aspirant to buddhahood.

12 In one case, AvŚ 2, it is a 'she'. The *Avadānaśataka* does provide some limited gender balance, with stories of women predicted to buddhahood and pratyekabuddhahood (though in both cases becoming male before that attainment) and ten tales of women attaining arhatship. On the latter, see Muldoon-Hules 2017.

13 *anena kuśalamūlena cittotpādena deyadharmaparityāgena ca trikalpāsaṃkhyeyasamudānītāṃ bodhiṃ samudānīya mahākaruṇāparibhāvitāḥ ṣaṭ pāramitāḥ paripūrya X nāma samyaksaṃbuddho bhaviṣyati daśabhir balaiś caturbhir vaiśāradyais tribhir āveṇikaiḥ smṛtyupasthānair mahākaruṇayā ca / ayam asya deyadharmo yo mamāntike cittaprasāda iti* (AvŚ 1; Speyer 1902: 7). Stories 2 and 4 have *cittasyābhiprasāda* instead of *cittaprasāda*, and 9 omits *deyadharmaparityāgena* in all but one of Speyer's manuscripts, and hence in his edition, perhaps because it is the only story in which the person receiving the prediction has not in fact made a gift, as discussed below. The formula also appears in AvŚ 20 when Śākyamuni predicts someone else to buddhahood. Translating the final phrase is tricky, and it is possible that the implication is that the attainment of *bodhi* is the 'gift' (*deyadharma*) received by the person with the faithful mind as a result of their meritorious deeds; my translation attempts to retain the ambiguity.

14 *tasmāt tarhi bhikṣava evaṃ śikṣitavyaṃ yac chāstāraṃ satkariṣyāmo gurukariṣyāmo mānayiṣyāmaḥ pūjayiṣyāmaḥ śāstāraṃ satkṛtya gurukṛtya mānayitvā pūjayitvopaniśritya vihariṣyāmaḥ ity evaṃ vo bhikṣavaḥ śikṣitavyam*

(AvŚ 1; Speyer 1902: 7). This formula is also found at the end of stories 11–20, as well as 21, 29, 35, 38, 53 and 54.

15 I try to give translations of names to demonstrate the frequent association between characters' names and their deeds. These are indicative only; indeed, in this case the *bhadra* could be translated in a number of ways, including 'fortunate' or even 'rich', while *pūrṇa* also encompasses a range of meanings.

16 AvŚ 5 is missing from all Sanskrit sources, though it is present in the Tibetan and Chinese. A French translation of the Tibetan is included in Feer 1979 [1879], while an English translation of the Chinese is found in Fa Chow 1945: 37–41. An English translation of the Tibetan will be appended to Fiordalis forthcoming. The story recounts how a poor man offered the Buddha some yarn with which the Buddha then mended his robe, which spontaneously presented holes. The poor man, called Soma, was then predicted to buddhahood.

17 The exceptions are AvŚ 57 and 59. In AvŚ 57 the story nonetheless ends with a teaching from the Buddha.

18 Here the term used is *satyopayācana*, which is not readily translated as Act of Truth, though the mechanism is the same as when Pāli characters perform a *saccakiriyā* (on which, see Kong 2012). The power of a declaration of truth is also used in AvŚ 31, when the king (the Buddha-to-be) declares his intention to become a curative fish: here the act is not given a specific term either, but the king declares *satyena satyavacanena* and later *satyena satyavākyena* – 'by this truth, by this declaration of truth'. Likewise, in AvŚ 37 the Bodhisattva hare brings rain through a true utterance. On the connection between Acts of Truth and miracles, see also Fiordalis 2008: 101–7.

19 See note 13.

20 *yan na śakyaṃ suśikṣitena karmakāreṇa karmāntevāsinā vā kartum yathāpi tad buddhānāṃ buddhānubhāvena devatānāṃ ca devānubhāvena* (AvŚ 2; Speyer 1902: 9).

21 For more on the importance of conversion in these ten stories, see Fifield 2008.

22 For a study of the characterization of Śakra across Buddhist, Jain and Brahmanical Hindu narrative, see Appleton 2017: ch. 2.

23 For the *Buddhavaṃsa*, see Jayawickrama 1974; Horner 1975. For the parallel portions of the *Mahāvastu*, see Senart 1882–97: vol. 1, 46ff., vol. 3, 224–50; Jones 1949–56: vol. 1, 39ff., vol. 3, 219–39. Tournier (2017) provides French translations of the relevant passages of the *Mahāvastu* as well as a thorough study thereof. For the Gandhāran text, see Salomon 2018: 265–94.

24 The term is not used in this chapter, but does feature in AvŚ 31, 36, 37 and 38; see below.

25 The *buddhas* are called Bhāgīratha, Brahmā, Candana, Candra, Indradamana, Ratnaśaila, Prabodhana, Indradhvaja, Kṣemaṃkara and

Pūrṇa. Of these, the *Mahāvastu* pays some attention to Indradhvaja, and Candana and Bhāgīratha are mentioned in the same text's long list of *buddhas* before Dīpaṅkara, which directly follows the account of Indradhvaja (Senart 1882–97: vol. 3, 226–40). The names are not found in lists of *buddhas* since Dīpaṅkara, and hence are not in the Gandhāran *Many Buddhas Sūtra* nor the *Buddhavaṃsa*. On these lists, see Tournier 2017: ch. 2, especially the helpful comparative tables on pp. 158 and 180. This may indicate that the stories are intended to take us back to times before these *buddhas*.

26 While the structure, with a frame story in the 'present' of the Buddha and a past-life in a time of no *buddhas*, is similar to the *Jātakatthavaṇṇanā*, the contents have little overlap, for the stories are more aligned with *avadāna* and northern *jātaka* repertoires. For example, there is substantial overlap with Haribhaṭṭa's *Jātakamālā* (Khoroche 2017): the past-life stories of AvŚ 31, 32, 37 and 40 (including the embedded story of Subhadra) are found in Haribhaṭṭa's text. Āryaśūra's *Jātakamālā* (Khoroche 1989), by contrast, is closer to the Pāli tradition in terms of its range of stories and has little in common with the Avadānaśataka; the stories of Śibi and the Hare, which form the only potential overlap, are very different in each text.

27 This type of deed forms a subgenre in the *Mahāvastu*, in which it is associated with the idea that, during the third stage of the path towards buddhahood (the third *bhūmi*), the Bodhisattva will do anything to access even a single verse of wisdom (*subhāṣitā gāthā*): Senart 1882–97: vol. 1, 91–5; Jones 1949–56: vol. 1, 72–5. A version of the story of Surūpa, which forms AvŚ 35, is found here.

28 The role of tester-of-virtues is one he occupies in Jain and Brahminical Hindu narrative too; see Appleton 2017: ch. 2.

29 Even in the Pāli tradition, where this idea came to dominate conceptions of the *jātaka* genre, it is not actually prominent in the early sources; see Appleton 2010: esp. ch. 5.

30 The six perfections are mentioned elsewhere in the *Avadānaśataka* as part of formulaic lists of the qualities of buddhahood, but they are not discussed.

31 Instead the text clearly considers them *avadānas*. For a discussion on why we might still usefully consider them to be *jātakas* as well as *avadānas*, or as a special subset of *jātaka-avadānas*, see Appleton 2015.

32 *kim atra bhikṣava āścaryaṃ yad idānīṃ tathāgato vigatarāgo vigatadveṣo vigatamohaḥ parimukto jātijarāvyādhimaraṇaśokaparidevaduḥkhadaurmanasyopāyāsebhyaḥ sarvajñaḥ sarvākārajñaḥ sarvajñānajñeyavaśiprāpto yat tv aham atīte 'dhvani sarāgaḥ sadveṣaḥ samoho 'parimukto jātijarāvyādhimaraṇaśokaparidevaduḥkhadaurmanasyopāyāsebhyo . . .* (AvŚ 34; Speyer 1902: 183). Versions of this passage also occur in AvŚ 33, 36, 37, 38 and 40.

33 Support for parents is a more important monastic value than we might assume, however: see Clarke 2014 for a discussion of family-friendly Buddhist monasticism.
34 *ko loke puṇyakāma* (AvŚ 34; Speyer 1902: 182–3).
35 *anena te pāṇinā trīṇi kalpāsaṃkhyeyāni dānaśīlakṣāntivīryadhyānaprajñā upacitāḥ* (AvŚ 34; Speyer 1902: 183).
36 The story says that the Buddha stopped 'in order to demonstrate the consequences of actions, and in order to abstain from taking what is not given' (*karmaṇāmavipraṇāśasaṃdarśanārtham adattādānavairamaṇyārthaṃ*; Speyer 1902: 223), leaving open the possibility that it was his own choice.
37 See discussions in Walters 1990; Cutler Mellick 1997; and Strong 2012.
38 This remains the standard translation despite the possibility — argued by Norman (1983) — that the term originally referred to someone 'awakened by signs', as appears to be the meaning in early Jain sources. As discussed below, signs of impermanence are an important part of the wider pool of *pratyekabuddha* narratives. For a counterargument to Norman, see Anālayo 2010: esp. 11–12.
39 For a general overview of the category, see the classic study by Louis de La Vallée Poussin (1908–27) and more recent discussions by Harvey (2007) and Ray (1994), as well as Kloppenborg (1974) for the Pāli tradition.
40 Perhaps the same response is meant to be implied in the subsequent stories too, but this is unclear.
41 Indian Buddhism includes *dharma* teaching as one of the possible forms of miracles or wonders, and indeed it is often said to be the most powerful of all possible miracles. For further discussion, see Fiordalis 2010.
42 The Buddha's ability to provide transformative encounters is also evident from the four stories of predictions to *pratyekabodhi* in the *Divyāvadāna*, where the recipients are a girl (4), a man (5), a bull (11) and two parrot chicks (16). The inclusion of animals suggests an impressively potent field of merit, though importantly the predictions in these cases include intervening births in various heaven realms.
43 Such themes are particularly prominent in the stories accompanying the rhinoceros horn verses of the *Sutta Nipāta* and in Pāli *jātaka* stories. See Appleton 2019a.
44 For a full discussion of this network of stories, see Appleton 2017: ch. 6.
45 With the woman taking centre stage as *pratyekabuddha*-to-be, we also see a more inclusive vision of this attainment, though of course she is predicted to become a *male pratyekabuddha*, as is the young woman in story 23. One wonders if there was a conscious decision on the part of the narrators to reverse the imagery here: instead of a woman with bracelets featuring as a sign of the dangers of worldly life, she is able to quit worldly life herself. I am indebted to Karen Muldoon-Hules for this latter suggestion.
46 *eṣānanda dārako 'nena kuśalamūlena cittotpādena deyadharmaparityāgena ca pañcadaśa kalpān vinipātaṃ na gamiṣyati divyamānuṣasukham anubhūya*

padmottaro nāma pratyekabuddho bhaviṣyati | ayam asya deyadharmo yo mamāntike cittaprasādaḥ (AvŚ 22; Speyer 1902: 128).

47 For a thorough discussion of the roles of miracles in early Buddhist literature, see Fiordalis 2008; and on the ability of the Buddha to generate *prasāda*, see Rotman 2009. On how AvŚ 1–10 function as conversion stories involving the use of miracles to generate *prasāda*, see Fifield 2008.

48 On the limitations of future vision within Buddhist narrative, see Appleton 2014: ch. 4.

49 The composers of the *avadānamālās* evidently thought so too, since they generally skipped over the fourth decade when compiling their texts; see further discussion on page 48.

50 Strong (1979) presents an interesting analysis, though one more applicable to the stories of the final four decades than the ones under discussion here, while more extensive work in this area is being undertaken by Fiordalis (2008, 2010, forthcoming).

51 For discussion of this trope, which is also found in other Buddhist texts, see Fiordalis forthcoming. Collett (2006) discusses the formula, among others, in relation to the function of the formulae overall and the possible oral composition of the text.

52 For a full translation, see pages 68–71; and for an alternative translation and interesting discussion, see Fiordalis 2008: 28–30.

53 *tad yadi bhagavān atītaṃ karma vyākartukāmo bhavati bhagavataḥ pṛṣṭhato 'ntardhīyante | anāgataṃ vyākartukāmo bhavati purastād antardhīyante | narakopapattiṃ vyākartukāmo bhavati pādatale 'ntardhīyante | tiryagupapattiṃ vyākartukāmo bhavati pārṣṇyām antardhīyante | pretopapattiṃ vyākartukāmo bhavati pādāṅguṣṭhe 'ntardhīyante | manuṣyopapattiṃ vyākartukāmo bhavati jānunor antardhīyante | balacakravartirājyaṃ vyākartukāmo bhavati vāme karatale 'ntardhīyante | cakravartirājyaṃ vyākartukāmo bhavati dakṣiṇe karatale 'ntardhīyante | devopapattiṃ vyākartukāmo bhavati nābhyām antardhīyante | śrāvakabodhiṃ vyākartukāmo bhavati āsye 'ntardhīyante | pratyekabodhiṃ vyākartukāmo bhavati ūrṇāyām antardhīyante | anuttarāṃ samyaksaṃbodhiṃ vyākartukāmo bhavati uṣṇīṣe antardhīyante* (for example, AvŚ 1; Speyer 1902: 5–6, following his emendations).

54 Other options are available in other texts: in the *Aśokāvadāna* the rays of light enter the Buddha's left palm, and he predicts that Aśoka will become an armed wheel-turning king (Strong 1983b: 201–4); in the story of Rudrāyaṇa in the *Divyāvadāna* the light enters the Buddha's foot and he predicts a hellish rebirth (Rotman 2017: 321–6).

55 Fifteen if you count AvŚ 5, which is missing from the Sanskrit but present in the Tibetan, where the formula appears.

56 AvŚ 3, 6, 13, 14, 15, 17, 18 and 23. Also 50, 56, 79, 80, 81 and 92.

57 For a full translation, see pages 77–8.

58 *dvātriṃśatā mahāpuruṣalakṣaṇaiḥ samalaṃkṛtam aśītyā cānuvyaṃjanair virājitagātraṃ vyāmaprabhālaṃkṛtaṃ sūryasahasrātirekaprabhaṃ jaṅgamam*

iva ratnaparvataṃ samantato bhadrakam (for example, AvŚ 1; Speyer 1902: 3).

59 *tathāgato 'rhan samyaksaṃbuddho vidyācaraṇasaṃpannaḥ sugato lokavid anuttaraḥ puruṣadamyasārathiḥ śāstā devamanuṣyāṇāṃ buddho bhagavān* (for example, AvŚ 11; Speyer 1902: 65).

60 *tatra bhagavato 'cirābhisaṃbuddhabodher yaśasā ca sarvaloka āpūrṇaḥ* (AvŚ 1; Speyer 1902: 2).

61 See discussion in Feer 1979: xvi–xxvii and Strong 1983b: 160–1, while Fiordalis 2019 helpfully reviews the current state of scholarship on the *avadānamālā*s, with a particular focus on the *Kalpadrumāvadānamālā*.

62 This concern to neutralize the threat of independent *buddhas* is not unique to the *Avadānaśataka*. Other textual collections grappled with the same challenge, and several came to the same conclusion as here: that it is best to subordinate them to the Buddha through a network of devotional encounters. In a series of verses in the Pāli *Apadāna* (Lilley 1925–27: vol. I, 7–14), for example, the Buddha tells his disciple Ānanda how *paccekabuddhas* came to achieve awakening, explaining that they served former *buddhas* but did not achieve awakening in that time. Following this tradition, some of the commentarial stories that accompany the *Sutta Nipāta* verses on the rhinoceros horn note the past lives of some *paccekabuddhas* in the time of the Buddha Kassapa; however, most have no such backstory (see Bodhi 2017: 401–96). The Pāli *Jātakatthavaṇṇanā*, meanwhile, appears instead to celebrate the independence of *paccekabuddhas*, who achieve awakening through their own efforts, and often teach others, including the Bodhisatta. Nonetheless, the *Jātakatthavaṇṇanā* still offers various ways to subordinate these figures to the Buddha, if not also to the Bodhisatta (see Appleton 2019a). For an interesting, if not entirely convincing, historical hypothesis about how early Buddhism dealt with the existence of previous awakened beings in part through the notion of the *pratyekabuddha*, see Wiltshire 1990. Ray (1994) also offers some valuable historical speculations on this matter.

63 This hypothesis is further illuminated by story 27, with which we began this study, and in which the Buddha's ability to ferry *arhats* is contrasted with the ferryman predicted to become a *pratyekabuddha*.

64 This sentiment is expressed in AvŚ 80, 89, 90, 96, 98 and 99. The *Divyāvadāna* goes further and has the Buddha end such stories with a reminder that the aspirants have indeed got what they wished for, as he is 'more distinguished than hundreds and thousands and millions of solitary buddhas' (in Rotman's translation, for example, 2008: 240). Another intriguing *Divyāvadāna* story from the perspective of hierarchies is found in the *Kanakavarṇa-avadāna* (20; Rotman 2017: 87–92). Here we are told that a certain *bodhisattva* becomes fed up with the world and so becomes a *pratyekabuddha*. This *pratyekabuddha* then performs the standard function of a field of merit by receiving King Kanakavarṇa's last

measure of food. Kanakavarṇa is subsequently identified as the Buddha in a past life.

65 In contrast to the *buddhas* of the past who feature in chapter 2, these are all well-known past *buddhas* since Dīpaṅkara, and their names were familiar across Buddhist schools.

66 For example, AvŚ 86 and 87 both feature two past *buddhas*, while AvŚ 88–90 each feature a *pratyekabuddha* and the past *buddha* Kāśyapa; AvŚ 88 also features the past *buddha* Vipaśyin, while AvŚ 90 includes a third past-life story in which the *arhat*-to-be encounters a brahmin teacher.

67 *dānto dāntaparivāraḥ śāntaḥ śāntaparivāro mukto muktaparivāra āśvasta āśvastaparivāro vinīto vinītaparivāro 'rhann arhatparivāro vītarāgo vītarāgaparivāraḥ prāsādikaḥ prāsādikaparivāro vṛṣabha iva gogaṇaparivṛto gaja iva kalabhagaṇaparivṛtaḥ siṃha iva daṃṣṭrigaṇaparivṛto haṃsa iva haṃsagaṇaparivṛto suparṇīva pakṣigaṇaparivṛto vipra iva śiṣyagaṇaparivṛtaḥ svaśva iva turagagaṇaparivṛtaḥ śūra iva yodhagaṇaparivṛto deśika ivādhvagagaṇaparivṛtaḥ sārthavāha iva vaṇiggaṇaparivṛtaḥ śreṣṭhīva pauragaṇaparivṛtaḥ koṭṭarāja iva mantrigaṇaparivṛtaś cakravartīva putrasahasraparivṛtaś candra iva nakṣatragaṇaparivṛtaḥ sūrya iva raśmisahasraparivṛto dhṛtarāṣṭra iva gandharvagaṇaparivṛto virūḍha iva kumbhāṇḍagaṇaparivṛto virūpākṣa iva nāgagaṇaparivṛto dhanada iva yakṣagaṇaparivṛto vemacitrīvāsuragaṇaparivṛtaḥ śakra iva tridaśagaṇaparivṛto brahmā iva brahmakāyikaparivṛtaḥ stimita iva jalanidhiḥ sajala iva jaladharo vimada iva gajapatiḥ* (AvŚ 19; Speyer 1902: 108).

68 For the latest research into the origins and characteristics of early Mahāyāna, see Harrison 2018.

69 For a translation, see Walters 2018.

70 According to some interpretations, he also had superior wisdom to his disciples, or superior powers. For a helpful discussion of the tension within Theravāda thought, see Endo 1997 and, more broadly, Nattier 2004.

PART B

Translation

Note on the translation

The translation in this volume is from the edition by J.S. Speyer, published between 1902 and 1909, and reprinted in 1958. I have also consulted Vaidya's 1958 edition, which is largely a reprint of Speyer with some emendations (of which some are helpful, others considerably less so). The GRETIL edition, input by Klaus Wille and based on these two editions, has been invaluable as I have continued to work on this text over the years. Notes – which have been kept to a minimum – indicate places where my readings have moved away from Speyer, alongside other additional information of primary interest to scholars. A Glossary provides key terms and definitions.

I find Speyer's edition to be readable and of a high standard, and my policy has been to translate what is there. I have not made any efforts to consult manuscripts or other versions of the text, such as the Tibetan or Chinese translations (though I have made some use of Feer's French translation). This is in large part pragmatism: I am not well qualified for such a task, and neither am I interested in it. My aim is to present a readable yet loyal rendering of the text – a text that has been available in a high-quality printed edition for over 100 years – to enable others to enjoy and study the stories and teachings within it. If my translation is superseded by other more text-critical work in due course, I will be delighted to see the *Avadānaśataka* finally getting the attention it deserves.

In general I have translated the text in full including the many repeated formulae. The only exception to this is the formulaic description of the Buddha's smile. Although I find this passage to be fantastically interesting and valuable (see discussion above), it appears ten times in chapter 1 and eight in chapter 3, and including it in full each time would lengthen the volume considerably, thereby adding to its expense. As such, this passage appears in full only the first time it occurs in each chapter. Subsequent occurrences are abbreviated, indicated by '. . .' and a reference to the story in which the complete version may be found. Some readers may find themselves wishing that I had abbreviated more of the formulae, but to them I would urge reading the text aloud, imagining themselves into a performance of this magnificent text.

I keep names in Sanskrit, but for characters of past and future times I often provide a translation in parenthesis, since these names often have a close relation to the deeds or gifts associated with that character. These translations should be viewed as speculative and indicative only.

As noted in the Preface, my translation is greatly indebted to Karen Muldoon-Hules, Andy Rotman, David Fiordalis and Justin Fifield, with whom I have had lengthy discussions about how to translate the *Avadānaśataka* and in particular its formulaic passages, and who have shared their own renderings of other chapters. Rotman's *Divyāvadāna* translation (Wisdom, 2008, 2017), which shares many of the same motifs and formulae, has also been invaluable, and I have followed his renderings of several key terms and names, and his formatting of one pleasingly numerical formula. All remaining errors and infelicities are, of course, my own responsibility.

First Decade

(Stories 1–10)

1. Pūrṇabhadra

The Buddha, the Blessed One, was honoured, revered, respected and worshipped by kings, ministers, the wealthy, the townsfolk, merchants, caravan leaders, gods, *nāgas*, *yakṣas*, antigods, heavenly birds, *kinnaras* and great snakes. That Buddha, the Blessed One, who was venerated as such by gods, *nāgas*, *yakṣas*, antigods, heavenly birds, *kinnaras*, and great snakes, who was famous and possessed of great merit, and who was provided with the requisites — robes, bowls, bedding, seats, and medicine to cure the sick — took residence with his community of disciples near Rājagṛha, in Kalandakanivāpa in the Veṇu Grove. At that time the whole world was filled with the glory of the Blessed One's recent awakening as a *buddha*.

In that country, among the southern hills, there lived a great brahmin householder named Saṃpūrṇa (Complete). He was rich, of great wealth and property, and extensive, wide holdings. He possessed the wealth of Vaiśravaṇa, rivalling Vaiśravaṇa in wealth. And he was devout and good, of virtuous disposition, dedicated to the good of others as well as his own benefit, compassionate, great-hearted, devoted to the *dharma*, and affectionate towards people. He delighted in giving, loved giving gifts, engaged in gift-giving and extensive donation. Once he undertook to hold a sacrifice for all the heretics, at which many hundreds of thousands of heretics would be fed.

When King Bimbisāra and his assembly were converted by the Blessed One, on account of his training many hundreds of thousands of beings were attracted to the discipline. And some kinsmen of Pūrṇa who were visiting from Rājagṛha began to speak in praise of the Buddha, *dharma* and *saṅgha* in front of Pūrṇa. Hearing of the extensive qualities of the Blessed One, Pūrṇa, that great brahmin householder, experienced great faith. He climbed up onto his roof and, facing Rājagṛha, knelt with both knees on the ground. He threw flowers, incense and water, and entreated the Blessed One: 'May the Blessed One come to my sacrificial ground to enjoy my sacrifice!' And those flowers, through the power of the Buddha and the power of gods, flew to the Buddha and remained above the Blessed One like a flower pavilion. The incense became like a towering cloud and the water like a sliver of beryl.

Then Venerable Ānanda joined his hands in respect and asked the Blessed One, 'Where does this invitation come from?' The Blessed one answered, 'Ānanda, in the southern hills of the country lives a great brahmin householder called Saṃpūrṇa. Let us go there. The monks should get ready.'

The Blessed One, with a retinue of a thousand monks, journeyed through the southern hills of the country. When he came close to the sacrificial ground of that great brahmin householder Pūrṇa, he thought, 'What if I were to convert this brahmin Pūrṇa with a miraculous display?' Then the Blessed One made his thousand monks invisible, and stood near Pūrṇa alone, with his monastic bowl in his hands. That great brahmin householder Pūrṇa saw the Blessed One adorned with the thirty-two marks of a great man and the eighty secondary marks, his body shining, arrayed with light that extended a fathom, radiance in excess of a thousand suns, like a living mountain of jewels, handsome in his entirety. And having seen him he hastily approached the Blessed One and said to him, 'Welcome, Blessed One! May the Blessed One be seated, may he accept a seat as a favour to me.' The Blessed One said, 'If you have a gift, it may be placed in this bowl.' Then Pūrṇa, that great brahmin householder, surrounded by his five hundred pupils, began to fill the Blessed One's bowl with food: various foods both hard and soft, and cordials, drinks and broths and so on. But the Blessed One transferred the food from his own bowl into the bowls of his monks. When the Blessed One knew that the monks' bowls were full, then he allowed his own bowl to appear full.[1] Then he revealed the thousand monks with their bowls full, arranged in the shape of a half-moon. The gods in the sky cried out: 'The bowls of the Blessed One and the thousand monks are full!'

As a result of this miraculous display, Pūrṇa became faithful, and he was thrilled, delighted and pleased, his mind uplifted with joy. He fell at the Blessed One's feet like a tree felled at the roots and made this fervent aspiration: 'By this root of virtue, the arising of this thought and this properly given gift, may I become a *buddha* in this dark world that is leaderless and without a guide. May I carry across those beings who have not crossed over, liberate those who are not liberated, console those in need of consolation, bring to complete *nirvāṇa* those who have not entered complete *nirvāṇa*.'

Then the Blessed One, understanding the succession of causes and the succession of actions of that householder, smiled. Now, according to the natural order of things, when *buddhas* display a smile then blue, yellow, red and white rays issue from his mouth and some go upwards and some downwards. Those that go downwards, they go to the hells – the Saṃjīva (Reviving), Kālasūtra (Black Thread), Saṃghāta (Crushing), Raurava (Shrieking), Mahāraurava (Loud Shrieking), Tapana (Heat), Pratāpana (Extreme Heat), Avīci (Endless Torture), Arbuda (Blistering), Nirarbuda (Blisters Bursting),

Aṭaṭa (Chattering Teeth), Hahava (Ugh!), Huhuva (Brrr!), Utpala (Blue Lotus), Padma (Lotus), and Mahāpadma (Great Lotus). Those that descend into the hot hells become cool, and those that descend into the cold hells become warm, and in this way they alleviate the various sufferings of the beings there, such that it occurs to them, 'Friends, can it be that we have left this place and arisen elsewhere?' Then, in order to make them develop faith, the Blessed One emits an image of himself, and seeing this image they realize, 'No, friends, we have not left this place nor arisen elsewhere. There is this being, not seen before, whose power is easing our various sufferings.' Their minds become faithful towards this image, and they cast off the karma still to be experienced in hell, and take rebirth among gods and men, where they become vessels for the truths.

Those [rays of light] that go upwards, they go to the gods — the Cāturmahārājika (Four Groups of the Great Kings), Trāyastriṃśa (Thirty-three), Yāma (Of Yama), Tuṣita (Content), Nirmāṇarati (Delighting in Creation), Paranirmitavaśavartin (Masters of Others' Creations), Brahmakāyika (Brahmā's Assembly), Brahmapurohita (Brahmā's Priests), Mahābrahma (Great Brahmā), Parittābhā (Limited Splendour), Apramāṇābhā (Immeasurable Splendour), Abhāsvara (Radiant), Parittaśubha (Limited Beauty), Apramāṇaśubha (Immeasurable Beauty), Śubhakṛtsna (Complete Beauty), Anabhraka (Unclouded), Puṇyaprasava (Merit Born), Bṛhatphala (Great Result), Abṛha (Not Vast), Atapa (Serene), Sudṛśa (Good-Looking), Sudarśana (Clear Sighted) and Akaniṣṭha (Supreme). They shout out, 'Impermanent! Suffering! Empty! Not-Self!' and speak two verses:

> 'Exert yourselves! Go forth!
> Take up the Buddha's teaching!
> Shake the army of death
> like an elephant shakes a reed-hut!
>
> Whoever diligently follows
> this *dharma* and discipline,
> will abandon the cycle of rebirths
> and make an end to suffering.'

Then those rays of light, having roamed through the great trichiliocosm, assemble behind the Blessed One. If the Blessed One wishes to explain past actions, they disappear into the Blessed One's back; if he wishes to explain future actions, they vanish into his front. If he wishes to predict arising in a hell, they disappear into the soles of his feet, while if he wants to predict arising as an animal, they enter his heel, and if he wants to predict arising as a hungry ghost, they vanish into his big toe, and if he desires to predict arising as a human, they disappear into his knee. If he wishes to predict rule as an armed wheel-turning king, they enter the palm of his left hand, while if he wishes to predict rule as a wheel-turning king, they disappear into the palm of his right hand. If he wishes to predict arising as a god, they vanish into his navel. If he wishes to predict awakening as a disciple, they enter his mouth, while if he wants to predict awakening as a *pratyekabuddha*, they vanish into the circle of hair between his eyebrows, and if he wants to predict unsurpassed and perfect full buddhahood, they disappear into his *uṣṇīṣa*.

And those rays of light circumambulated the Blessed One three times and disappeared into the Blessed One's *uṣṇīṣa*. Then Venerable Ānanda joined his hands in respect and asked the Blessed One:

> 'A collection of a thousand bright-coloured rays of various
> kinds
> is expelled from the inside of your mouth,
> completely illuminating the directions
> as if from the rising of the sun.'

And he spoke these verses:

> '*Buddhas* have cut off rebirth, abandoned affliction and
> enjoyment,
> and become the cause of what is best in the world.
> Not without reason do victors, their enemies conquered,
> exhibit a smile, white as a conch-shell or lotus-fibre.
>
> Hero, ascetic, the best of victors, you know at once
> through your own intelligence, the wishes of your listeners.
> Bull among sages, remove the doubt that has arisen,

with splendid, wise and superior speech.

It is not without reason that perfect *buddhas*, protectors
firm as the ocean or the king of the mountains, exhibit a
smile.
A multitude of people yearn to hear
the reason why wise ones exhibit a smile.'

The Blessed One said, 'It is like this, Ānanda. It is like this. It is not without cause or without reason, Ānanda, that *tathāgatas* who are *arhats* and perfectly and fully awakened display a smile. Ānanda, this great brahmin householder Pūrṇa, through this root of virtue, the arising of this thought, and this properly given gift, after three incalculable aeons he will attain awakening, and having fulfilled the six perfections that are pervaded with great compassion he will become a full and perfect *buddha* named Pūrṇabhadra (Completely Good), with the ten powers, four confidences, three special applications of mindfulness and great compassion. This is the gift of one who has a faithful thought towards me.'

When Pūrṇa the great brahmin householder had been predicted to unsurpassed perfect and full buddhahood by the Blessed One, he provided the Blessed One and his community of monks with food for three months in his sacrificial ground. Through this he planted even more roots of virtue.[2]

'Therefore, monks, you should train in this way: "We will honour, revere, respect and worship the teacher. And having honoured, revered, respected and worshipped the teacher, we will live in reliance on him." In this way, monks, you should train.'

This was said by the Blessed One, and the monks were delighted and praised the Blessed One's speech.

2. Yaśomatī

The Buddha, the Blessed One, was honoured, revered, respected and worshipped by kings, ministers, the wealthy, the townsfolk, merchants, caravan leaders, gods, *nāgas*, *yakṣas*, antigods, heavenly birds, *kinnaras* and great snakes. That Buddha, the Blessed One, who was venerated as such by gods, *nāgas*, *yakṣas*, antigods, heavenly birds, *kinnaras* and great snakes, who was famous and possessed of great merit, and who was provided with the requisites — robes, bowls, bedding, seats, and medicine to cure the sick — took up residence with his community of monks near Vaiśālī, in the upper hall on the banks of Markaṭahrada.

In the morning, the Blessed One got dressed and, taking his robe and bowl, surrounded by a group of monks and attended by the monastic community, he entered Vaiśālī for alms. Having wandered through Vaiśālī in proper order for alms, he arrived at the house of General Siṃha (Lion). He entered and sat on a seat that had been prepared.

Now General Siṃha had a daughter-in-law called Yaśomatī (Glorious), who was beautiful, good-looking and pleasing. She saw the Blessed One's body, splendid with the various marks, and became extremely faithful. She asked her father-in-law, 'How can I get these qualities?' Then it occurred to General Siṃha, 'Oh, my daughter is intent on greatness! She will achieve this end if she makes a fervent aspiration to unsurpassed full and perfect awakening.' Knowing this, he said, 'Daughter, if you are intent on taking on this cause, in this way you too will become a Blessed One like this.' Then, in order to increase Yaśomatī's faith, the General Siṃha gave her lots of gold, silver and jewels. His daughter Yaśomatī invited the Blessed One and his community of monks to take their meal in the house the following day, and the Blessed One agreed, in order to benefit her.

Then the girl Yaśomatī had flowers made from gold, silver and jewels, assembled lots of perfumes, garlands and ointments, and prepared food of a hundred flavours. Then a servant announced to the Blessed One that it was time: 'Venerable one, the food is ready, so the Blessed One should know that it is now time.' The Blessed One, surrounded by a group of monks and attended by the monastic community, approached the General Siṃha's house, and sat on a seat that had been prepared, at the head of the community of monks. Then the girl Yaśomatī, seeing that the monastic community with the Buddha at their head was seated comfortably, served them food of a hundred flavours with her own hands, and threw flowers over the Blessed One. Those flowers remained above the Blessed One like a jewelled peaked-roof, or a jewelled parasol, or a jewelled pavilion. This is something that is not possible through careful training or hard work or as the result of previous actions,[3] but only by *buddhas* through their *buddha*-power, and by gods through their god-power.

Having seen this extremely wonderful miracle that humbled gods and men, that girl Yaśomatī threw her whole body at the Blessed One's feet, like a tree felled at the roots, and made this fervent aspiration: 'By this root of virtue, the arising of this thought and this properly given gift, may I become a *buddha* in this dark world that is leaderless and without a guide. May I carry across those beings who have not crossed over, liberate those who are not liberated, console those in need of consolation, bring to complete *nirvāṇa* those who have not entered complete *nirvāṇa*.'

Then the Blessed One, understanding the succession of causes and the succession of actions of that girl Yaśomatī, smiled. . . . [as story 1].

The Blessed One said, 'It is like this, Ānanda. It is like this. It is not without cause or without reason, Ānanda, that *tathāgatas* who are *arhats* and perfectly and fully awakened display a smile. Did you see, Ānanda, how this girl Yaśomatī honoured me in this way?' 'Yes, sir.' 'Ānanda, this girl Yaśomatī, through this root of virtue, the arising of this thought, and this properly given gift, after three incalculable aeons will attain awakening, and having fulfilled the six perfections that are pervaded with great compassion she will become a full and perfect *buddha* named Ratnamati (Bejewelled), with the ten powers, four confidences, three special applications of mindfulness and great compassion.[4] This is the gift of one who has a faithful thought towards me.'

This was said by the Blessed One, and the monks were delighted and praised the Blessed One's speech.

3. Lazybones (*Kusīda*)

The Buddha, the Blessed One, was honoured, revered, respected and worshipped by kings, ministers, the wealthy, the townsfolk, merchants, caravan leaders, gods, *nāgas*, *yakṣas*, antigods, heavenly birds, *kinnaras* and great snakes. That Buddha, the Blessed One, who was venerated as such by gods, *nāgas*, *yakṣas*, antigods, heavenly birds, *kinnaras* and great snakes, who was famous and possessed of great merit, and who was provided with the requisites — robes, bowls, bedding, seats, and medicine to cure the sick — was staying with his community of monks in Anāthapiṇḍada's park, the Jeta Grove in Śrāvastī.

In Śrāvastī there lived a certain guildsman, who was rich, of great wealth and property, and extensive, wide holdings. He possessed the wealth of Vaiśravaṇa, rivaling Vaiśravaṇa in wealth. He took a wife from a suitable family, and together with her he played, enjoyed himself and made love, but despite that play, love-making and enjoyment he had neither son nor daughter. Resting his cheek in his hand he became lost in thought: 'I have a house full of riches, but I have no son or daughter. After my death, having declared me sonless the king will appropriate all my property.'

Ascetics, brahmins, soothsayers, friends, relatives and family members told him: 'You should entreat the gods!' For there is this saying in the world, that sons and daughters are born because of entreaties. But this is not so, for if it were the case then each person would have a thousand sons just like a wheel-turning king. Rather, sons and daughters are born from the coming-together of three favourable conditions. Which three? The mother and father unite in love-making, the mother is healthy and in her fertile period, and a *gandharva* is standing by. Sons and daughters are born from the coming-together of these three favourable conditions.

But being misled by the ascetics, brahmins, soothsayers, friends, relatives and family members, because he had no son and desired a son, he entreated Śiva, Varuṇa, Kubera, Śakra, Brahmā and so on, as well as various other deities, namely the gods of the grove, the gods of the forest, the gods of four-way crossroads, the gods of three-way crossroads, and the gods who receive oblations. He also implored his lineage gods, the gods who shared his nature, and his tutelary gods. He continued entreating them in this way, and a certain being came out from a certain group of beings and descended into his wife's womb.

There are five particular characteristics of any wise woman. What are the five? She knows when a man is enamoured and when he is indifferent. She knows the right time, for she knows when she is in her fertile period. She knows when she has conceived, and she knows who has impregnated her. She knows when it is a boy and when it is a girl, for if it is a boy it lies on the right side of her womb and stays there, and if it is a girl it lies on the left side of her womb and stays there.

She was thrilled and delighted and addressed her husband, 'You are fortunate, noble lord! I have become pregnant. And because it lies on the right side of my womb it will certainly be a boy!' He too was thrilled and delighted, and he puffed out his chest and stretched out his right arm, and uttered this joyous speech: 'O that I might see the face of a son, desired for a long time! May he not be born unworthy of me! May he do his duty! Having been supported by me, may he be my support! May he claim his inheritance, and may my family lineage last a long time! And when we are gone, may he give gifts large or small and perform rites, saying, "May this follow these two, wherever they have gone or arisen" and thereby dedicate it in our names!'

Knowing that she was pregnant, he kept her on the upper storey of a lofty palace, unrestrained, with everything necessary for the cold when it was cold, and everything necessary for the heat when it was hot. She was provided with food as prescribed by the doctors, neither too bitter nor too sour, neither too salty nor too sweet, neither too sharp nor too astringent, with food that was free from bitterness, sourness, saltiness, sweetness, sharpness and astringence. She was adorned with strings of pearls, and like a celestial nymph roving the Nandana Grove she moved from bed to bed and from seat to seat without descending to the ground below.[5] And she did not hear any unpleasant sound while her foetus was maturing.

After eight or nine months had passed she gave birth. A boy was born who was well formed, beautiful and pleasing, and the family was delighted at his birth. After he was born they celebrated his birth-festival and fixed the naming ceremony: 'What should be this boy's name?' His kinsmen said, 'Since the whole family was delighted at his birth, the boy should be named Nanda (Delight).' And so he was given the name Nanda.

The boy Nanda was given eight nurses: two nurses to carry him, two nurses to feed him, two nurses to clean him and two nurses to play with him. He was raised by the eight nurses and nourished with milk, curds, fresh butter, clarified butter, the residue of the clarified butter and other foods of excellent, beneficial characteristics, so he grew quickly like a lotus in a pool.

When he had grown bigger, about five or six years old, he became lazy, extremely lazy, and did not want to get up from his bed or chair. But because of his sharp and eager mind, he studied the *śāstra*s even though he stayed indoors. And that guildsman thought, 'Somehow, through honouring the gods, a son has been born to me. But he is lazy, extremely lazy, and won't even get up from his bed or chair. What use to me is the birth of a son like this, who has a healthy body yet lives like an animal?'

Now that guildsman had faith in Pūraṇa, and he invited eight heretic teachers to his home: 'Surely my son, on seeing them, will be filled with respect and get up from his seat or bed!' But that lazy son, on seeing those teachers, did not even raise his eyes to look at them, to say nothing of standing up or respectfully greeting them or offering them a seat! When the householder saw this situation he became even more upset. Resting his cheek in his hand, he became lost in thought.

Now there is nothing that is unknown, unseen, unrecognized and unobserved by the *buddhas*, blessed ones. Indeed, being greatly compassionate and devoted to benefitting the world, *buddhas*, blessed ones:

> have one protector,
> dwell in calm and insight,
> are skilled in the threefold self-control,
> have overcome the four floods,
> have conduct grounded in the four bases of supernormal power,
> have long practised the four articles of attraction,
> lack the five [bad] qualities,
> have gone beyond the five realms,
> are endowed with the six qualities [of equanimity],
> have accomplished the six perfections,
> abound in the flowers that are the seven factors of awakening,
> are guides on the eightfold path,
> are skilled in the nine successive attainments [of meditation],
> are mighty with the ten powers,
> with splendour that fully pervades the ten directions,
> and more distinguished than ten times a hundred rulers.

It is a rule that when they survey the world with their *buddha*-vision for three days and three nights, knowledge and perception arise: ‘Who is falling? Who is flourishing? Who has met with pain? Who is in danger? Who is afflicted? Who has met with pain, danger and affliction? Who is headed for a state of woe? Who is inclined towards a state of evil? Who is bent on a bad destiny? Whom can I raise up from bad states and establish in heaven and liberation? Who, mired in sense pleasures, might I raise up with my hands? Who, deprived of them, could I establish in mastery over and excellence in the noble treasures? Whose unplanted roots of virtue should I plant? Whose planted [roots] should I bring to maturity? And whose matured [roots] should I bring to liberation?' And it is said:

> Though the ocean, abode of monsters,
> may pass over the shore,
> A *buddha* cannot pass over the opportunity
> of young people in need of training.

The Blessed One saw: 'This lazy boy, on seeing me, will become energized, such that he will develop an intention towards unsurpassed perfect and full awakening.' Then, in order to destroy the pride and conceit of the heretics, and also to produce roots of virtue in the boy, the Blessed One emitted golden rays of light that were brighter than a thousand suns, and which illuminated the whole house. And he emitted beams of loving-kindness, cultivated during thousands of aeons, which delight the body at the merest touch. And he [the boy] began to look here and there: 'Whose power has delighted my body?' Then the Blessed One, surrounded by a group of monks, entered the house. The lazy boy saw the Buddha, the Blessed One adorned with the thirty-two marks of a great man and the eighty secondary marks, his body shining, arrayed with light that extended a fathom, radiance in excess of a thousand suns, like a living mountain of jewels, handsome in his entirety. And on seeing him he became extremely faithful, and immediately got up and prepared a seat for the Blessed One, saying, 'Come, Blessed One, you are welcome, Blessed One! May the Blessed One be seated on his prepared seat.' Seeing this unprecedented marvel, his parents and other relatives were filled with great wonder.

Then the lazy boy, his eyes wide with joy, honoured the Blessed One's feet and sat to one side in order to hear the *dharma*. The Blessed One spoke of the many ill qualities of indolence, and praised vigour and exertion. He offered him a sandalwood stick: 'Child, hit this stick.' He started to hit it, and as he beat that stick he heard a pleasing sound and saw a treasury of various jewels. He thought, 'Oh this is the great distinction of being energetic! What if I were to cultivate vigour to a greater degree?' Then he had a bell rung in Śrāvastī and announced himself to be a caravan leader, and he crossed the great ocean six times. Having acquired a great hoard of jewels, with his boat still in one piece, he fed the Blessed One and his community of monks in his home, and he made a fervent aspiration for unsurpassed perfect and full awakening.

Then the Blessed One, understanding the succession of causes and the succession of actions of that lazy boy, smiled. . . . [as story 1].

The Blessed One said, 'It is like this, Ānanda. It is like this. It is not without cause or without reason, Ānanda, that *tathāgatas* who are *arhats* and perfectly and fully awakened display a smile. Did you see, Ānanda, how this lazy boy did me service in this way?' 'Yes, sir.' 'Ānanda, this lazy boy, through this root of virtue, the arising of this thought, and this properly given gift, after three incalculable aeons will attain awakening, and having fulfilled the six perfections that are pervaded with great compassion he will become a full and perfect *buddha* named Atibalavīryaparākrama (Hero of Very Powerful Vigour), with the ten powers, four confidences, three special applications of mindfulness and great compassion. This is the gift of one who has a faithful thought towards me.'

This was said by the Blessed One, and the monks were delighted and praised the Blessed One's speech.

4. The Caravan Leader (*Sārthavāha*)

The Buddha, the Blessed One, was honoured, revered, respected and worshipped by kings, ministers, the wealthy, the townsfolk, merchants, caravan leaders, gods, *nāgas*, *yakṣas*, antigods, heavenly birds, *kinnaras* and great snakes. That Buddha, the Blessed One, who was venerated as such by gods, *nāgas*, *yakṣas*, antigods, heavenly birds, *kinnaras* and great snakes, who was famous and possessed of great merit, and who was provided with the requisites — robes, bowls, bedding, seats, and medicine to cure the sick — was staying with his community of monks in Anāthapiṇḍada's park, the Jeta Grove in Śrāvastī.

A certain great caravan leader from Śrāvastī had returned from the great ocean with his boat broken up. A second and a third time he entreated his gods and went out on the great ocean, and again came home with his boat broken. He became very depressed as a result, and thought to himself: 'By what means can I make money?' Then it occurred to him, 'There is a Buddha, a Blessed One, more distinguished than all the gods, dedicated to the good of others as well as his own benefit, compassionate, greatly devoted to the *dharma*, and affectionate towards the people. What if I were to cross the great ocean again, this time in his name? If I return with my ship intact, I will worship him with half my earnings.'

Having made this resolve, he set out on the great ocean again. And by the power of the Buddha he reached Jewel Island and amassed lots of jewels before returning home successfully. After recovering from the exhausting journey he began to inspect his goods. Seeing the jewels of various kinds there, he became very greedy, and he thought, 'Am I going to give half of the jewels of this quality to the ascetic Gautama? What if I were to sell them to my own wife, exchanging them for two coins, and then give the Blessed One some incense?' So he bought a little with his two coins and went to the Jeta Grove, and stood at the gate looking ashamed, burning his little bit of incense.

Then the Blessed One made that material into a performance through his supernormal power, by which the incense vapour rose up into the sky overhead and spread over all of Śrāvastī, and remained like a huge towering thundercloud. Seeing this extremely wonderful miracle that humbled gods and men, he [the caravan leader] became very faithful. He said to himself, 'If I don't honour the Blessed One with jewels, then I will not become like him.'

That caravan leader invited the Blessed One, along with his community of monks, to his house for a meal. There he served them with excellent food, and showered them with jewels. And those jewels rose up into the sky overhead and remained above the Blessed One's head like a jewelled peaked-roof, or a jewelled parasol, or a jewelled pavilion. This is something that is possible not through careful training or hard work or as the result of previous actions, but only by *buddhas* through their *buddha*-power, and by gods through their god-power.

Seeing this miracle, the caravan leader became doubly faithful and fell at the Blessed One's feet, like a tree felled at the roots. He made this fervent aspiration: 'By this root of virtue, the arising of this thought and this properly given gift, may I become a *buddha* in this dark world that is leaderless and without a guide. May I carry across those beings who have not crossed over, liberate those who are not liberated, console those in need of consolation, bring to complete *nirvāṇa* those who have not entered complete *nirvāṇa*.'

Then the Blessed One, understanding the succession of causes and the succession of actions of that caravan leader, smiled. . . . [as story 1].

The Blessed One said, 'It is like this, Ānanda. It is like this. It is not without cause or without reason, Ānanda, that *tathāgatas* who are *arhats* and perfectly and fully awakened display a smile. Did you see, Ānanda, how this caravan leader honoured me in this way?' 'Yes, sir.' 'Ānanda, this caravan leader, through this root of virtue, the arising of this thought, and this properly given gift, after three incalculable aeons will attain awakening, and having fulfilled the six perfections that are pervaded with great compassion he will become a full and perfect *buddha* named Ratnottama (Supreme Jewel), with the ten powers, four confidences, three special applications of mindfulness and great compassion. This is the gift of one who has a faithful thought towards me.'

This was said by the Blessed One, and the monks were delighted and praised the Blessed One's speech.

5. Soma

[missing from the Sanskrit text][6]

6. Vaḍika

The Buddha, the Blessed One, was honoured, revered, respected and worshipped by kings, ministers, the wealthy, the townsfolk, merchants, caravan leaders, gods, *nāgas*, *yakṣas*, antigods, heavenly birds, *kinnaras* and great snakes. That Buddha, the Blessed One, who was venerated as such by gods, *nāgas*, *yakṣas*, antigods, heavenly birds, *kinnaras* and great snakes, who was famous and possessed of great merit, and who was provided with the requisites — robes, bowls, bedding, seats, and medicine to cure the sick — was staying with his community of monks in Anāthapiṇḍada's park, the Jeta Grove in Śrāvastī.

In Śrāvastī there lived a certain householder guildsman, who was rich, of great wealth and property, and extensive, wide holdings. He possessed the wealth of Vaiśravaṇa, rivaling Vaiśravaṇa in wealth. He took a wife from a suitable family, and together with her he played, enjoyed himself and made love. As a result of that playing, love-making and enjoyment, a being entered into his wife's womb. After nine months she gave birth, and a boy was born who was well formed, beautiful and pleasing. They performed the naming ceremony at his birth and his father gave him the name Vaḍika.

The boy Vaḍika was given eight nurses: two nurses to carry him, two nurses to feed him, two nurses to clean him and two nurses to play with him. He was raised by the eight nurses and nourished with milk, curds, fresh butter, clarified butter, the residue of the clarified butter and other foods of excellent, beneficial characteristics, so he grew quickly like a lotus in a pool. When he was bigger, about five or six years old, he was assigned to a teacher, and studied all the *śāstras*. He had a sharp mind, and quickly mastered all the *śāstras*.

Immediately after that, as a result of some actions done in a past life, Vaḍika's body was struck by a physical pain. That afflicted being wondered, 'What evil deeds did I do, that my body experiences this physical pain?' And his father, seeing his son's physical affliction, was very anxious, and tortured by the fear his son would die. With his face covered in tears of grief he quickly summoned a doctor and showed him his son's disease. 'What is the disease, and what has caused it to occur in my son's body?' he asked. The doctor looked at the symptoms of the disease and started a treatment, but this did not calm the illness; instead, it got worse.

His father saw his son's illness get stronger, and thinking his son would certainly die since it was impossible even for the doctor to cure his illness, he fell on the ground in a faint. Seeing this, his son became even more anxious, his mind even more agitated by worry. The boy, afflicted by illness, almost unable to speak, somehow said to his father, 'Father, do not give up! Hold onto your courage and stand up! You must not become afraid for my life like I am. Worship the gods in my name, and give gifts. Then I will become well.' Hearing his son's words, the householder worshipped all the gods and gave gifts to all the brahmins and heretics and renouncers. But even then his illness did not ease, and so he became even more troubled: 'My father has worshipped all the gods and given gifts, yet I am not better.' Then he recalled the qualities of the Tathāgata and began to pay homage to the Buddha.

Now there is nothing that is unknown, unseen, unrecognized and unobserved by the *buddhas*, blessed ones. Indeed, being greatly compassionate and devoted to benefitting the world, *buddhas*, blessed ones:

> have one protector,
> dwell in calm and insight,
> are skilled in the threefold self-control,
> have overcome the four floods,

have conduct grounded in the four bases of supernormal
power,
have long practised the four articles of attraction,
lack the five [bad] qualities,
have gone beyond the five realms,
are endowed with the six qualities [of equanimity],
have accomplished the six perfections,
abound in the flowers that are the seven factors of
awakening,
are guides on the eightfold path,
are skilled in the nine successive attainments [of
meditation],
are mighty with the ten powers,
with splendour that fully pervades the ten directions,
and more distinguished than ten times a hundred
rulers.

It is a rule that when they survey the world with their *buddha*-vision for three days and three nights, knowledge and perception arise: 'Who is falling? Who is flourishing? Who has met with pain? Who is in danger? Who is afflicted? Who has met with pain, danger and affliction? Who is headed for a state of woe? Who is inclined towards a state of evil? Who is bent on a bad destiny? Whom can I raise up from bad states and establish in heaven and liberation? Who, mired in sense pleasures, might I raise up with my hands? Who, deprived of them, could I establish in mastery over and excellence in the noble treasures? Whose unplanted roots of virtue should I plant? Whose planted [roots] should I bring to maturity? And whose matured [roots] should I bring to liberation?' And it is said:

Though the ocean, abode of monsters,
may pass over the shore,
A *buddha* cannot pass over the opportunity
of young people in need of training.

The Blessed One, seeing the condition of that householder's son Vaḍika, emitted golden rays of light that were brighter than a thousand suns, and which illuminated the whole house. And he emitted beams of loving-kindness, cultivated during thousands of aeons, which delight the body at the merest touch. Then the Blessed One arrived at the gate, and the doorkeeper announced that the Blessed One was standing at the door. Vaḍika the son of the guildsman became faithful and was comforted. He said, 'Come in, Blessed One! The Blessed One is welcome. I wish to see the Blessed One.' The Blessed One entered and sat on a prepared seat.

Once seated, the Blessed One said to Vaḍika, 'What troubles you, Vaḍika?' Vaḍika replied, 'I have pain in my body and in my mind.' Then the Blessed One taught him about having loving-kindness towards all beings: 'This will counteract the mental pain.' And then he had a worldly thought: 'Oh, that Śakra the king of the gods should bring medicinal herbs from the Gandhamādana Mountain!' And with the Blessed One's thought, Śakra the king of the gods brought medicinal herbs from Gandhamādana Mountain and gave them to the Blessed One. And the Blessed One, with his own hands, gave them to Vaḍika saying, 'This will calm the fiery pain in your body.'

With his body calmed and made comfortable, he developed faithful thoughts towards the Blessed One. With faithful mind, he informed King Prasenajit, and offered food to the Blessed One together with his community of disciples, clothed them with a hundred thousand cloths, and honoured them with garlands of all sorts of flowers. Then he developed an intention, and made a fervent aspiration: 'By this root of virtue, the arising of this thought and this properly given gift, just as the Blessed One, unsurpassed king of doctors, healed me, may I too in a future time become a *buddha* in this dark world that is leaderless and without a guide. May I carry across those beings who have not crossed over, liberate those who are not liberated, console those in need of consolation, bring to complete *nirvāṇa* those who have not entered complete *nirvāṇa*.'

Then the Blessed One, understanding the succession of causes and the succession of actions of Vaḍika, smiled. . . . [as story 1].

The Blessed One said, 'It is like this, Ānanda. It is like this. It is not without cause or without reason, Ānanda, that *tathāgatas* who are *arhats* and perfectly and fully awakened display a smile. Did you see,

Ānanda, how this householder's son Vaḍika honoured me in this way?' 'Yes, sir.' 'Ānanda, this householder's son Vaḍika, through this root of virtue, the arising of this thought, and this properly given gift, after three incalculable aeons will attain awakening, and having fulfilled the six perfections that are pervaded with great compassion he will become a full and perfect *buddha* named Śākyamuni, with the ten powers, four confidences, three special applications of mindfulness and great compassion. This is the gift of one who has a faithful thought towards me.'

This was said by the Blessed One, and the monks were delighted and praised the Blessed One's speech.

7. Lotus (*Padma*)

The Buddha, the Blessed One, was honoured, revered, respected and worshipped by kings, ministers, the wealthy, the townsfolk, merchants, caravan leaders, gods, *nāgas*, *yakṣas*, antigods, heavenly birds, *kinnaras* and great snakes. That Buddha, the Blessed One, who was venerated as such by gods, *nāgas*, *yakṣas*, antigods, heavenly birds, *kinnaras* and great snakes, who was famous and possessed of great merit, and who was provided with the requisites – robes, bowls, bedding, seats, and medicine to cure the sick – was staying with his community of monks in Anāthapiṇḍada's park, the Jeta Grove in Śrāvastī.

Before the Blessed One had arisen in the world, King Prasenajit worshipped gods and heretics with flowers, incense, perfumes, garlands and unguents. But when the Blessed One arose in the world, King Prasenajit was converted by the relating of the *Dahara Sūtra*[7] and developed faith in the teachings of the Blessed One. Then he was delighted and joyful, and three times approached the Blessed One and worshipped him with flowers, incense, perfumes, garlands and unguents.

A certain gardener had picked a fresh lotus and entered Śrāvastī seeking King Prasenajit. A heretical layperson saw him and asked, 'Is this lotus for sale?' He replied, 'Yes.' Just then the householder Anāthapiṇḍada arrived at that spot wishing to buy it. He offered twice the price, and then they each kept increasing their offer until the price was one hundred thousand. It occurred to the gardener, 'This householder Anāthapiṇḍada is steadfast and unshakeable. Surely there is a reason for that!' And having this doubt he asked the person who was a follower of the heretics, 'Sir, for whose sake do you increase your offer in this way?' He replied, 'I do so for the sake of the Blessed One Nārāyaṇa.' Anāthapiṇḍada said, 'I do so for the sake of the Blessed One, the Buddha.' The gardener said, 'What is this name "Buddha"?' Then Anāthapiṇḍada explained the many qualities of the Buddha, and the gardener said to Anāthapiṇḍada, 'Householder, I would like to worship the Blessed One myself.'

Then the householder Anāthapiṇḍada took the gardener and approached the place where the Blessed One was. The gardener saw the Buddha, the Blessed One adorned with the thirty-two marks of a great man and the eighty secondary marks, his body shining, arrayed with light that extended a fathom, radiance in excess of a thousand suns, like a living mountain of jewels, handsome in his entirety. And on seeing him the gardener threw that lotus towards the Blessed One. Just where it was thrown it became as big as a cart-wheel, and remained above the Blessed One.

Seeing that miracle, the gardener fell at the Blessed One's feet like a tree felled at the roots, and with hands joined in respect he developed an intention and undertook to make a fervent aspiration: 'By this root of virtue, the arising of this thought and this properly given gift, may I become a *buddha* in this dark world that is leaderless and without a guide. May I carry across those beings who have not crossed over, liberate those who are not liberated, console those in need of consolation, bring to complete *nirvāṇa* those who have not entered complete *nirvāṇa*.'

Then the Blessed One, understanding the succession of causes and the succession of actions of that gardener, smiled. . . . [as story 1].

The Blessed One said, 'It is like this, Ānanda. It is like this. It is not without cause or without reason, Ānanda, that *tathāgatas* who are *arhats* and perfectly and fully awakened display a smile. Did you see, Ānanda, how this gardener became faithful and worshipped me in this way?' 'Yes, sir.' 'Ānanda, this gardener, through this root of virtue, the arising of this thought, and this properly given gift, after three incalculable aeons will attain awakening, and having fulfilled the six perfections that are pervaded with great compassion he will become a full and perfect *buddha* named Padmottama (Supreme Lotus), with the ten powers, four confidences, three special applications of mindfulness and great compassion. This is the gift of one who has a faithful thought towards me.'

This was said by the Blessed One, and the monks were delighted and praised the Blessed One's speech.

8. Pañcāla

The Buddha, the Blessed One, was honoured, revered, respected and worshipped by kings, ministers, the wealthy, the townsfolk, merchants, caravan leaders, gods, *nāgas*, *yakṣas*, antigods, heavenly birds, *kinnaras* and great snakes. That Buddha, the Blessed One, who was venerated as such by gods, *nāgas*, *yakṣas*, antigods, heavenly birds, *kinnaras* and great snakes, who was famous and possessed of great merit, and who was provided with the requisites – robes, bowls, bedding, seats, and medicine to cure the sick – was staying with his community of monks in Anāthapiṇḍada's park, the Jeta Grove in Śrāvastī.

At that time the king of North Pañcāla and the king of South Pañcāla were at war.[8] King Prasenajit the Kośalan went to visit the Blessed One. Having approached, he honoured the Blessed One's feet with his head and sat to one side. Seated to one side, King Prasenajit the Kośalan said to the Blessed One, 'Sir, the Blessed One is certainly an unsurpassed king of *dharma*, a saviour for beings who have fallen into evil, and a soother of hostility between enemies. This king of North Pañcāla is at war with the king of South Pañcāla, and they are killing one another's people. Let the Blessed One soothe their long-standing hostility through compassion.' The Blessed One consented to King Prasenajit the Kośalan through his silence. King Prasenajit the Kośalan understood from the Blessed One's silence that he had consented, and having honoured the Blessed One's feet with his head, he got up from his seat and left.

The very next morning the Blessed One got dressed, and taking his robe and bowl he set out on the journey towards Vārāṇasī, the city of the Kāśi people. Wandering on this journey in due course he reached Vārāṇasī and took up residence in Vārāṇasī, in the deer-park at Ṛṣipatana. At that, the two [kings] understood: 'The Blessed One has come to conquer us.'

The Blessed One frightened the King of North Pañcāla by creating the image of a fourfold army through his supernormal power. Alarmed, he mounted a single chariot and approached the Blessed One. The Blessed One gave a *dharma* teaching in order to calm his hostility, and on hearing the *dharma* he went forth in the presence of the Blessed One. By applying himself, striving and exerting, he abandoned all defilements and attained the state of arhatship.

And the king of South Pañcāla invited the Blessed One with his community of disciples and fed them with food of a hundred flavours for three months, and he clothed them with a hundred thousand cloths. Then he made a fervent aspiration: 'By this root of virtue, the arising of this thought and this properly given gift, may I become a *buddha* in this dark world that is leaderless and without a guide. May I carry across those beings who have not crossed over, liberate those who are not liberated, console those in need of consolation, bring to complete *nirvāṇa* those who have not entered complete *nirvāṇa*.'

Then the Blessed One, understanding the succession of causes and the succession of actions of that king of South Pañcāla, smiled. . . . [as story 1].

The Blessed One said, 'It is like this, Ānanda. It is like this. It is not without cause or without reason, Ānanda, that *tathāgatas* who are *arhats* and perfectly and fully awakened display a smile. Did you see, Ānanda, how this king of South Pañcāla honoured me in this way?' 'Yes, sir.' 'Ānanda, this king of South Pañcāla, through this root of virtue, the arising of this thought, and this properly given gift, after three incalculable aeons will attain awakening, and having fulfilled the six perfections that are pervaded with great compassion he will become a full and perfect *buddha* named Vijaya (Victor), with the ten powers, four confidences, three special applications of mindfulness and great compassion. This is the gift of one who has a faithful thought towards me.'

This was said by the Blessed One, and the monks were delighted and praised the Blessed One's speech.

9. Incense (*Dhūpa*)

The Buddha, the Blessed One, was honoured, revered, respected and worshipped by kings, ministers, the wealthy, the townsfolk, merchants, caravan leaders, gods, *nāgas*, *yakṣas*, antigods, heavenly birds, *kinnaras* and great snakes. That Buddha, the Blessed One, who was venerated as such by gods, *nāgas*, *yakṣas*, antigods, heavenly birds, *kinnaras* and great snakes, who was famous and possessed of great merit, and who was provided with the requisites – robes, bowls, bedding, seats, and medicine to cure the sick – was staying with his community of monks in Anāthapiṇḍada's park, the Jeta Grove in Śrāvastī.

At that time in Śrāvastī there were two guildsmen, and they were enemies of one another. One was a follower of Pūraṇa, and the the other of the Buddha, the Blessed One. When they were discussing and debating with one another, the disciple of Pūraṇa said, 'Pūraṇa is more distinguished than the Buddha!' and the disciple of the Buddha said, 'The Blessed One, the completely awakened Buddha, is most distinguished!' Then they made a wager of all their belongings.

King Prasenajit heard about this and ordered his courtiers: 'These two should be examined!' And so the courtiers proclaimed with a bell throughout the country: 'In seven days there will be an examination of the disciples of the Buddha and of a heretic! All who wish to see a marvel should come!' Then on the seventh day many hundreds of thousands of beings gathered on an extensive piece of ground, and many thousands of gods assembled in the vault of the sky, and the circle of cow-dung was laid out.

The disciple of the heretics first gathered together his garlands and incense, and then made his entreaty of truth: 'By this truth – that the six teachers with Pūraṇa at their head are chief in the world – by this truth may these flowers and this incense and this water go towards them!' At this declaration, the flowers fell to the floor, the fire went out, and the water completely vanished, disappearing into the earth. That great body of people cried out loudly with roars of joy, and seeing that the disciple of the heretics became silent and began to shake, his shoulders drooping, his face downcast and his confidence gone. He became very pensive, and placing his cheek in his hand he became lost in thought.

Then the disciple of the Blessed One was uplifted with joy, and with his eyes widened with faith, he arranged his upper robe on one shoulder, placed his right knee on the ground, and made his entreaty of truth: 'By this truth – the Blessed One is the best of all beings – by this truth may these flowers and this incense and water go towards the Blessed One!' And at that declaration they set off in the sky towards the Jeta Grove, the flowers like a flock of geese, the incense like a towering thundercloud, and the water like a sliver of beryl. Seeing this miracle the great body of the people cried out loudly with roars of joy, and followed behind those things.

Then those flowers remained above the Blessed One, and the water and incense in front of him. The great body of the people became faithful and worshipped the Blessed One's feet before sitting to one side to listen to the *dharma*. Then the Blessed One spoke this *sūtra*:

'Brahmins and householders, there are these three teachings about what is foremost. Which three? Teaching about the Buddha, and teaching about the *dharma* and about the *saṅgha*. What is the teaching about what is foremost about the Buddha? Brahmins and householders: the Tathāgata, the *arhat* who is a fully awakened Buddha is declared foremost among any beings, whether they have no feet or two feet or many feet, whether they have bodies or not, whether they have consciousness or not, or even those neither conscious nor unconscious.[9] Those who have faith in the Buddha, they have faith in the foremost. And the results for those who have faith in the foremost are also foremost, and should be expected as gods among the gods, or humans among humans. This, brahmins and householders, is the teaching about what is foremost with regard to the Buddha. And what is the teaching about what is foremost about the *dharma*? Whatever *dharma*s there are, ornamented or plain,[10] the *dharma* of dispassion is declared foremost of all these. Whoever has faith in the *dharma* has faith in the foremost. And the results for those who have faith in the foremost are also foremost, and should be expected as gods among the gods, or humans among humans. This, brahmins and householders, is the teaching about what is foremost with regard to the *dharma*. And what is the teaching about what is foremost about the *saṅgha*? Whatever *saṅgha*s there are, groups or assemblies or councils, the *saṅgha* of disciples of the Tathāgata is declared to be foremost of them all. Whoever has faith in the *saṅgha* has faith in the foremost. And the results for those who have faith in the foremost are also foremost, and should be expected as gods among the gods, or humans among humans. This, brahmins and householders, is the teaching about what is foremost with regard to the *saṅgha*.'

While this teaching was under way, some of those brahmins and householders gained faith in the Buddha, *dharma* and *saṅgha*, some took refuge and undertook the precepts, and some went forth. Those ones understood that this fivefold wheel of rebirth is in constant motion, rejected all conditioned things as being characterized by decay, decline, destruction and ruin, and through destroying all defilements achieved the state of arhatship.

And the disciple of the heretics gained faith in the Tathāgata and fell at his feet like a tree felled at the roots. He made this fervent aspiration: 'By this root of virtue, the arising of this thought and this properly given gift, may I become a *buddha* in this dark world that is leaderless and without a guide. May I carry across those beings who have not crossed over, liberate those who are not liberated, console those in need of consolation, bring to complete *nirvāṇa* those who have not entered complete *nirvāṇa*.'

Then the Blessed One, understanding the succession of causes and the succession of actions of that follower of the heretics, smiled. . . . [as story 1].

The Blessed One said, 'It is like this, Ānanda. It is like this. It is not without cause or without reason, Ānanda, that *tathāgatas* who are *arhats* and perfectly and fully awakened display a smile. Did you see, Ānanda, how this follower of the heretics honoured me in this way?' 'Yes, sir.' 'Ānanda, this follower of the heretics, through this root of virtue and the arising of this thought,[11] after three incalculable aeons will attain awakening, and having fulfilled the six perfections that are pervaded with great compassion he will become a full and perfect *buddha* named Acala (Unshakeable), with the ten powers, four confidences, three special applications of mindfulness and great compassion. This is the gift of one who has a faithful thought towards me.'

This was said by the Blessed One, and the monks were delighted and praised the Blessed One's speech.

10. The King (*Rājā*)

The Buddha, the Blessed One, was honoured, revered, respected and worshipped by kings, ministers, the wealthy, the townsfolk, merchants, caravan leaders, gods, *nāgas*, *yakṣas*, antigods, heavenly birds, *kinnaras* and great snakes. That Buddha, the Blessed One, who was venerated as such by gods, *nāgas*, *yakṣas*, antigods, heavenly birds, *kinnaras* and great snakes, who was famous and possessed of great merit, and who was provided with the requisites — robes, bowls, bedding, seats, and medicine to cure the sick — was staying with his community of monks in Anāthapiṇḍada's park, the Jeta Grove in Śrāvastī.

At that time, King Prasenajit the Kośalan and King Ajātaśatru were one another's enemies, and King Ajātaśatru prepared his fourfold army — elephants, horses, chariots and infantry — and marched out to war against King Prasenajit the Kośalan. King Prasenajit the Kośalan heard: 'King Ajātaśatru has readied his fourforld army of elephants, horses, chariots and infantry and has marched out to war!' Hearing this, he prepared his fourfold army of elephants, horses, chariots and infantry and marched out to war with King Ajātaśatru. And all of the elephant division of King Prasenajit the Kośalan were routed by King Ajātaśatru, and likewise the cavalry, chariots and infantry were routed. King Prasenajit the Kośalan, conquered and defeated, broken and frightened, turned back and entered Śrāvastī in a single chariot. This happened three times.

Then King Prasenajit the Kośalan went to his grieving room and resting his cheek in his hand he became lost in thought. There was a certain guildsman in Śrāvastī, who was rich, of great wealth and property, and extensive, wide holdings. He possessed the wealth of Vaiśravaṇa, rivaling Vaiśravaṇa in wealth. He heard that King Prasenajit the Kośalan had turned back, defeated and destroyed, and returned on a single chariot. Having heard this, he approached King Prasenajit the Kośalan. Having approached, he greeted King Prasenajit the Kośalan with 'Victory!' and 'Long life!' and said, 'Why does his majesty grieve? I offer his majesty gold, as much as is necessary to achieve his majesty's wishes.' Then he made a great heap of gold such that a seated person could not see a standing person, nor a standing person a seated one.

Then King Prasenajit the Kośalan sent out spies all over his kingdom: 'Listen to the talk of the people!' One day in the Jeta Grove there were two wrestlers chatting with one another: 'There is this formation called "lion" in which the cowardly men are placed at the front of the formation, the middling in the middle, and the best heroic men at the back.' This was reported to the king, and having heard it, King Prasenajit the Kośalan readied his fourfold army — elephants, cavalry, chariots and infantry — in this manner, and marched out to battle with King Ajātaśatru. And King Prasenajit the Kośalan routed all of the elephant division of King Ajātaśatru the son of Vaidehi, and likewise routed the cavalry, chariots and infantry. He captured alive King Ajātaśatru the son of Vaidehī, who was conquered and defeated, broken and frightened, and retreating. Taking him on a single chariot he went to where the Blessed One was. Having approached, he honoured the Blessed One's feet with his head and sat to one side. Seated to one side, King Prasenajit the Kośalan said to the Blessed One, 'Sir, this King Ajātaśatru has been hostile to me for a long time, though I am not hostile to him. He is my enemy though I am not his enemy. I do not want to deprive him of his life. Since he is the son of my friend, I will free him.' 'Then free him, great king,' said the Blessed One, and he spoke this verse at that time:

> 'Victory breeds hostility,
> The defeated sleep in pain;
> The peaceful sleep happy,
> Giving up victory and defeat.'

Then King Prasenajit the Kośalan thought, 'I secured my kingdom because of the faith of that guildsman. What if I were to reward him with a boon?' And King Prasenajit the Kośalan granted that guildsman a boon. He said, 'I wish my boon to be that you offer me the kingdom for my pleasure for seven days.' The king had it announced with gongs throughout his realm: 'I give this guildsman the kingdom for seven days!' Then the guildsman invited the community of monks with the Buddha at their head and fed them for seven days, as well as King Prasenajit and his retinue. And to those people who lived in Kāśi and Kośala he sent a messenger: 'For seven days you should each do as you wish and live in comfort. Having come here somehow, go for refuge with the Buddha, and with the *dharma* and the *saṅgha*. Enjoy my own food and honour the Tathāgata.' Hence the Blessed One, together with his community of disciples, was greatly honoured in this way for seven days, and many hundreds of thousands of beings were directed towards virtue.

When the seven days were over, he fell at the feet of the Blessed One, fostered an intention and made a fervent aspiration: 'By this root of virtue, the arising of this thought and this properly given gift, may I become a *buddha* in this dark world that is leaderless and without a guide. May I carry across those beings who have not crossed over, liberate those who are not liberated, console those in need of consolation, bring to complete *nirvāṇa* those who have not entered complete *nirvāṇa*.'

Then the Blessed One, understanding the succession of causes and the succession of actions of that guildsman, smiled. . . . [as story 1].

The Blessed One said, 'It is like this, Ānanda. It is like this. It is not without cause or without reason, Ānanda, that *tathāgatas* who are *arhats* and perfectly and fully awakened display a smile. Did you see, Ānanda, how this guildsman honoured the Tathāgata and his community of followers in this way, and brought a great many people to goodness?' 'Yes, sir.' 'Ānanda, this guildsman, through this root of virtue, the arising of this thought, and this properly given gift, after three incalculable aeons will attain awakening, and having fulfilled the six perfections that are pervaded with great compassion he will become a full and perfect *buddha* named Abhayaprada (Giving Safety), with the ten powers, four confidences, three special applications of mindfulness and great compassion. This is the gift of one who has a faithful thought towards me.'

This was said by the Blessed One, and the monks were delighted and praised the Blessed One's speech.

Second Decade

(Stories 11–20)

11. The Boatmen (*Nāvikā*)

The Buddha, the Blessed One, was honoured, revered, respected and worshipped by kings, ministers, the wealthy, the townsfolk, merchants, caravan leaders, gods, *nāgas*, *yakṣas*, antigods, heavenly birds, *kinnaras* and great snakes. That Buddha, the Blessed One, who was venerated as such by gods, *nāgas*, *yakṣas*, antigods, heavenly birds, *kinnaras* and great snakes, who was famous and possessed of great merit, and who was provided with the requisites — robes, bowls, bedding, seats, and medicine to cure the sick — was staying together with his community of disciples in Śrāvastī, below a village of boatmen on the River Ajiravatī.

Those boatmen approached the Blessed One, and having approached they venerated the Blessed One's feet with their heads and sat to one side. The Blessed One taught, inspired, incited and delighted those boatmen seated to one side with discourses on the *dharma*. Having taught, inspired, incited and delighted them with many kinds of *dharma* discourse, he was silent. Then those boatmen rose from their seats, placed their outer garments on one shoulder, respectfully extended their hands towards the Blessed One and said to him, 'Let the Blessed One, along with his community of monks, consent to take tomorrow's meal with us on the banks of the River Ajiravatī. We will transport you across on a bridge of boats.'[12] The Blessed One consented to the boatmen through his silence.

Then the boatmen prepared the bank of the River Ajiravatī by removing all the gravel, pebbles and small stones. They raised up parasols, flags and banners, and scattered various flowers there, and perfumed it with incense sticks. They had excellent food prepared, and made lots of bouquets of flowers, and decorated the bridge of boats with flower pavilions.

A messenger announced to the Blessed One that it was time: 'It is the moment, sir. The food is prepared, so the Blessed One should know that it is time.' The Blessed One, surrounded by a group of monks and attended by the monastic community, approached the village of the boatmen. Having approached, he sat on a seat that had been prepared, in front of the community of monks. When the boatmen saw that the community of monks with the Buddha at their head were comfortably seated nearby, they served them with their own hands, delighting them with pure and excellent hard and soft foods. Having served them with their own hands and delighted them with various kinds of pure and excellent hard and soft foods, when they saw that the Blessed One had eaten, his hands were washed and the bowl removed, they took lower seats and sat in front of the Blessed One in order to hear the *dharma*.

And the Blessed One, understanding the dispositions, propensities, character and nature of those boatmen, furnished them with a *dharma* teaching of such a kind that penetrated the four noble truths. Having heard this some boatmen attained the fruit of stream-entry, others the fruit of once-returning, others the fruit of non-returning, some renounced and by abandoning all defilements realized arhatship, others produced a resolve to attain the awakening of a disciple, others a resolve to *pratyekabodhi*, and yet others a resolve to full and perfect buddhahood. And the whole assembly was established in commitment to the Buddha, inclination towards the *dharma*, and devotion to the *saṅgha*. And then with great reverence the boatmen transported the Blessed One across on the bridge of boats, along with his community of monks.

The monks, their minds overcome by seeing the honour paid to the Buddha, asked the Blessed One, the Buddha, 'Where were these virtuous roots planted by the Blessed One?' The Blessed One said, 'O monks, actions that the Tathāgata performed and accumulated[13] in other previous births have come to fullness and their conditions have matured. Their flood, being at hand, was unavoidable. That is why the Tathāgata is honoured in this way. Would you like to hear about it, monks?' 'Indeed, sir.' 'Then listen, monks: concentrate your minds properly and well, and I will explain:

'Formerly, monks, in a past time, a fully awakened one called Bhāgīratha arose in the world: a *tathāgata*, an *arhat*, fully and perfectly awakened, perfected in knowledge and conduct, a well-farer, an unsurpassed knower of the world, a tamer of people who should be tamed, a teacher of gods and humans, a *buddha*, a blessed one. Surrounded by sixty-two thousand *arhat*s, he wandered on a journey through the countryside, and reached the shore of the Ganges.

'At that time a caravan leader with a retinue of several hundred was transporting his goods across the River Ganges, and in that place there was great danger from thieves. The caravan leader saw the fully and perfectly awakened Bhāgīratha with his assembly of 62 thousand *arhat*s, and having seen him his mind was filled with faith. With mind full of faith, he addressed the Blessed One: "I will carry the Blessed One across first of all." The fully and perfectly awakened Bhāgīratha consented to the caravan leader through his silence, and then the caravan leader conveyed the fully and perfectly awakened Bhāgīratha and his assembly of sixty-two thousand *arhat*s across on a bridge of boats with great pomp. And having refreshed them with excellent food, he made a fervent aspiration to attain unsurpassed full and perfect awakening.'

The Blessed One said, 'What do you think, monks? The person who was the caravan leader at that time, on that occasion, that was me. I transported the fully and perfectly awakened Bhāgīratha across on a bridge of boats along with his retinue of sixty-two thousand *arhat*s, refreshed them with excellent food, and made the fervent aspiration. Because of the ripening of that action of mine I have experienced great happiness in the boundless cycle of rebirths, and now I have attained unsurpassed full and perfect awakening and receive great honour like this. Therefore, monks, you should train in this way: "We will honour, revere, respect and worship the teacher. And having honoured, revered, respected and worshipped the teacher, we will live in reliance on him." In this way, monks, you should train.'

This was said by the Blessed One, and the monks were delighted and praised the Blessed One's speech.

12. The Post (*Stambha*)

The Buddha, the Blessed One, was honoured, revered, respected and worshipped by kings, ministers, the wealthy, the townsfolk, merchants, caravan leaders, gods, *nāga*s, *yakṣa*s, antigods, heavenly birds, *kinnara*s and great snakes. That Buddha, the Blessed One, who was venerated as such by gods, *nāga*s, *yakṣa*s, antigods, heavenly birds, *kinnara*s and great snakes, who was famous and possessed of great merit, and who was provided with the requisites – robes, bowls, bedding, seats, and medicine to cure the sick – wandered with his community of disciples on a journey through the countryside among the Kauravyas and arrived at the city of Kauravya.

Now a multitude of Kauravya people were ripe for conversion by the Buddha, for they were generous-minded and delighted by giving. It occurred to the Blessed One: 'If I were to summon Śakra, king of the gods, surrounded by his retinue of Maruts, as a result of seeing him they would increase their roots of virtue.' So the Blessed

One had a worldly thought: 'Well now! If only Śakra the king of the gods, together with his retinue of Maruts, would come bringing a post of *gośīrṣa* sandalwood!' With the arising of this thought, Śakra the king of gods, surrounded by his retinue of Maruts, came there, as did Viśvakarman and the great kings of the four directions, surrounded by many gods, *nāgas*, *yakṣas* and *kumbhāṇḍas*, bringing a post of *gośīrṣa* sandalwood. They cried out loudly — 'Ha! Ha! Kila! Kila!' — and according to the Blessed One's intention they constructed a palace made of *gośīrṣa* sandalwood.[14] Then in that palace Śakra the king of the gods honoured, revered, respected and worshipped the Blessed One, along with his community of disciples, with divine food, divine beds and seats, and celestial perfumes, garlands and flowers.

The multitude of Kauravya people saw that divine magnificence[15] and then they were amazed and thought: 'Surely the Buddha, the Blessed One, is supreme in the world, for he is honoured by gods with their kings!' Their minds were overcome and they turned to the Blessed One. Having honoured the Blessed One's feet they sat to one side. Seated to one side in that palace, the group of Kauravya people became extremely faithful.

Then the Blessed One made that palace disappear and taught a *dharma* teaching about such things as attachment to transient objects. Hearing that, many people who lived in Kauravya attained the fruit of stream-entry. Others attained the fruit of once-returning, some the fruit of non-returning, and some renounced and by abandoning all defilements realized arhatship. Others produced a resolve to attain the awakening of a disciple, others a resolve to *pratyekabodhi*, and yet others a resolve to full and perfect buddhahood. And the whole assembly was established in commitment to the Buddha, inclination towards the *dharma*, and devotion to the *saṅgha*.

The monks, their minds overcome by seeing the divine honour paid to the Blessed One, asked the Buddha, the Blessed One: 'Where were these good roots planted by the Blessed One?' The Blessed One said, 'O monks, actions that the Tathāgata performed and accumulated in other previous births have come to fullness and their conditions have matured. Their flood, being at hand, was unavoidable. That is why the Tathāgata is honoured in this way. Would you like to hear about it, monks?' 'Indeed, sir.' 'Then listen, monks: concentrate your minds properly and well, and I will explain:

'Formerly, monks, in a past time, a fully awakened one called Brahmā arose in the world: a *tathāgata*, an *arhat*, fully and perfectly awakened, perfected in knowledge and conduct, a well-farer, an unsurpassed knower of the world, a tamer of people who should be tamed, a teacher of gods and humans, a *buddha*, a blessed one. Surrounded by sixty-two thousand *arhat*s he wandered on a journey through the countryside, and reached a certain royal city.

'The consecrated warrior king heard, "The fully and perfectly awakened Brahmā along with his retinue of sixty-two thousand *arhat*s, wandering on a journey through the countryside, has arrived in our realm." Hearing this, with great royal power and great regal pomp, he went to the place where the Blessed One, the fully and perfectly awakened Brahmā was. Having arrived he venerated the fully and perfectly awakened Brahmā's feet with his head and sat to one side. The Blessed One inspired that consecrated warrior king who was seated to one side with the qualities that bring about awakening.

'That king became faithful, and getting up from his seat he put his outer robe over one shoulder, respectfully extended his hands towards the Blessed One and said to the Blessed One, "May the Blessed One consent to live in this royal residence for the three-month rainy season. I will attend upon the Blessed One and his community of disciples with the requisite robes, almsbowls, beds, seats, and medicines for the sick." The fully and perfectly awakened Brahmā consented to the king through his silence. Then that consecrated king, according to the Blessed One's intention, had a palace constructed out of *gośīrṣa* sandalwood. He presented this, decorated with a myriad of cloths and ornaments, covered with various flowers and perfumed with incense sticks, to the Blessed One along with his community of disciples. For three months he entertained them with excellent food and clothed them with diverse kinds of cloths, and then made a fervent aspiration to full and perfect buddhahood.'

The Blessed One said, 'What do you think, monks? The person who was the consecrated warrior king at that time, on that occasion, that was me. I honoured the fully and perfectly awakened Brahmā, and because of the ripening of that action of mine I have experienced great happiness in the boundless cycle of rebirths, and now I have attained unsurpassed perfect and full awakening and receive great honour like this. Therefore, monks, you should train in this way: "We will honour, revere, respect and worship the teacher. And having honoured, revered, respected and worshipped the teacher, we will live in reliance on him." In this way, monks, you should train.'

This was said by the Blessed One, and the monks were delighted and praised the Blessed One's speech.

13. The Bath (*Snātra*)

The Buddha, the Blessed One, was honoured, revered, respected and worshipped by kings, ministers, the wealthy, the townsfolk, merchants, caravan leaders, gods, *nāgas*, *yakṣas*, antigods, heavenly birds, *kinnaras* and great snakes. That Buddha, the Blessed One, who was venerated as such by gods, *nāgas*, *yakṣas*, antigods, heavenly birds, *kinnaras* and great snakes, who was famous and possessed of great merit, and who was provided with the requisites – robes, bowls, bedding, seats, and medicine to cure the sick – was staying with his community of disciples in Anāthapiṇḍada's park, the Jeta Grove in Śrāvastī.

At that time in Śrāvastī, five hundred merchants had gone along a forest path, and having lost their way they ended up in a desert. Tormented by heat and exhaustion, their provisions used up, scorched by the hot rays of the midday sun, they rolled around on the earth like fish out of water, enduring painful feelings that were severe, harsh, sharp and unpleasant. They entreated thousands of deities, namely Śiva, Varuṇa, Kubera, Vāsava and so on, but none of them was able to rescue them. But one of them was a layman who recognized the Buddha's teachings, and that merchant said to them, 'Good sirs, go to the Buddha for refuge!' And they all, in a single cry, went to the Buddha for refuge.

Now there is nothing that is unknown, unseen, unrecognized and unobserved by the *buddhas*, blessed ones. Indeed, being greatly compassionate and devoted to benefitting the world, *buddhas*, blessed ones:

> have one protector,
> dwell in calm and insight,
> are skilled in the threefold self-control,
> have overcome the four floods,
> have conduct grounded in the four bases of supernormal power,
> have long practised the four articles of attraction,
> lack the five [bad] qualities,
> have gone beyond the five realms,
> are endowed with the six qualities [of equanimity],
> have accomplished the six perfections,
> abound in the flowers that are the seven factors of awakening,
> are guides on the eightfold path,
> are skilled in the nine successive attainments [of meditation],
> are mighty with the ten powers,
> with splendour that fully pervades the ten directions,
> and more distinguished than ten times a hundred rulers.

It is a rule that when they survey the world with their *buddha*-vision for three days and three nights, knowledge and perception arise: 'Who is falling? Who is flourishing? Who has met with pain? Who is in danger? Who is afflicted? Who has met with pain, danger and affliction? Who is headed for a state of woe? Who is inclined towards a state of evil? Who is bent on a bad destiny? Whom can I raise up from bad states and establish in heaven and liberation? Who, mired in sense pleasures, might I raise up with my hands? Who, deprived of them, could I establish in mastery over and excellence in the noble treasures? Whose unplanted roots of virtue should I plant? Whose planted [roots] should I bring to maturity? And whose matured [roots] should I bring to liberation?' And it is said:

> Though the ocean, abode of monsters,
> may pass over the shore,
> A *buddha* cannot pass over the opportunity
> of young people in need of training.

In this way the Blessed One saw the many merchants who had met with misfortune, danger and affliction. At the very looking of his eye he disappeared from the Jeta Grove with his retinue of monks and reached that place. The merchants saw the Blessed One with his community of monks, and seeing him they let forth a loud cry. Then this worldly thought occurred to the Blessed One: 'Well now! Śakra, king of the gods, let loose the rain of Great Indra, and send forth cold winds!' And with the arising of this thought in the Blessed One, Śakra let loose the rain of Great Indra and set in motion cold wind. In this way the thirst of those merchants was quenched, and their heat was calmed. Those merchants obtained clear knowledge, and with the Blessed One showing them the road they reached Śrāvastī.

Their fatigue from the journey dispelled, they turned to the Blessed One, and the Blessed One gave a *dharma* teaching of such a kind that penetrated the four noble truths. Hearing this, some attained the fruit of stream-entry, some attained the fruit of once-returning, some the fruit of non-returning, and some renounced and by abandoning all defilements realized arhatship. Others produced a resolve to attain the awakening of a disciple, others a resolve to *pratyekabodhi*, and yet others a resolve to full and perfect buddhahood. And the whole assembly was established in commitment to the Buddha, inclination towards the *dharma*, and devotion to the *saṅgha*.

The monks became doubtful and asked the Buddha, the Blessed One, who cuts through all doubt, 'It is a marvel, Blessed One, that these merchants were rescued from the path in the wilderness by the Blessed One, and that with the arising of a thought the rains of Great Indra rained down and cooling winds blew.' The Blessed One said, 'O monks, actions that the Tathāgata performed and accumulated in other previous births have come to fullness and their conditions have matured. Their flood, being at hand, was unavoidable. These actions have been done and accumulated by me, so who else would experience their fruition? Monks, actions that have been done and accumulated do not bear fruit outside, neither in the earth element, nor in the water element, nor in the fire element, nor in the wind element. Rather, deeds done, whether pure or impure, ripen when the aggregates, the physical elements and the sense bases have arisen.

> Actions never come to naught
> even through hundreds of millions of aeons.[16]
> Having reached fullness and at the proper time,
> they bear fruit without fail for embodied beings.

'Formerly, monks, in a past time, a fully awakened one called Candana arose in the world — a *tathāgata*, an *arhat*, fully and perfectly awakened, perfected in knowledge and conduct, a well-farer, an unsurpassed knower of the world, a tamer of people who should be tamed, a teacher of gods and humans, a *buddha*, a blessed one. The fully and perfectly awakened Candana wandered on a journey through the countryside and reached a certain royal city.

'The consecrated warrior king approached the place where the fully and perfectly awakened Candana was. Having approached he honoured the fully and perfectly awakened Candana's feet with his head and sat to one side. And the fully and perfectly awakened Candana inspired that consecrated warrior king who was seated to one side with the qualities that bring about awakening. Getting up from his seat, the consecrated warrior king put his upper robe over one shoulder, placed his right knee on the ground, respectfully extended his hands towards the fully and perfectly awakened Candana, and said to the fully and perfectly awakened Candana, "May the Blessed One consent to live in this royal residence for the three-month rainy season, along with his community of monks.'"The fully and perfectly awakened Candana consented to the king through his silence.

'Now at that time a great drought appeared, as a result of which it happened that the rivers and wells contained little water and the trees lost their flowers and fruits. The king made a request of the fully and perfectly awakened Candana: "Blessed One, I will have a lotus pool filled with perfumed water built in the middle of our city, in which the Blessed One together with his community of disciples will bathe. Surely as a result of the Blessed One's bath the god will rain in our country." The Blessed One, the fully and perfectly awakened Candana, consented to the king through his silence.

'Then that consecrated warrior king gave an order to his courtiers: "Sirs, make ready perfumed water and water pitchers made of jewels, with which we will bathe the Blessed One together with his community of disciples." Then the king, surrounded by his retinue of courtiers, arranged that the city be cleared of gravel, pebbles and small stones, had flags and banners put up, scattered various flowers, sprinkled fragrant water, and perfumed it with a variety of incense. And the lotus pool was prepared.

'Then the Blessed One, the fully and perfectly awakened Candana, in order to benefit everyone, stood in a single robe in the lotus pool. The king, surrounded by his retinue of courtiers, bathed the fully and perfectly awakened Candana together with his community of disciples with water that was infused with various perfumes. And with that bathing of Candana the fully and perfectly awakened one, Śakra the king of the gods sent forth rains of the Great Indra variety, which revived all the crops. And because of this a great mass of the people gained faith in the Buddha. the Blessed One, and some of them established a perfumed *stūpa*. All those who went to the fully and perfectly awakened Candana for refuge entered *nirvāṇa*, and I am the only one remaining.

'Therefore, monks, you should train in this way: "We will honour, revere, respect and worship the teacher. And having honoured, revered, respected and worshipped the teacher, we will live in reliance on him." In this way, monks, you should train.'

This was said by the Blessed One, and the monks were delighted and praised the Blessed One's speech.

14. The Plague (*Īti*)

The Buddha, the Blessed One, was honoured, revered, respected and worshipped by kings, ministers, the wealthy, the townsfolk, merchants, caravan leaders, gods, *nāgas*, *yakṣas*, antigods, heavenly birds, *kinnaras* and great snakes. That Buddha, the Blessed One, who was venerated as such by gods, *nāgas*, *yakṣas*, antigods, heavenly birds, *kinnaras* and great snakes, who was famous and possessed of great merit, and who was provided with the requisites — robes, bowls, bedding, seats, and medicine to cure the sick — took residence with his community of disciples near Rājagṛha, in Kalandakanivāpa in the Veṇu Grove.

At that time there was an epidemic among the inhabitants of Nāḍakanthā, and lots of people were afflicted with diseases. They entreated several thousand different deities, including Śiva, Varuṇa, Kubera, Vāsava and so on, but none calmed the plague. Now a certain layman lived in Nāḍakanthā, and he said to the brahmins and householders who lived in Nāḍakanthā, 'Come, you should go to the Buddha for refuge, and entreat the Blessed One to come here. Then the Blessed One would put an end to the epidemic and lessen our pain.' So the brahmins and householders of Nāḍakanthā began to entreat the Blessed One: 'May the Blessed One come and free us from our dangerous plight!'

Now there is nothing that is unknown, unseen, unrecognized and unobserved by the *buddhas*, blessed ones. Indeed, being greatly compassionate and devoted to benefitting the world, *buddhas*, blessed ones:

have one protector,
dwell in calm and insight,
are skilled in the threefold self-control,
have overcome the four floods,
have conduct grounded in the four bases of supernormal
  power,
have long practised the four articles of attraction,
lack the five [bad] qualities,
have gone beyond the five realms,
are endowed with the six qualities [of equanimity],
have accomplished the six perfections,
abound in the flowers that are the seven factors of
  awakening,
are guides on the eightfold path,
are skilled in the nine successive attainments [of
  meditation],
are mighty with the ten powers,
  with splendour that fully pervades the ten directions,
  and more distinguished than ten times a hundred
    rulers.

It is a rule that when they survey the world with their *buddha*-vision for three days and three nights, knowledge and perception arise: 'Who is falling? Who is flourishing? Who has met with pain? Who is in danger? Who is afflicted? Who has met with pain, danger and affliction? Who is headed for a state of woe? Who is inclined towards a state of evil? Who is bent on a bad destiny? Whom can I raise up from bad states and establish in heaven and liberation? Who, mired in sense pleasures, might I raise up with my hands? Who, deprived of them, could I establish in mastery over and excellence in the noble treasures? Whose unplanted roots of virtue should I plant? Whose planted [roots] should I bring to maturity? And whose matured [roots] should I bring to liberation?' And it is said:

Though the ocean, abode of monsters,
may pass over the shore,
A *buddha* cannot pass over the opportunity
of young people in need of training.

In the morning the Blessed One dressed and, taking his robe and bowl and, surrounded by a group of monks and attended by the monastic community, reached Nāḍakanthā. Then the Blessed One suffused the whole city with heartfelt loving-kindness, and as a result the epidemic was gone, and the plague calmed. Then, on account of seeing the Buddha, those brahmins and householders experienced great faith, and those in whom faith had arisen served the Blessed One and his community of disciples with the requisite robes, almsbowls, beds, seats, and medicines for the sick. Then the Blessed One gave a *dharma* teaching of such a kind that penetrated the four noble truths. Hearing this, some of the brahmins and householders attained the fruit of stream-entry, some attained the fruit of once-returning, some the fruit of non-returning, and some renounced and by abandoning all defilements realized arhatship. And the whole city was established in commitment to the Buddha, inclination towards the *dharma*, and devotion to the *saṅgha*.

The monks became doubtful and asked the Blessed One, the Buddha, who cuts through all doubt, 'It is a marvel, sir, that these beings who had experienced calamity, through faith in the Blessed One were completely freed from their plight.' The Blessed One said, 'O monks, actions that the Tathāgata performed and accumulated in other previous births have come to fullness and their conditions have matured. Their flood, being at hand, was unavoidable. These actions have been done and accumulated by me, so who else would experience their fruition? Monks, actions that have been done and accumulated do not bear fruit outside, neither in the earth element, nor in the water element, nor in the fire element, nor in the wind element. Rather, deeds done, whether pure or impure, ripen when the aggregates, the physical elements and the sense bases have arisen.

> Actions never come to naught
> even through hundreds of millions of aeons.
> Having reached fullness and at the proper time,
> they bear fruit without fail for embodied beings.

'Formerly, monks, in a past time, a fully awakened one called Candra arose in the world: a *tathāgata*, an *arhat*, fully and perfectly awakened, perfected in knowledge and conduct, a well-farer, an unsurpassed knower of the world, a tamer of people who should be tamed, a teacher of gods and humans, a *buddha*, a blessed one. The fully and perfectly awakened Candra wandered on a journey through the countryside and reached a certain royal city.

'The consecrated warrior king heard: "A fully and perfectly awakened one has arrived in our realm." Having heard this, with great royal power and great regal pomp he went to the place where the fully and perfectly awakened Candra was. Having arrived, he honoured the fully and perfectly awakened Candra's feet with his head and sat to one side. The fully and perfectly awakened Candra inspired that consecrated warrior king who was seated to one side with the qualities that bring about awakening. Then that consecrated warrior king became faithful, and getting up from his seat he placed his robe on his shoulder, put his right knee on the ground, respectfully extended his hands towards the fully and perfectly awakened Candra, and said to the fully and perfectly awakened Candra: "May the Blessed One consent to live here with his community of monks for the three-month rainy season. I will attend upon the Blessed One with the requisite robes, almsbowls, beds, seats, and medicines for the sick." The fully and perfectly awakened Candra consented to the king through his silence.

'At that time in the king's city there was a great epidemic among the populace, and a plague that seriously afflicted a great body of people. The king, for the sake of appeasing the sickness, requested of Candra the fully and perfectly awakened one, "It would be good, Blessed One, if you were able by some means to calm the epidemic." Then the Blessed One, the fully and perfectly awakened Candra, said to the king, "Go, great king! Having fastened this robe on the top of a banner, have it paraded about in your realm with great reverence and make a great festival for it. And instruct all the many people to keep their minds on the Buddha. It will be for your benefit."

'So the king did everything as he had been instructed, and by that means and for that reason all the diseases were calmed. Then a body of people became faithful and the citizens and royal courtiers went to the Buddha for refuge, also taking refuge in the *dharma* and the *saṅgha*.'

The Blessed One said, 'What do you think, monks? The person who was the king at that time, on that occasion, that was me. I greatly honoured the fully and perfectly awakened Candra, and because of the ripening of that action of mine I have experienced great happiness in the cycle of rebirths. It caused me to attain divine and human birth, and because of it I am now powerful. All this was attained because of that thought and according to that wish. Therefore, monks, you should train in this way: "We will honour, revere, respect and worship the teacher. And having honoured, revered, respected and worshipped the teacher, we will live in reliance on him." In this way, monks, you should train.'

This was said by the Blessed One, and the monks were delighted and praised the Blessed One's speech.

15. The Miracle (*Prātihārya*)

The Buddha, the Blessed One, was honoured, revered, respected and worshipped by kings, ministers, the wealthy, the townsfolk, merchants, caravan leaders, gods, *nāgas*, *yakṣas*, antigods, heavenly birds, *kinnaras* and great snakes. That Buddha, the Blessed One, who was venerated as such by gods, *nāgas*, *yakṣas*, antigods, heavenly birds, *kinnaras* and great snakes, who was famous and possessed of great merit, and who was provided with the requisites – robes, bowls, bedding, seats, and medicine to cure the sick – took residence with his community of disciples near Rājagṛha, in Kalandakanivāpa in the Veṇu Grove.

When King Ajātaśatru, under the influence of Devadatta, put an end to the life of his father, a righteous and just monarch, and established himself as king, faithlessness became strong and faithfulness became weak. A certain senior courtier had no faith and was hostile to the teaching of the Blessed One, and he began to commission sacrifices from brahmins. Several hundred thousand brahmins assembled and made a resolution that nobody should approach the ascetic Gautama. Then those skilled brahmins, all in agreement, began to supplicate Śakra in the middle of the street with rites and utterances from the *Vedas* — 'Come, come, Lover of Ahalyā!'

Now there is nothing that is unknown, unseen, unrecognized and unobserved by the *buddhas*, blessed ones. Indeed, being greatly compassionate and devoted to benefitting the world, *buddhas*, blessed ones:

> have one protector,
> dwell in calm and insight,
> are skilled in the threefold self-control,
> have overcome the four floods,
> have conduct grounded in the four bases of supernormal power,
> have long practised the four articles of attraction,
> lack the five [bad] qualities,
> have gone beyond the five realms,
> are endowed with the six qualities [of equanimity],
> have accomplished the six perfections,
> abound in the flowers that are the seven factors of awakening,
> are guides on the eightfold path,
> are skilled in the nine successive attainments [of meditation],
> are mighty with the ten powers,
> with splendour that fully pervades the ten directions,
> and more distinguished than ten times a hundred rulers.

It is a rule that when they survey the world with their *buddha*-vision for three days and three nights, knowledge and perception arise: 'Who is falling? Who is flourishing? Who has met with pain? Who is in danger? Who is afflicted? Who has met with pain, danger and affliction? Who is headed for a state of woe? Who is inclined towards a state of evil? Who is bent on a bad destiny? Whom can I raise up from bad states and establish in heaven and liberation? Who, mired in sense pleasures, might I raise up with my hands? Who, deprived of them, could I establish in mastery over and excellence in the noble treasures? Whose unplanted roots of virtue should I plant? Whose planted [roots] should I bring to maturity? And whose matured [roots] should I bring to liberation?' And it is said:

> Though the ocean, abode of monsters,
> may pass over the shore,
> A *buddha* cannot pass over the opportunity
> of young people in need of training.

The Blessed One saw: 'These brahmins formerly planted virtuous roots and seized the path to liberation, desiring their own welfare and well disposed towards *nirvāṇa*, indifferent towards the cycle of rebirths. But now, because of lacking a spiritual guide they are hostile towards my teaching. I should approach eagerly for the purpose of training them.'

Then the Blessed One made himself look like Śakra, and shining forth with the appearance of a god he began to descend into the sacrificial arena. As a result, those brahmins were thrilled, pleased and delighted, becoming intensely joyful and happy, and all as one said: 'Come, come, Blessed One! You are welcome Blessed One!' Then the Blessed One, bearing the appearance of Śakra, sat on the seat that had been prepared.

Word spread throughout the city of Rājagṛha: 'During a sacrifice Śakra the king of the gods has descended!' Hearing this, many hundreds of thousands of beings assembled. Then after the humbled brahmins had honoured him in this way, the Blessed One removed his disguise as Śakra and resumed once again the appearance of the Buddha. He gave a *dharma* teaching of the kind that penetrates the four noble truths, hearing which sixty thousand brahmins, having split apart with the thunderbolt of knowledge the mountain of wrong views about individuality that rises up with twenty peaks, realized the fruit of stream-entry, and many hundreds of thousands of beings gained faith in the Blessed One.

Then the monks became doubtful and asked the Blessed One, the Buddha, who cuts through all doubt, 'It is a marvel, sir, that having come to the Blessed One these brahmins were made to see the truth, and that many hundreds of thousands of beings became greatly faithful.' The Blessed One said, 'O monks, actions that the Tathāgata performed and accumulated in other previous births have come to fullness and their conditions have matured. Their flood, being at hand, was unavoidable. These actions have been done and accumulated by me, so who else would experience their fruition? Monks, actions that have been done and accumulated do not bear fruit outside, neither in the earth element, nor in the water element, nor in the fire element, nor in the wind element. Rather, deeds done, whether pure or impure, ripen when the aggregates, the physical elements and the sense bases have arisen.

> Actions never come to naught
> even through hundreds of millions of aeons.
> Having reached fullness and at the proper time,
> they bear fruit without fail for embodied beings.

'Formerly, monks, in a past time, a fully awakened one called Indradamana arose in the world — a *tathāgata*, an *arhat*, fully and perfectly awakened, perfected in knowledge and conduct, a well-farer, an unsurpassed knower of the world, a tamer of people who should be tamed, a teacher of gods and humans, a *buddha*, a blessed one. He wandered on a journey through the countryside and reached a certain royal city. That royal city supported heretics.

'A certain consecrated warrior king heard, "The fully and perfectly awakened Indradamana has arrived in our realm." Having heard this, with great royal power and great regal pomp he went to the place where the fully and perfectly awakened Indradamana was. Having arrived he honoured the feet of the Blessed One, the fully and perfectly awakened Indradamana, with his head and sat to one side. The fully and perfectly awakened Indradamana inspired that consecrated warrior king who was seated to one side with the qualities that bring about awakening. Then that king gained faith, and getting up from his seat he placed his robe on his shoulder, put his right knee on the ground, and respectfully extending his hands towards the fully and perfectly awakened Indradamana he said this to the fully and perfectly awakened Indradamana: "May the Blessed One consent to live here for the three-month rainy season. I will attend upon the Blessed One with the requisite robes, almsbowls, beds, seats, and medicines for the sick."

'The Blessed One said, "Great King, is there any monastery in this realm in which monks who are coming or going can stay?" The King said, "There is not, Blessed One. But may the Blessed One stay! I will have a monastery built, in which monks who are coming and going may make their abode." Then the king had a monastery built according to the wishes of the Tathāgata, with solid walls and an arched doorway, adorned with round windows, turrets, half-moon-shaped lattice windows and balconies, and furnished with sleeping mats. It had abundant streams and was filled with groves of trees that contained various flowers and fruits. And when it was made it was presented to the Blessed One and his community of disciples, and the Blessed One was requested to perform a great miracle in return. Entreated by the king the Blessed One, the fully and perfectly awakened Indradamana, displayed a great miracle in which a multitude of *buddhas* became apparent. As a result of seeing this, the king, together with his courtiers and the town and country folk and the whole city, became very faithful and extremely devoted to the teaching.

'What do you think, monks? The one who was the king at that time, on that occasion, that was me. I honoured the fully and perfectly awakened Indradamana in this way, and because of the ripening of that action I experienced boundless happiness in the cycle of rebirths, and now being a *tathāgata* I have this brilliant teaching. Therefore, monks, you should train in this way: "We will honour, revere, respect and worship the teacher. And having honoured, revered, respected and worshipped the teacher, we will live in reliance on him." In this way, monks, you should train.'

This was said by the Blessed One, and the monks were delighted and praised the Blessed One's speech.

16. The Quinquennial Festival (*Pañcavārṣika*)

The Buddha, the Blessed One, was honoured, revered, respected and worshipped by kings, ministers, the wealthy, the townsfolk, merchants, caravan leaders, gods, *nāgas*, *yakṣas*, antigods, heavenly birds, *kinnaras* and great snakes. That Buddha, the Blessed One, who was venerated as such by gods, *nāgas*, *yakṣas*, antigods, heavenly birds, *kinnaras* and great snakes, who was famous and possessed of great merit, and who was provided with the requisites — robes, bowls, bedding, seats, and medicine to cure the sick — took residence with his community of disciples near Rājagṛha, in Kalandakanivāpa in the Veṇu Grove.

When that deluded person Devadatta had done a thousand evils with regard to the Blessed One's teaching, but was unable even to move a hair of the Blessed One, he addressed King Ajātaśatru: 'One should make a resolution that nobody in Rājagṛha is to approach the ascetic Gautama, or give him alms. Then, getting no goods and no honour, surely he will move on to another country.' The king did this.

Then those laypeople who had seen the truth began to lament: 'Oh it is dreadful that the city of Rājagṛha has no protector! For it is not possible to approach the Blessed One, the Buddha, whose appearance is as rare as the flower of the *udumbara* tree, and make provision for him.' Word of this passed on from person to person and was heard by the monks. Venerable Ānanda heard it and announced it to the Blessed One. The Blessed One said, 'Do not worry, Ānanda. In this matter the *tathāgatas* know the seasons. As long as there is my teaching, as before and now, there will be no insufficiency in the service of the disciples.'

Now it happened that Śakra, the king of the gods, came to know about this matter, and saw the alteration with regard to the Blessed One's teaching. For the sake of strengthening the generous givers, highlighting the greatness of the arising of a *buddha*, breaking the pride and arrogance of Ajātaśatru and Devadatta, and increasing his own faith, he manifested with splendour and nobility and made a loud announcement to the whole of Rājagṛha: 'Today I will serve the Blessed One together with his community of disciples with divine requisite robes, almsbowls, beds, seats, and medicines for the sick.'

Having announced this, he approached the Blessed One. Once he had approached he venerated the Blessed One's feet with his head and stood to one side. Then Śakra the king of the gods said this to the Blessed One: 'May the Blessed One consent that in this city of Rājagṛha I will serve the Blessed One with divine requisite robes, almsbowls, beds, seats, and medicines for the sick.' The Blessed One replied, 'Enough, Kauśika. It is sufficient to make your mind fully faithful, for there are many in the world who desire merit.'

Śakra said, 'May the Blessed One consent to stay for five years. I will make the quinquennial festival for the sake of the Tathāgata.' The Blessed One replied, 'Enough, Kauśika. It is sufficient to make your mind fully faithful, for there are many in the world who desire merit.'

Śakra said, 'May the Blessed One consent to five days.' Then the Blessed One, for the sake of displaying the strength of his own virtue, and in order to benefit Śakra the king of the gods, and to ensure the continuity of future quinquennial festivals, consented through his silence.

Then Śakra the king of the gods, understanding that the Blessed One had consented through his silence, made that Veṇu Grove look like Vaijayanta Palace with divine seats, heavenly lotus pools and divine food. The Blessed One sat on the seat that had been prepared. Śakra the king of the gods, seeing that the Buddha first of all and also the community of monks were happily seated, served and waited on them with his own hands, surrounded by several thousand deities. Having served him in various ways and waited on him with his own hands, understanding that the Blessed One had eaten, his hands washed and the bowl removed, he took a lower seat and sat before the Blessed One in order to hear the *dharma*. Then the Blessed One taught, inspired, incited and delighted Śakra the king of the gods and his retinue with a *dharma* discourse.

King Ajātaśatru, who had gone out on the palace roof terrace, saw this worship of the Blessed One in the Veṇu Grove, and having seen it he was remorseful and experienced great faith. The citizens who lived in Rājagṛha became agitated for the *dharma* and having approached the king they spoke thus: 'Great king, your majesty, the citizens who live in Rājagṛha have been robbed, for the gods, despite being heedless and delighting in intoxication, have abandoned their divine realm and worship the Blessed One. It would be good, your majesty, to undo the resolution.' Then King Ajātaśatru undid the resolution and proclaimed with a gong: 'Honour should be paid to the Blessed One as desired!'

The citizens who lived in Rājagṛha and their followers were thrilled, pleased and delighted, became intensely joyful and happy, and approached in order to see the Blessed One, bringing perfumes, garlands and flowers. Then the gods and humans paid great honour to the Blessed One, and the Blessed One gave a *dharma* talk of the kind that penetrates the four noble truths for the gods and humans standing there. Hearing this, many of the gods and humans saw the truth.

Seeing the honour paid to the Blessed One, the monks became doubtful and asked the Blessed One, 'It is a marvel, sir, that there be a festival of this kind in the Blessed One's dispensation.' The Blessed One said, 'O monks, actions that the Tathāgata performed and accumulated in other previous births have come to fullness and their conditions have matured. Their flood, being at hand, was unavoidable. These actions have been done and accumulated by me, so who else would experience their fruition? Monks, actions that have been done and accumulated do not bear fruit outside, neither in the earth element, nor in the water element, nor in the fire element, nor in the wind element. Rather, deeds done, whether pure or impure, ripen when the aggregates, the physical elements and the sense bases have arisen.

> Actions never come to naught
> even through hundreds of millions of aeons.
> Having reached fullness and at the proper time,
> they bear fruit without fail for embodied beings.

'Formerly, monks, in a past time, a fully awakened one named Ratnaśaila arose in the world: a *tathāgata*, an *arhat*, fully and perfectly awakened, perfected in knowledge and conduct, a well-farer, an unsurpassed knower of the world, a tamer of people who should be tamed, a teacher of gods and humans, a *buddha*, a blessed one. He wandered on a journey through the countryside and reached a certain royal city.

'In that royal city a king called Dharmaśuddhi (Pure Dharma) ruled the kingdom. And in that royal city there was a great epidemic, so that king offered the Blessed One and his community of disciples food for three months, in order to cure the epidemic. With the passing of three months the epidemic was pacified, and so the king and the citizens, their minds converted, made the quinquennial festival for the Tathāgata and his community of disciples.'

And he said:

> 'Ānanda, Ratnaśaila of great splendour, entreated by the king
> who desired peace, carried out the quinquennial festival.'

'What do you think, monks? He who at that time, on that occasion, was the king, that was me. I carried out the quinquennial festival for the Tathāgata Ratnaśaila, and because of that I experienced great happiness in the cycle of rebirths, and for that reason now I am honoured in this manner as a *tathāgata*. And when I am fully liberated there will be many hundreds of quinquennial festivals in my dispensation. Therefore, monks, you should train in this way: "We will honour, revere, respect and worship the teacher. And having honoured, revered, respected and worshipped the teacher, we will live in reliance on him." In this way, monks, you should train.'

This was said by the Blessed One, and the monks were delighted and praised the Blessed One's speech.

17. The Eulogy (*Stuti*)

The Buddha, the Blessed One, was honoured, revered, respected and worshipped by kings, ministers, the wealthy, the townsfolk, merchants, caravan leaders, gods, *nāgas*, *yakṣas*, antigods, heavenly birds, *kinnaras* and great snakes. That Buddha, the Blessed One, who was venerated as such by gods, *nāgas*, *yakṣas*, antigods, heavenly birds, *kinnaras* and great snakes, who was famous and possessed of great merit, and who was provided with the requisites – robes, bowls, bedding, seats, and medicine to cure the sick – was staying with his community of disciples in Anāthapiṇḍada's park, the Jeta Grove in Śrāvastī.

On that occasion, five hundred musicians were living in Śrāvastī as a company. At that time a king among musicians, named Supriya, arrived, and his power was of such a kind that he produced seven notes and twenty-one modes[17] on a single string. Proclaiming loudly that there were no skilled musicians in the six great cities, he arrived in Śrāvastī. The residents of Śrāvastī and the musicians reported this to the king. The king said, 'Do not worry, gentlemen. We will know what to do.'

Then Supriya the king of musicians thought this: 'It is often heard that King Prasenajit is very skilled in music. I should propose a contest with him.' So Supriya the king of musicians approached King Prasenajit the Kośalan, and having approached he said this to King Prasenajit the Kośalan: 'I have heard, king, that you are skilled in music. If you are without a teacher, you should be examined.' King Prasenajit put him off, saying, 'I have an accomplished teacher, an unsurpassed king of musicians, stationed in the Jeta Grove. Come, we should go to his presence.' Then King Prasenajit the Kośalan went to the Jeta Grove surrounded by the five hundred musicians, along with Supriya the king of musicians and many hundreds of thousands of beings.

Now there is nothing that is unknown, unseen, unrecognized and unobserved by the *buddhas*, blessed ones. Indeed, being greatly compassionate and devoted to benefitting the world, *buddhas*, blessed ones:

> have one protector,
> dwell in calm and insight,
> are skilled in the threefold self-control,
> have overcome the four floods,
> have conduct grounded in the four bases of supernormal power,
> have long practised the four articles of attraction,
> lack the five [bad] qualities,
> have gone beyond the five realms,
> are endowed with the six qualities [of equanimity],
> have accomplished the six perfections,
> abound in the flowers that are the seven factors of awakening,
> are guides on the eightfold path,
> are skilled in the nine successive attainments [of meditation],
> are mighty with the ten powers,
> with splendour that fully pervades the ten directions,
> and more distinguished than ten times a hundred rulers.

It is a rule that when they survey the world with their *buddha*-vision for three days and three nights, knowledge and perception arise: 'Who is falling? Who is flourishing? Who has met with pain? Who is in danger? Who is afflicted? Who has met with pain, danger and affliction? Who is headed for a state of woe? Who is inclined towards a state of evil? Who is bent on a bad destiny? Whom can I raise up from bad states and establish in heaven and liberation? Who, mired in sense pleasures, might I raise up with my hands? Who, deprived of them, could I establish in mastery over and excellence in the noble treasures? Whose unplanted roots of virtue should I plant? Whose planted [roots] should I bring to maturity? And whose matured [roots] should I bring to liberation?' And it is said:

> Though the ocean, abode of monsters,
> may pass over the shore,
> A *buddha* cannot pass over the opportunity
> of young people in need of training.

Then the Blessed One had a worldly thought to benefit those beings in need of training: 'Oh, that Pañcaśikha, the son of a *gandharva*, would enter my presence, with his retinue of seven thousand *gandharvas* and bringing his lute with its neck of beryl.' With the arising of that thought, Pañcaśikha the son of a *gandharva* with his retinue of seven thousand *gandharvas* was there, duly praising the Blessed One and bringing his lute with its neck of beryl for the Blessed One.

Then Supriya the king of musicians began to play the lute before the Blessed One, and he began to produce seven notes and twenty-one modes on a single string. On hearing this, King Prasenajit and a large body of the people were filled with intense wonder. Then the Blessed One also played the lute with its neck of beryl, such that he displayed several different notes and many kinds of modes on each string, yet making them appear empty.[18] And he showed that the body is like a lute, the notes like the sense organs and the modes like the heart element.

On hearing this, Supriya the king of musicians was humbled, and leaving his lute in the perfumed chamber he went forth in the presence of the Blessed One. And by applying himself, striving and exerting, he understood that this fivefold wheel of rebirth is in constant motion. Having rejected all conditioned things as being characterized by decay, decline, destruction and ruin, through destroying all the defilements he achieved the state of arhatship. Having become an *arhat* he was dispassionate towards the triple world. He considered a clod of earth the same as gold, and empty space the same as the palm of his hand, indifferent alike to an axe and sandal-paste. Having attained the knowledges, supernormal knowledges and special knowledges, he turned away from honours, desires, possessions and continued existence. He became worthy of worship, respect and veneration by the gods including Indra and Upendra.

Then the gods, *nāgas*, *yakṣas*, antigods, heavenly birds, *kinnara*s and great snakes were converted and began to be protectors of the Blessed One's teaching. The five hundred musicians became happy and glad, and it occurred to them: 'We are living in a low occupation and in a condition of suffering. What if, after asking the king, we were to invite the Blessed One together with his community of disciples into the city?' And accordingly those musicians gained permission and invited the Blessed One together with his community of disciples into the city, and the Blessed One accepted the invitation of those musicians through his silence. Then those musicians, along with the king, his courtiers, the citizens and countryfolk, removed the gravel, pebbles and small stones from the whole city of Śrāvastī, sprinkled it with perfumed water, scattered various flowers, perfumed it with various scents, and decorated it with heaps of flowers. And then those musicians, each carrying his own lute, and with various drums, flutes and cymbals, approached and served the Blessed One and his community of disciples with excellent food.

Then the Blessed One smiled. Now according to the natural order of things, when *buddha*s display a smile then blue, yellow, red and white rays issue from his mouth and some go upwards and some downwards. Those that go downwards, they go to the hells — the Saṃjīva (Reviving), Kālasūtra (Black Thread), Saṃghāta (Crushing), Raurava (Shrieking), Mahāraurava (Loud Shrieking), Tapana (Heat), Pratāpana (Extreme Heat), Avīci (Endless Torture), Arbuda (Blistering), Nirarbuda (Blisters Bursting), Aṭaṭa (Chattering Teeth), Hahava (Ugh!), Huhuva (Brrr!), Utpala (Blue Lotus), Padma (Lotus) and Mahāpadma (Great Lotus). Those that descend into the hot hells become cool, and those that descend into the cold hells become warm, and in this way they alleviate the various sufferings of the beings there, such that it occurs to them, 'Friends, can it be that we have left this place and arisen elsewhere?' Then, in order to make them develop faith, the Blessed One emits an image of himself, and seeing this image they realize, 'No, friends, we have not left this place nor arisen elsewhere. There is this being, not seen before, whose power is easing our various sufferings.' Their minds become faithful towards this image, and they cast off the karma still to be experienced in hell, and take rebirth among gods and men, where they become vessels for the truths.

Those [rays of light] that go upwards, they go to the gods — the Cāturmahārājika (Four Groups of the Great Kings), Trāyastriṃśa (Thirty-three), Yāma (Of Yama), Tuṣita (Content), Nirmāṇarati (Delighting in Creation), Paranirmitavaśavartin (Masters of Others' Creations), Brahmakāyika (Brahmā's Assembly), Brahmapurohita (Brahmā's Priests), Mahābrahma (Great Brahmā), Parittābhā (Limited Splendour), Apramāṇābhā (Immeasurable Splendour), Abhāsvara (Radiant), Parittaśubha (Limited Beauty), Apramāṇaśubha (Immeasurable Beauty), Śubhakṛtsna (Complete Beauty), Anabhraka (Unclouded), Puṇyaprasava (Merit Born), Bṛhatphala (Great Result), Abṛha (Not Vast), Atapa (Serene), Sudṛśa (Good-Looking), Sudarśana (Clear-Sighted) and Akaniṣṭha (Supreme). They shout out, 'Impermanent! Suffering! Empty! Not-Self!' and speak two verses:

> 'Exert yourselves! Go forth!
> Take up the Buddha's teaching!
> Shake the army of death
> like an elephant shakes a reed-hut!
>
> Whoever diligently follows
> this *dharma* and discipline,
> will abandon the cycle of rebirths
> and make an end to suffering.'

Then those rays of light, having roamed through the great trichiliocosm, assemble behind the Blessed One. If the Blessed One wishes to explain past actions, they disappear into the Blessed One's back; if he wishes to explain future actions, they vanish into his front. If he wishes to predict arising in a hell, they disappear into the soles of his feet, while if he wants to predict arising as an animal, they enter his heel, and if he wants to predict arising as a hungry ghost, they vanish into his big toe, and if he desires to predict arising as a human, they disappear into his knee. If he wishes to predict rule as an armed wheel-turning king, they enter the palm of his left hand, while if he wishes to predict rule as a wheel-turning king, they disappear into the palm of his right hand. If he wishes to predict arising as a god, they vanish into his navel. If he wishes to predict awakening as a disciple, they enter his mouth, while if he wants to predict awakening as a *pratyekabuddha*, they vanish into the circle of hair between his eyebrows, and if he wants to predict unsurpassed and perfect full buddhahood, they disappear into his *uṣṇīṣa*.

And those rays of light circumambulated the Blessed One three times and disappeared into the circle of hair between the Blessed One's eyebrows. Then Venerable Ānanda joined his hands in respect and asked the Blessed One:

> 'A collection of a thousand bright coloured rays of various
> kinds
> is expelled from the inside of your mouth,
> completely illuminating the directions
> as if from the rising of the sun.'

And he spoke these verses:

> '*Buddhas* have cut off rebirth, abandoned affliction and
> enjoyment,
> and become the cause of what is best in the world.
> Not without reason do victors, their enemies conquered,
> exhibit a smile, white as a conch-shell or lotus-fibre.
>
> Hero, ascetic, the best of victors, you know at once
> through your own intelligence, the wishes of your listeners.
> Bull among sages, remove the doubt that has arisen,
> with splendid, wise and superior speech.

It is not without reason that perfect *buddhas*, protectors
firm as the ocean or the king of the mountains, exhibit a
smile.
A multitude of people yearn to hear
the reason why wise ones exhibit a smile.'

The Blessed One said, 'It is like this, Ānanda. It is like this. It is not without cause or without reason, Ānanda, that *tathāgatas* who are *arhats* and perfectly and fully awakened display a smile. Did you see, Ānanda, the way these musicians paid me honour? Thus, Venerable Ānanda, these musicians, because of this root of virtue, the arising of this thought, and this properly given gift, when the time comes they will acquire *pratyekabodhi*, and become *pratyekabuddhas* called Varṇasvarā (Glorious Tones) in a future time. They will feel compassion for the wretched and miserable, and take their food, bed and seat in a lonely place, and be the only ones worthy of veneration in the world. This is the gift of those who have a faithful thought towards me.'

The monks became doubtful and asked the Blessed One, the Buddha, who cuts through all doubt, 'Sir, what were the virtuous roots planted by the Blessed One that produced this?' The Blessed One said, 'O monks, actions that the Tathāgata performed and accumulated in other previous births have come to fullness and their conditions have matured. Their flood, being at hand, was unavoidable. These actions have been done and accumulated by me, so who else would experience their fruition? Monks, actions that have been done and accumulated do not bear fruit outside, neither in the earth element, nor in the water element, nor in the fire element, nor in the wind element. Rather, deeds done, whether pure or impure, ripen when the aggregates, the physical elements and the sense bases have arisen.

Actions never come to naught
even through hundreds of millions of aeons.
Having reached fullness and at the proper time,
they bear fruit without fail for embodied beings.

'Formerly, monks, in a past time, a fully awakened one named Prabodhana arose in the world: a *tathāgata*, an *arhat*, fully and perfectly awakened, perfected in knowledge and conduct, a well-farer, an unsurpassed knower of the world, a tamer of people who should be tamed, a teacher of gods and humans, a *buddha*, a blessed one. He wandered on a journey through the countryside and reached a certain royal city.

'The king's park was endowed with all that was suitable, so the Blessed One entered that park and in order to benefit the king he sat down near a certain tree. Having arranged his seat, he attained the fire-element meditation. Then the consecrated warrior king entered the park with women playing music on instruments, and walking through that park the king saw the Blessed One Prabodhana, the fully and perfectly awakened one who engenders faith in those who would be faithful, calm of mind, endowed with the highest degree of calmness and control of the mind, like a pillar of gold, radiant and blazing. And having seen him the king became faithful and, with his harem, woke[19] the Blessed One from his meditative state by playing various musical instruments. He served him with excellent food, and made an aspiration to unsurpassed full and perfect buddhahood.

'What do you think, monks? The person who at that time, on that occasion, was the king, that was me. I honoured the fully and perfectly awakened Prabodhana, and as a result of that I have been praised in this way by the musicians. Therefore, monks, you should train in this way: "We will honour, revere, respect and worship the teacher. And having honoured, revered, respected and worshipped the teacher, we will live in reliance on him." In this way, monks, you should train.'

This was said by the Blessed One, and the monks were delighted and praised the Blessed One's speech.

18. The Boon (*Varada*)

The Buddha, the Blessed One, was honoured, revered, respected and worshipped by kings, ministers, the wealthy, the townsfolk, merchants, caravan leaders, gods, *nāgas*, *yakṣas*, antigods, heavenly birds, *kinnaras* and great snakes. That Buddha, the Blessed One, who was venerated as such by gods, *nāgas*, *yakṣas*, antigods, heavenly birds, *kinnaras* and great snakes, who was famous and possessed of great merit, and who was provided with the requisites – robes, bowls, bedding, seats, and medicine to cure the sick – was staying with his community of disciples in Anāthapiṇḍada's park, the Jeta Grove in Śrāvastī.

In Śrāvastī a certain philanderer was intent on doing bad deeds. He was seized by the king's men and brought before the king. The king declared him a criminal, and gave him the death sentence. With his neck ornamented by a garland of oleander flowers, he was proclaimed a criminal on the roads and at crossroads and junctions by the king's men, who were dressed in blue garments and holding their swords aloft, and then led through the southern gate of the city.

Now there is nothing that is unknown, unseen, unrecognized and unobserved by the *buddhas*, blessed ones. Indeed, being greatly compassionate and devoted to benefitting the world, *buddhas*, blessed ones:

have one protector,
dwell in calm and insight,
are skilled in the threefold self-control,
have overcome the four floods,
have conduct grounded in the four bases of supernormal
    power,
have long practised the four articles of attraction,
lack the five [bad] qualities,
have gone beyond the five realms,
are endowed with the six qualities [of equanimity],
have accomplished the six perfections,

abound in the flowers that are the seven factors of
    awakening,
are guides on the eightfold path,
are skilled in the nine successive attainments [of
    meditation],
are mighty with the ten powers,
    with splendour that fully pervades the ten directions,
    and more distinguished than ten times a hundred
        rulers.

It is a rule that when they survey the world with their *buddha*-vision for three days and three nights, knowledge and perception arise: 'Who is falling? Who is flourishing? Who has met with pain? Who is in danger? Who is afflicted? Who has met with pain, danger and affliction? Who is headed for a state of woe? Who is inclined towards a state of evil? Who is bent on a bad destiny? Whom can I raise up from bad states and establish in heaven and liberation? Who, mired in sense pleasures, might I raise up with my hands? Who, deprived of them, could I establish in mastery over and excellence in the noble treasures? Whose unplanted roots of virtue should I plant? Whose planted [roots] should I bring to maturity? And whose matured [roots] should I bring to liberation?' And it is said:

Though the ocean, abode of monsters,
may pass over the shore,
A *buddha* cannot pass over the opportunity
of young people in need of training.

In the morning the Blessed One dressed, and taking his bowl and robe he entered Śrāvastī for alms. That man saw the Buddha, the Blessed One, adorned with the thirty-two marks of a great man and the eighty secondary marks, his body shining, arrayed with light that extended a fathom, radiance in excess of a thousand suns, like a living mountain of jewels, handsome in his entirety. And having seen him he threw himself at the Blessed One's feet and said to the Blessed One: 'I am worthy of a boon, Blessed One. Grant me my life, as I wish.'

The Blessed One addressed Venerable Ānanda: 'Ānanda, go to King Prasenajit and say, "Offer me this man, I will make him a monk."' Venerable Ānanda approached King Prasenajit the Kośalan. Having approached, he spoke the Blessed One's words to King Prasenajit the Kośalan: 'Grant that the Blessed One ordain this man.'

Saying, 'So be it', King Prasenajit the Kośalan consented, and the man was received and ordained by the Blessed One. And by applying himself, striving and exerting, he understood that this fivefold wheel of rebirth is in constant motion. Having rejected all conditioned things as being characterized by decay, decline, destruction and ruin, through destroying all the defilements he achieved the state of arhatship. Having become an *arhat*, he was dispassionate towards the triple world. He considered a clod of earth the same as gold, and empty space the same as the palm of his hand, indifferent alike to an axe and sandal-paste. Having attained the knowledges, supernormal knowledges and special knowledges, he turned away from honours, desires, possessions and continued existence. He became worthy of worship, respect and veneration by the gods including Indra and Upendra.

The monks became doubtful and questioned the Blessed One, who cuts through all doubt, 'It is a marvel, sir, that all intentions prosper through the Blessed One.' The Blessed One said, 'O monks, actions that the Tathāgata performed and accumulated in other previous births have come to fullness and their conditions have matured. Their flood, being at hand, was unavoidable. These actions have been done and accumulated by me, so who else would experience their fruition? Monks, actions that have been done and accumulated do not bear fruit outside, neither in the earth element, nor in the water element, nor in the fire element, nor in the wind element. Rather, deeds done, whether pure or impure, ripen when the aggregates, the physical elements and the sense bases have arisen.

> Actions never come to naught
> even through hundreds of millions of aeons.
> Having reached fullness and at the proper time,
> they bear fruit without fail for embodied beings.

'Formerly, monks, in a past time, a fully awakened one named Indradhvaja arose in the world: a *tathāgata*, an *arhat*, fully and perfectly awakened, perfected in knowledge and conduct, a well-farer, an unsurpassed knower of the world, a tamer of people who should be tamed, a teacher of gods and humans, a *buddha*, a blessed one. He wandered on a journey through the countryside and reached a certain royal city.

'In that royal city a brahmin who had mastered the *Veda*s and the Vedic expositions had a seat of honour with the king. In the morning, Indradhvaja the fully and perfectly awakened one dressed himself and, taking his bowl and robe, entered that royal city for alms. That brahmin saw Indradhvaja the fully and perfectly awakened one, adorned with the thirty-two marks of a great man and the eighty secondary marks, his body shining, arrayed with light that extended a fathom, radiance in excess of a thousand suns, like a living mountain of jewels, handsome in his entirety. And having seen him, he was like a tree cut off at the roots, and throwing himself at the Blessed One's feet he said, "I am worthy of a boon, Well-Farer. May the Blessed One sit on the seat of honour." Then the Blessed One, the fully and perfectly awakened Indradhvaja, wishing to benefit him, sat on the seat of honour. And the brahmin praised Indradhvaja the fully and perfectly awakened one, seated in that seat of honour, in a hundred verses,[20] and served him with excellent food, and made a fervent aspiration to unsurpassed full and perfect buddhahood. And because of this the king, courtiers and citizens were converted.

'What do you think, monks? The one who was that brahmin on that occasion at that time, that was me. It was me that honoured the Tathāgata Indradhvaja, and because of this I have experienced boundless happiness in the cycle of rebirths, and that wish, that aspiration, all came to fruition. Therefore, monks, you should train in this way: "We will honour, revere, respect and worship the teacher. And having honoured, revered, respected and worshipped the teacher, we will live in reliance on him." In this way, monks, you should train.'

This was said by the Blessed One, and the monks were delighted and praised the Blessed One's speech.

19. The Cloth of Kāśi (*Kāśikavastra*)

The Buddha, the Blessed One, was honoured, revered, respected and worshipped by kings, ministers, the wealthy, the townsfolk, merchants, caravan leaders, gods, *nāgas*, *yakṣas*, antigods, heavenly birds, *kinnaras* and great snakes. That Buddha, the Blessed One, who was venerated as such by gods, *nāgas*, *yakṣas*, antigods, heavenly birds, *kinnaras* and great snakes, who was famous and possessed of great merit, and who was provided with the requisites — robes, bowls, bedding, seats, and medicine to cure the sick — was staying with his community of disciples near Rājagṛha, in Kalandakanivāpa in the Veṇu Grove.

When King Bimbisāra, along with many hundreds of thousands of beings, had comprehended the truths, then in order to display his gratitude, for the sake of promoting worship of the Buddha, in order to display the extent of his house, and in order to make known the value of the arising of a *buddha*, he invited the Blessed One together with his community of monks to take a meal in the royal palace. And he commanded the citizens of Magadha, 'At the entrance to the city the Blessed One is to be honoured with garlands, flowers, perfumes and ointments, and the whole city of Rājagṛha should be prepared by removing the gravel, pebbles and small stones. Various flowers should be scattered and flags and banners raised up all the way from the Veṇu Grove to Rājagṛha, and the whole of the road in between should be covered with cloths.' And all this was arranged by the courtiers. Then King Bimbisāra himself held the hundred-ribbed parasol [of state] over the Blessed One's head, and the remaining citizens did the same for the community of monks.

Now the Blessed One — restrained and surrounded by restrained people, peaceful and surrounded by the peaceful, freed and surrounded by the freed, calmed and surrounded by the calm, tamed and surrounded by the tamed, an *arhat* surrounded by *arhats*, dispassionate and surrounded by the dispassionate, an agent of faith and surrounded by agents of faith, like a bull among a herd of cattle, like an elephant among a group of young elephants, like a lion among a group of predators, like a goose among a flock of geese, like a *suparṇa* among a flock of birds, like a sage surrounded by a group of students, like a good horse among a herd of horses, like a hero among a group of warriors, like a guide among a band of travellers, like a caravan leader among a caravan of merchants, like a guildsman among a group of city-dwellers, like the ruler of a castle among a group of courtiers, like a wheel-turning monarch surrounded by his thousand sons, like the moon among the collection of stars, like the sun surrounded by its thousand rays, like Dhṛtarāṣṭra among a troop of *gandharvas*, like Virūḍa among a group of *kumbhāṇḍas*, like Virūpākṣa surrounded by a troop of *nāgas*, like Dhanada among a group of *yakṣas*, like Vemacitri surrounded by a group of antigods, like Śakra among the group of thirty gods, like Brahmā surrounded by Brahmā's retinue, like the tranquil ocean, like a watery thundercloud, like a lord of elephants free from rut — the Blessed One entered that city walking with proper steady deportment, with senses completely restrained, filled with the many special qualities of a *buddha*.

And when the Blessed One's foot was placed on the threshold, the great earth trembled in six ways, and when the Blessed One entered the city many other wonders of such a kind occurred. That is to say: small things became broad, elephants called out, horses neighed, bulls bellowed, various musical instruments that were in the houses played by themselves, the blind recovered their sight, the deaf their hearing, mutes became able to speak, those who were deficient in the other sense organs had their senses completely restored, those who were horribly drunk became sober, those who had taken poison were freed from it, those who were enemies with one another became friendly, pregnant women gave birth successfully, those bound in fetters were freed, the poor received riches, and the atmospheric deities, gods, antigods, heavenly birds, *kinnaras* and great snakes let loose divine flowers.

Then the Blessed One began to enter the royal palace with supernormal power of this kind, and King Bimbisāra himself stood in the courtyard outside the door. He took foot-washing water fragranced with *gośīrṣa* sandalwood and washed the feet of the Blessed One and his community of monks. Having seen that the community of monks with the Buddha at their head were happily seated nearby, he presented them with food of a hundred flavours, and after they had eaten he clothed them in *kāśi* cloths. And because of this the citizens of Magadha were converted.

Then the monks became doubtful and asked the Blessed One, the Buddha, who cuts through all doubt, 'Where was this virtuous root of the Blessed One planted, on account of which the Blessed One and the community of monks have been honoured in such a fashion?' The Blessed One said, 'O monks, actions that the Tathāgata performed and accumulated in other previous births have come to fullness and their conditions have matured. Their flood, being at hand, was unavoidable. These actions have been done and accumulated by me, so who else would experience their fruition? Monks, actions that have been done and accumulated do not bear fruit outside, neither in the earth element, nor in the water element, nor in the fire element, nor in the wind element. Rather, deeds done, whether pure or impure, ripen when the aggregates, the physical elements and the sense bases have arisen.

> Actions never come to naught
> even through hundreds of millions of aeons.
> Having reached fullness and at the proper time,
> they bear fruit without fail for embodied beings.

'Formerly, monks, in a past time, a fully awakened one named Kṣemaṃkara arose in the world: a *tathāgata*, an *arhat*, fully and perfectly awakened, perfected in knowledge and conduct, a well-farer, an unsurpassed knower of the world, a tamer of people who should be tamed, a teacher of gods and humans, a *buddha*, a blessed one.

He wandered on a journey through the countryside and reached a certain royal city.

'The consecrated warrior king heard, "Kṣemaṃkara the fully and perfectly awakened one, wandering on a journey through the countryside, has reached our royal city." And hearing this, with great royal power and great regal pomp he approached the place where the Blessed One, the fully and perfectly awakened Kṣemaṃkara, was. Having arrived, he honoured the fully and perfectly awakened Kṣemaṃkara's feet with his head and sat to one side. The fully and perfectly awakened Kṣemaṃkara inspired that consecrated warrior king who was seated to one side with the qualities that bring about awakening. Then that king gained faith, and having invited the fully and perfectly awakened Kṣemaṃkara to the royal palace he presented him with food of a hundred flavours and clothed him with a cloth worth a hundred thousand. And when he had attained complete *nirvāṇa* he had a *stūpa* constructed that was a *krośa* high and a *yojana* in every direction.

'What do you think, monks? He who was at that time and on that occasion the king, that was me. It was me that paid the fully and perfectly awakened Kṣemaṃkara honour in that way. For that reason I experienced boundless happiness in the cycle of rebirths, and now I receive honour of such a kind from King Bimbisāra. Therefore, monks, you should train in this way: "We will honour, revere, respect and worship the teacher. And having honoured, revered, respected and worshipped the teacher, we will live in reliance on him." In this way, monks, you should train.'

This was said by the Blessed One, and the monks were delighted and praised the Blessed One's speech.

20. Divine Food (*Divyabhojana*)

The Buddha, the Blessed One, was honoured, revered, respected and worshipped by kings, ministers, the wealthy, the townsfolk, merchants, caravan leaders, gods, *nāgas*, *yakṣas*, antigods, heavenly birds, *kinnaras* and great snakes. That Buddha, the Blessed One, who was venerated as such by gods, *nāgas*, *yakṣas*, antigods, heavenly birds, *kinnaras* and great snakes, who was famous and possessed of great merit, and who was provided with the requisites — robes, bowls, bedding, seats, and medicine to cure the sick — was staying with his community of disciples in Rājagṛha, in Kalandakanivāpa in the Veṇu Grove.

There was a certain guildsman who was rich, of great wealth and property, and extensive, wide holdings, who possessed the wealth of Vaiśravaṇa, rivaling Vaiśravaṇa in wealth, and who was a follower of the heretics. He was converted to the [Buddhist] teaching by Venerable Mahāmaudgalyāyana and developed great faith in the Blessed One. And that householder, having a strong inclination towards generosity, said to Venerable Mahāmaudgalyāyana, 'Be a friend to me. I wish to pay honour to the Blessed One.' Venerable Mahāmaudgalyāyana consented to that householder through his silence.

Then Venerable Mahāmaudgalyāyana took the householder and went to where the Blessed One was. Having arrived, he honoured the Blessed One's feet with his head and sat to one side. Seated to one side, Venerable Mahāmaudgalyāyana said this to the Blessed One, 'Sir, this householder wishes to feed the Blessed One together with his community of monks. So let the Blessed One, feeling compassion, consent to this.' The Blessed One consented to the householder through his silence.

Then that householder, understanding that the Blessed One had consented through his silence, brought together food of a hundred flavours as well as ointments, garlands, perfumes and flowers. And Venerable Mahāmaudgalyāyana requested of the king of gods

Śakra, 'This householder should be assisted.' So Śakra the king of gods magically made the Veṇu Grove into the Nandana Grove, and a thousand elephants resembling Airāvaṇa and Supratiṣṭhita . . . fanned with a yak-tail fan.[21] Several thousand *gandharvas*, beginning with Supriya, Pañcaśikha and Tumburu, were brought near, played music on musical instruments of various kinds, and prepared divine food and elixirs. Then that householder, with the assistance of the spirit-deities, approached the Blessed One, threw his whole body at the Blessed One's feet and made a fervent aspiration: 'By this root of virtue, the arising of this thought and this properly given gift, may I become a *buddha* in this dark world that is leaderless and without a guide. May I carry across those beings who have not crossed over, liberate those who are not liberated, console those in need of consolation, bring to complete *nirvāṇa* those who have not entered complete *nirvāṇa*.'

Then the Blessed One, understanding the succession of causes and the succession of actions of that householder, smiled. Now, according to the natural order of things, when *buddhas* display a smile then blue, yellow, red and white rays issue from his mouth and some go upwards and some downwards. Those that go downwards, they go to the hells – the Saṃjīva (Reviving), Kālasūtra (Black Thread), Saṃghāta (Crushing), Raurava (Shrieking), Mahāraurava (Loud Shrieking), Tapana (Heat), Pratāpana (Extreme Heat), Avīci (Endless Torture), Arbuda (Blistering), Nirarbuda (Blisters Bursting), Aṭaṭa (Chattering Teeth), Hahava (Ugh!), Huhuva (Brrr!), Utpala (Blue Lotus), Padma (Lotus) and Mahāpadma (Great Lotus). Those that descend into the hot hells become cool, and those that descend into the cold hells become warm, and in this way they alleviate the various sufferings of the beings there, such that it occurs to them, 'Friends, can it be that we have left this place and arisen elsewhere?' Then, in order to make them develop faith, the Blessed One emits an image of himself, and seeing this image they realize, 'No, friends, we have not left this place nor arisen elsewhere. There is this being, not seen before, whose power is easing our various sufferings.' Their minds become faithful towards this image, and they cast off the karma still to be experienced in hell, and take rebirth among gods and men, where they become vessels for the truths.

Those [rays of light] that go upwards, they go to the gods – the Cāturmahārājika (Four Groups of the Great Kings), Trāyastriṃśa (Thirty-three), Yāma (Of Yama), Tuṣita (Content), Nirmāṇarati (Delighting in Creation), Paranirmitavaśavartin (Masters of Others' Creations), Brahmakāyika (Brahmā's Assembly), Brahmapurohita (Brahmā's Priests), Mahābrahma (Great Brahmā), Parittābhā (Limited Splendour), Apramāṇābhā (Immeasurable Splendour), Abhāsvara (Radiant), Parittaśubha (Limited Beauty), Apramāṇaśubha (Immeasurable Beauty), Śubhakṛtsna (Complete Beauty), Anabhraka (Unclouded), Puṇyaprasava (Merit Born), Bṛhatphala (Great Result), Abṛha (Not Vast), Atapa (Serene), Sudṛśa (Good-Looking), Sudarśana (Clear-Sighted) and Akaniṣṭha (Supreme). They shout out, 'Impermanent! Suffering! Empty! Not-Self!' and speak two verses:

> 'Exert yourselves! Go forth!
> Take up the Buddha's teaching!
> Shake the army of death
> like an elephant shakes a reed-hut!
>
> Whoever diligently follows
> this *dharma* and discipline,
> will abandon the cycle of rebirths
> and make an end to suffering.'

Then those rays of light, having roamed through the great trichiliocosm, assemble behind the Blessed One. If the Blessed One wishes to explain past actions, they disappear into the Blessed One's back; if he wishes to explain future actions, they vanish into his front. If he wishes to predict arising in a hell, they disappear into the soles of his feet, while if he wants to predict arising as an animal, they enter his heel, and if he wants to predict arising as a hungry ghost, they vanish into his big toe, and if he desires to predict arising as a human, they disappear into his knee. If he wishes to predict rule as an armed wheel-turning king, they enter the palm of his left hand, while if he wishes to predict rule as a wheel-turning king, they disappear into the palm of his right hand. If he wishes to predict arising as a god, they vanish into his navel. If he wishes to predict awakening as a disciple, they enter his mouth, while if he wants to predict awakening as a *pratyekabuddha*, they vanish into the circle of hair between his eyebrows, and if he wants to predict unsurpassed and perfect full buddhahood, they disappear into his *uṣṇīṣa*.

And those rays of light circumambulated the Blessed One three times and disappeared into the Blessed One's *uṣṇīṣa*. Then Venerable Ānanda joined his hands in respect and asked the Blessed One:

> 'A collection of a thousand bright-coloured rays of various kinds
> is expelled from the inside of your mouth,
> completely illuminating the directions
> as if from the rising of the sun.'

And he spoke these verses:

> '*Buddha*s have cut off rebirth, abandoned affliction and enjoyment,
> and become the cause of what is best in the world.
> Not without reason do victors, their enemies conquered,
> exhibit a smile, white as a conch-shell or lotus-fibre.
>
> Hero, ascetic, the best of victors, you know at once
> through your own intelligence, the wishes of your listeners.
> Bull among sages, remove the doubt that has arisen,
> with splendid, wise and superior speech.
>
> It is not without reason that perfect *buddha*s, protectors
> firm as the ocean or the king of the mountains, exhibit a smile.
> A multitude of people yearn to hear
> the reason why wise ones exhibit a smile.'

The Blessed One said, 'It is like this, Ānanda. It is like this. It is not without cause or without reason, Ānanda, that *tathāgata*s who are *arhat*s and perfectly and fully awakened display a smile. Did you see, Ānanda, the way this householder paid me honour? Thus, Venerable Ānanda, this householder, because of this root of virtue, the arising of this thought, and this properly given gift, after three incalculable aeons he will attain awakening, and having fulfilled the six perfections that are pervaded with great compassion he will become a full and perfect *buddha* named Divyānnada (Giver of Divine Food), with the ten powers, four confidences, three special applications of mindulness and great compassion. This is the gift of one who has a faithful thought towards me.' And having heard this explanation, King Bimbisāra and his attendants the Magadhans were greatly astonished.

The monks became doubtful and asked the Blessed One, the Buddha, who cuts through all doubt, 'See, Blessed One, how this householder worshipped the Blessed One and his community of monks with spirit-deities and supernormal powers.' The Blessed One said, 'O monks, actions that the Tathāgata performed and accumulated in other previous births have come to fullness and their conditions have matured. Their flood, being at hand, was unavoidable. These actions have been done and accumulated by me, so who else would experience their fruition? Monks, actions that have been done and accumulated do not bear fruit outside, neither in the earth element, nor in the water element, nor in the fire element, nor in the wind element. Rather, deeds done, whether pure or impure, ripen when the aggregates, the physical elements and the sense bases have arisen.

> Actions never come to naught
> even through hundreds of millions of aeons.
> Having reached fullness and at the proper time,
> they bear fruit without fail for embodied beings.

'Formerly, monks, in a past time, a fully awakened one named Pūrṇa arose in the world: a *tathāgata*, an *arhat*, fully and perfectly awakened, perfected in knowledge and conduct, a well-farer, an unsurpassed knower of the world, a tamer of people who should be tamed, a teacher of gods and humans, a *buddha*, a blessed one. Pūrṇa the fully and perfectly awakened one wandered on a journey through the countryside and reached a certain royal city.

'The consecrated warrior king heard, "Pūrṇa the fully and perfectly awakened one, wandering on a journey through the countryside, has reached our royal city." And hearing this, with great royal power and great regal pomp he approached the place where the fully and perfectly awakened Pūrṇa was. Having arrived he honoured the fully and perfectly awakened Pūrṇa's feet with his head and sat to one side. The fully and perfectly awakened Pūrṇa inspired that consecrated warrior king who was seated to one side with the qualities that bring about awakening.

'Then that consecrated warrior king offered to provide the fully and perfectly awakened Pūrṇa together with his community of monks with the requisite robes, almsbowls, beds, seats, and medicines for the sick for three months. The fully and perfectly awakened Pūrṇa consented to the king through his silence. Then the consecrated warrior king understood that the fully and perfectly awakened Pūrṇa had consented through his silence and attended them with the requisite robes, almsbowls, beds, seats, and medicines for the sick for three months. He had an image of the Blessed One made of jewels and carried out the Buddha-Joy [festival],[22] such that several hundred thousand beings attained great faith, and for that reason and through that cause they attained complete *nirvāṇa*.

'What do you think, monks? The one who was the king at that time and on that occasion, that was me. It was me that honoured the fully and perfectly awakened Pūrṇa in such a fashion, and thus I experienced boundless happiness in the cycle of rebirths, and for that reason as Tathāgata I was honoured in this way by the guildsman and by Śakra. Therefore, monks, you should train in this way: "We will honour, revere, respect and worship the teacher. And having honoured, revered, respected and worshipped the teacher, we will live in reliance on him." In this way, monks, you should train.'

This was said by the Blessed One, and the monks were delighted and praised the Blessed One's speech.

Third Decade

(Stories 21–30)

21. Candana

The Buddha, the Blessed One, was honoured, revered, respected and worshipped by kings, ministers, the wealthy, the townsfolk, merchants, caravan leaders, gods, *nāgas*, *yakṣas*, antigods, heavenly birds, *kinnaras* and great snakes. That Buddha, the Blessed One, who was venerated as such by gods, *nāgas*, *yakṣas*, antigods, heavenly birds, *kinnaras* and great snakes, who was famous and possessed of great merit, and who was provided with the requisites — robes, bowls, bedding, seats, and medicine to cure the sick — wandered together with his community of disciples among the Magadhan people and arrived at the bank of the Ganges.

Now at that time, not far from the banks of the Ganges, there was a ruined *stūpa*, totally destroyed by wind and heat. The monks saw this and asked the Blessed One, 'Whose is this *stūpa*?' The Blessed One replied, 'There was a *pratyekabuddha* called Candana, and it is his.' The monks said, 'Blessed One, how did the *pratyekabuddha* Candana arise, and how did his name come about?' The Blessed One said, 'Do you wish to hear, monks, how the *pratyekabuddha* Candana arose, and how his name came about?' 'Yes, sir.' 'Then listen, monks: concentrate your minds properly and well, and I will explain:

'Formerly, monks, in times past, a king called Brahmadatta ruled his kingdom in the city of Vārāṇasī. It was prosperous and flourishing, peaceful and abundantly supplied, and crowded with many people. Strife, quarrels, riots and tumult had ceased, thieves and disease had departed, and it had plenty of rice, sugar cane, cows and buffaloes. That virtuous king was just, and ruled his kingdom righteously. Being childless and desiring a son, he honoured Śiva, Varuṇa, Kubera, Śakra, Brahmā and so on, as well as various other deities, namely the gods of the grove, the gods of the forest, the gods of four-way crossroads, the gods of three-way crossroads and the gods who receive oblations. He also implored his lineage gods, the gods who shared his nature, and his tutelary gods. For there is a saying in the world that sons and daughters are born through entreating the gods. But this is not so. If it were so, each person would have a thousand sons like a wheel-turning king. Rather, sons and daughters are born from the coming-together of three favourable conditions. Which three? The mother and father unite in love-making, the mother is healthy and in her fertile period, and a *gandharva* is present. Sons and daughters are born from the coming-together of these three favourable conditions.

'But he persevered in worshipping in this way, and a great lotus — an extraordinarily big lotus — appeared in the park. Day after day it grew, but it did not open. The park keeper made it known to the king, and the king said, "This lotus should be watched." And then at a later date, at sunrise, that lotus flower opened, and right in the centre of that lotus was a boy, seated cross-legged. And he was handsome and good-looking, attractive, brilliant, golden-coloured, with a parasol-shaped head, pendulous arms, a broad forehead, a loud voice, eyebrows that joined and a prominent nose, adorned with the thirty-two marks of a great man and the eighty minor marks, his body glorious. The air that came from his mouth was scented like a lotus and his body had the fragrance of sandalwood.

'The park keeper announced this to the king, and the king, along with his courtiers and womenfolk, went to that park. The moment he saw him, the boy said to the king, "Come, Father. I am a son for you, who had no child." The king, thrilled, pleased and delighted, replied, 'Let it be just as you say, son!' Then the king plunged into the lotus pond, took the boy from the centre of the lotus, and placed him on the palm of his hand. And wherever that boy placed his feet, lotuses sprang up. Because of this, he was given the name Candana (Sandalwood).

'When the boy Candana in due course grew up, the citizens informed the king: "Your majesty, there is a holiday in our city here. It would be appropriate, your majesty, to let Prince Candana come out. He will experience the holiday with us, and he will decorate the whole town with lotuses." The king replied, "Let it be so." Then Candana, adorned with all ornaments, surrounded by the sons of courtiers and accompanied by the playing of various musical instruments, went outside the royal palace to experience the holiday. And as he went there, footstep by footstep lotuses appeared, and they were beautiful and charming. But merely by being touched by the rays of the sun, they faded and withered. And seeing this a fundamental mental concentration arose in that noble-hearted pure being, whose roots of goodness were planted with previous *buddhas*: "Just as these lotuses shine at the moment they arise, but, burnt by the rays of the sun, fade and wither, so too is the body." He thought about that and weighed it up, and while examining it the thirty-seven factors of awakening became manifest. And even as he stood right there in the middle of the crowd of people he realized *pratyekabodhi*. At that the gods of the pure abodes presented him with an ochre robe, and having put this on he rose up into the vault of the sky and performed various miracles. Seeing this, the king, courtiers and citizens attained great faith, and planted various roots of virtue.'

The Blessed One said, 'And that is how the *pratyekabuddha* Candana arose, and how his name came about.' The monks questioned the

Blessed One: 'Sir, what deeds had the *pratyekabuddha* Candana done in order to have a sweet-smelling body and keen senses?' The Blessed One said, 'He was a renouncer under the Buddha Kāśyapa, and he sprinkled perfume on a *stūpa* of his hair and nails, as well as placing flowers there. The path to *pratyekabodhi* was produced by that. Therefore, monks, you should train in this way: "We will honour, revere, respect and worship the teacher. And having honoured, revered, respected and worshipped the teacher, we will live in reliance on him." In this way, monks, you should train.'

This was said by the Blessed One, and the monks were delighted and praised the Blessed One's speech.

22. The Lotus (*Padma*)

The Buddha, the Blessed One, was honoured, revered, respected and worshipped by kings, ministers, the wealthy, the townsfolk, merchants, caravan leaders, gods, *nāga*s, *yakṣa*s, antigods, heavenly birds, *kinnara*s and great snakes. That Buddha, the Blessed One, who was venerated as such by gods, *nāga*s, *yakṣa*s, antigods, heavenly birds, *kinnara*s and great snakes, who was famous and possessed of great merit, and who was provided with the requisites – robes, bowls, bedding, seats, and medicine to cure the sick – was staying with his community of disciples in Anāthapiṇḍada's park, the Jeta Grove in Śrāvastī.

It was common practice in the Middle Country for gardeners to collect lotuses and go to sell them in the streets. Now in the morning the Blessed One dressed himself, and taking his robe and bowl he went into Śrāvastī for alms. And a certain woman, carrying a boy in her arms, was coming down the street. And that boy saw the Buddha, the Blessed One, adorned with the thirty-two marks of a great man and the eighty secondary marks, his body shining, arrayed with light that extended a fathom, radiance in excess of a thousand suns, like a living mountain of jewels, handsome in his entirety. And immediately upon seeing him, he became faithful. He stretched out his arms, seized a lotus from a nearby gardener, and threw it at his head, and that lotus, becoming as large as a cartwheel, remained in the sky above him. When the Blessed One moved, it followed, and when he stood it stayed. Then the Blessed One let loose light the same colour as the lotus, which illuminated the whole of Śrāvastī. And because of that the king, courtiers and citizens were humbled.

Then the Blessed One smiled. Now according to the natural order of things, when *buddhas* display a smile then blue, yellow, red and white rays issue from his mouth and some go upwards and some downwards. Those that go downwards, they go to the hells – the Saṃjīva (Reviving), Kālasūtra (Black Thread), Saṃghāta (Crushing), Raurava (Shrieking), Mahāraurava (Loud Shrieking), Tapana (Heat), Pratāpana (Extreme Heat), Avīci (Endless Torture), Arbuda (Blistering), Nirarbuda (Blisters Bursting), Aṭaṭa (Chattering Teeth), Hahava (Ugh!), Huhuva (Brrr!), Utpala (Blue Lotus), Padma (Lotus) and Mahāpadma (Great Lotus). Those that descend into the hot hells become cool, and those that descend into the cold hells become warm, and in this way they alleviate the various sufferings of the beings there, such that it occurs to them, 'Friends, can it be that we have left this place and arisen elsewhere?' Then in order to make them develop faith, the Blessed One emits an image of himself, and seeing this image they realize, 'No, friends, we have not left this place nor arisen elsewhere. There is this being, not seen before, whose power is easing our various sufferings.' Their minds become faithful towards this image, and they cast off the karma still to be experienced in hell, and take rebirth among gods and men, where they become vessels for the truths.

Those [rays of light] that go upwards, they go to the gods – the Cāturmahārājika (Four Groups of the Great Kings), Trāyastriṃśa (Thirty-three), Yāma (Of Yama), Tuṣita (Content), Nirmāṇarati (Delighting in Creation), Paranirmitavaśavartin (Masters of Others' Creations), Brahmakāyika (Brahmā's Assembly), Brahmapurohita (Brahmā's Priests), Mahābrahma (Great Brahmā), Parittābhā (Limited Splendour), Apramāṇābhā (Immeasurable Splendour),

Abhāsvara (Radiant), Parittaśubha (Limited Beauty), Apramāṇaśubha (Immeasurable Beauty), Śubhakṛtsna (Complete Beauty), Anabhraka (Unclouded), Puṇyaprasava (Merit Born), Bṛhatphala (Great Result), Abṛha (Not Vast), Atapa (Serene), Sudṛśa (Good-Looking), Sudarśana (Clear-Sighted) and Akaniṣṭha (Supreme). They shout out, 'Impermanent! Suffering! Empty! Not-Self!' and speak two verses:

'Exert yourselves! Go forth!
Take up the Buddha's teaching!
Shake the army of death
like an elephant shakes a reed-hut!

Whoever diligently follows
this *dharma* and discipline,
will abandon the cycle of rebirths
and make an end to suffering.'

Then those rays of light, having roamed through the great trichiliocosm, assemble behind the Blessed One. If the Blessed One wishes to explain past actions, they disappear into the Blessed One's back; if he wishes to explain future actions, they vanish into his front. If he wishes to predict arising in a hell, they disappear into the soles of his feet, while if he wants to predict arising as an animal, they enter his heel, and if he wants to predict arising as a hungry ghost, they vanish into his big toe, and if he desires to predict arising as a human, they disappear into his knee. If he wishes to predict rule as an armed wheel-turning king, they enter the palm of his left hand, while if he wishes to predict rule as a wheel-turning king, they disappear into the palm of his right hand. If he wishes to predict arising as a god, they vanish into his navel. If he wishes to predict awakening as a disciple, they enter his mouth, while if he wants to predict awakening as a *pratyekabuddha*, they vanish into the circle of hair between his eyebrows, and if he wants to predict unsurpassed and perfect full buddhahood, they disappear into his *uṣṇīṣa*.

And those rays of light circumambulated the Blessed One three times and disappeared into the circle of hair between the Blessed

One's eyebrows. Then Venerable Ānanda joined his hands in respect and asked the Blessed One:

'A collection of a thousand bright coloured rays of various
kinds
is expelled from the inside of your mouth,
completely illuminating the directions
as if from the rising of the sun.'

And he spoke these verses:

'*Buddhas* have cut off rebirth, abandoned affliction and
enjoyment,
and become the cause of what is best in the world.
Not without reason do victors, their enemies conquered,
exhibit a smile, white as a conch-shell or lotus-fibre.

Hero, ascetic, the best of victors, you know at once
through your own intelligence, the wishes of your listeners.
Bull among sages, remove the doubt that has arisen,
with splendid, wise and superior speech.

It is not without reason that perfect *buddhas*, protectors
firm as the ocean or the king of the mountains, exhibit a
smile.
A multitude of people yearn to hear
the reason why wise ones exhibit a smile.'

The Blessed One said, 'It is like this, Ānanda. It is like this. It is not without cause or without reason, Ānanda, that *tathāgatas* who are *arhats* and perfectly and fully awakened display a smile. Did you see, Ānanda, the way this boy became faithful and threw a lotus at the Tathāgata?' 'Yes, sir.' 'This boy, Ānanda, through this root of virtue, the arising of this thought, and this properly given gift, will not fall into misfortune for fifteen aeons. Having experienced the happiness of heavenly and human births, he will become a *pratyekabuddha* called Padmottara (Supreme Lotus). This is the gift of one who has a faithful thought towards me. Therefore, monks, you should train in this way: "Let us pay homage towards *buddhas*, *pratyekabuddhas* and disciples." In this way, monks, you should train.'

This was said by the Blessed One, and the monks were delighted and praised the Blessed One's speech.

23. The Disc (*Cakra*)

The Buddha, the Blessed One, was honoured, revered, respected and worshipped by kings, ministers, the wealthy, the townsfolk, merchants, caravan leaders, gods, *nāgas*, *yakṣas*, antigods, heavenly birds, *kinnaras* and great snakes. That Buddha, the Blessed One, who was venerated as such by gods, *nāgas*, *yakṣas*, antigods, heavenly birds, *kinnaras* and great snakes, who was famous and possessed of great merit, and who was provided with the requisites – robes, bowls, bedding, seats, and medicine to cure the sick – was staying with his community of disciples in Rājagṛha, in Kalandakanivāpa in the Veṇu Grove.

In Rājagṛha a certain caravan leader had gone over the great ocean. He had a young wife, and she longed for her husband and undertook ascetic practices, but her husband did not return. She prostrated herself before Nārāyaṇa and vowed, 'If my husband returns quickly, I will present you with a golden disc.' Then her husband returned safe and well from the great ocean, so she had a golden disc made. Surrounded by serving girls, she took the golden disc, as well as perfume, incense and flowers, and stood near to the temple.

Now there is nothing that is unknown, unseen, unrecognized and unobserved by the *buddhas*, blessed ones. Indeed, being greatly compassionate and devoted to benefitting the world, *buddhas*, blessed ones:

> have one protector,
> dwell in calm and insight,
> are skilled in the threefold self-control,
> have overcome the four floods,
> have conduct grounded in the four bases of supernormal
> power,

have long practised the four articles of attraction,
lack the five [bad] qualities,
have gone beyond the five realms,
are endowed with the six qualities [of equanimity],
have accomplished the six perfections,
abound in the flowers that are the seven factors of
awakening,
are guides on the eightfold path,
are skilled in the nine successive attainments [of
meditation],
are mighty with the ten powers,
with splendour that fully pervades the ten directions,
and more distinguished than ten times a hundred
rulers.

It is a rule that when they survey the world with their *buddha*-vision for three days and three nights, knowledge and perception arise: 'Who is falling? Who is flourishing? Who has met with pain? Who is in danger? Who is afflicted? Who has met with pain, danger and affliction? Who is headed for a state of woe? Who is inclined towards a state of evil? Who is bent on a bad destiny? Whom can I raise up from bad states and establish in heaven and liberation? Who, mired in sense pleasures, might I raise up with my hands? Who, deprived of them, could I establish in mastery over and excellence in the noble treasures? Whose unplanted roots of virtue should I plant? Whose planted [roots] should I bring to maturity? And whose matured [roots] should I bring to liberation?' And it is said:

Though the ocean, abode of monsters,
may pass over the shore,
A *buddha* cannot pass over the opportunity
of young people in need of training.

The Blessed One saw, 'This girl, upon seeing me, will be made to plant the virtuous root of *pratyekabodhi*.' So in the morning he dressed himself and taking his robe and bowl, surrounded by a group of monks and attended by the monastic community, he set out to enter Rājagṛha for alms. And that girl saw the Buddha, the

Blessed One, adorned with the thirty-two marks of a great man and the eighty secondary marks, his body shining, arrayed with light that extended a fathom, radiance in excess of a thousand suns, like a living mountain of jewels, handsome in his entirety. And upon seeing him, she became faithful and began to throw the golden disc towards the Blessed One, but she was restrained by a maidservant: 'This is not Nārāyaṇa!' Though held back, her mind was overcome with intense faith and she threw the golden disc above the Buddha, the Blessed One, and gave him a perfumed garland.

Then the Blessed One smiled . . . [as story 22].

The Blessed One said, 'It is like this, Ānanda. It is like this. It is not without cause or without reason, Ānanda, that *tathāgatas* who are *arhats* and perfectly and fully awakened display a smile. Did you see, Ānanda, the way this girl threw a golden disc at the Tathāgata?' 'Yes, sir.' 'This girl, Ānanda, through this root of virtue, the arising of this thought, and this properly given gift, will not fall into misfortune for fifteen aeons. Having experienced the happiness of heavenly and human births, she will become a *pratyekabuddha* called Cakrāntara (Disc Interior). This is the gift of one who has a faithful thought towards me. Therefore, monks, you should train in this way: "Let us pay homage towards *buddhas*, *pratyekabuddhas* and disciples." In this way, monks, you should train.'

This was said by the Blessed One, and the monks were delighted and praised the Blessed One's speech.

24. Daśaśiras

The Buddha, the Blessed One, was honoured, revered, respected and worshipped by kings, ministers, the wealthy, the townsfolk, merchants, caravan leaders, gods, *nāgas*, *yakṣas*, antigods, heavenly birds, *kinnaras* and great snakes. That Buddha, the Blessed One, who was venerated as such by gods, *nāgas*, *yakṣas*, antigods, heavenly birds, *kinnaras* and great snakes, who was famous and possessed of great merit, and who was provided with the requisites – robes, bowls, bedding, seats, and medicine to cure the sick – wandered together with his community of disciples among the Magadhan people, and arrived, along with his community of monks, at the bank of the Ganges.

And the monks saw from afar an old *stūpa*, broken and destroyed by years of wind and heat. And having seen this, they asked the Blessed One, 'Whose is this *stūpa*, sir?' The Blessed One said, 'It belongs to the *pratyekabuddha* Daśaśiras.' The monks said, 'Sir, how did the *pratyekabuddha* Daśaśiras arise, and how did his name come about?' The Blessed One said, 'Would you like to hear about this, monks?' They replied, 'Yes, sir.' 'Then listen, monks: concentrate your minds properly and well, and I will explain:

'Formerly, monks, in times past, a king called Brahmadatta ruled in the city of Vārāṇasī. It was prosperous and flourishing, peaceful and abundantly supplied, and crowded with many people. Strife, quarrels, riots and tumult had ceased, thieves and disease had departed, and it had plenty of rice, sugar cane, cows and buffaloes. That virtuous king was just, and ruled his kingdom righteously. Being childless and desiring a son, he honoured Śiva, Varuṇa, Kubera, Śakra, Brahmā and so on, as well as various other deities, namely the gods of the grove, the gods of the forest, the gods of four-way crossroads, the gods of three-way crossroads and the gods who receive oblations. He also implored his lineage gods, the gods who shared his nature, and his tutelary gods.

'He persevered in worshipping in this way. In his park there was a large lotus pool, a lotus pool that was covered in blue, red and white lotuses, and adorned with birds such as geese, *cakravāka*s and ducks. There an immense lotus, free of impediments, suddenly arose. Day after day it grew, but it did not open. The park keeper made it known to the king, and the king said, 'This lotus should be watched.' And then at a later date, at sunrise, that lotus flower opened, and right in the centre of that lotus was a boy, seated cross-legged. And he was handsome and good-looking, attractive, brilliant, golden-coloured, with a parasol-shaped head, pendulous arms, a broad forehead, a loud voice, eyebrows that joined and a prominent nose, adorned with the thirty-two marks of a great man and the eighty minor marks, his body glorious. Having seen this, park keeper announced it to the king. The king, having heard this, went to that park along with his courtiers and womenfolk. The king saw him shining in the centre of the lotus, and having seen this he was thrilled, pleased and delighted, and he became intensely happy and affectionate. He plunged into the lotus pool, picked him up and took him to his own home with great pomp, then presented him to the ascetics, brahmins and soothsayers. Three weeks — twenty-one days — after his birth he celebrated the birth-festival and gave him the name Daśaśiras (Ten-Headed).

'The boy Daśaśiras was given eight nurses: two nurses to carry him, two nurses to feed him, two nurses to clean him and two nurses to play with him. He was raised by the eight nurses and nourished with milk, curds, fresh butter, clarified butter, the residue of the clarified butter and other foods of excellent, beneficial characteristics, so he grew quickly like a lotus in a pool. And that prince was devout and good, of virtuous disposition, dedicated to the good of others as well as his own benefit, compassionate, great-hearted, devoted to the *dharma*, and affectionate towards the people. He saw that his father, established in kingly *dharma*, carried out actions that were blameable and worthy of censure. Seeing that, the agitated prince entreated his father, "Grant me permission, father: I will go forth in the well-proclaimed *dharma* and discipline." Permitted to do this by his father, he removed his hair and beard, clothed himself in ochre robes, and properly and gladly went forth from home into homelessness. Then without instruction, he realized the thirty-seven factors of awakening, and realized *pratyekabodhi*. He flew up into the sky and made various miraculous displays in the presence of his father. Then for three months the king offered him alms. Exhausted by carrying the burden of a body, he displayed various miracles and reached extinction like a fire that has run out of fuel. This is his *stūpa*.'

The monks became doubtful and asked the Blessed One, the Buddha, who cuts through all doubt, 'What deeds were done by Daśaśiras, sir, on account of which he did not arise in a woman's womb but arose in a lotus?' The Blessed One replied, 'Monks, actions that this very Daśaśiras performed and accumulated in other previous births obtained to fullness and their conditions matured; their flood, being at hand, was unavoidable. These actions were done and accumulated by Daśaśiras, so who else would experience their fruition? Monks, actions that have been done and accumulated do not bear fruit outside, neither in the earth element, nor in the water element, nor in the fire element, nor in the wind element. Rather, deeds done, whether pure or impure, ripen when the aggregates, the physical elements and the sense bases have arisen.

> Actions never come to naught
> even through hundreds of millions of aeons.
> Having reached fullness and at the proper time,
> they bear fruit without fail for embodied beings.

'Formerly, monks, in the ninety-first aeon in the past, a fully awakened one named Vipaśyin appeared in the world. He was perfected in knowledge and conduct, a well-farer, an unsurpassed knower of the world, a tamer of people who should be tamed, a teacher of gods and humans, a *buddha*, a blessed one. He was living near the capital city, Bandhumatī. Now the fully awakened Buddha Vipaśyin in the morning got dressed, and taking his robe and bowl, surrounded by a group of monks and attended by the monastic community, entered the city of Bandhumatī for alms. And a certain caravan leader arrived in the street carrying a lotus. He saw Vipaśyin, the fully awakened one, adorned with the thirty-two marks of a great man and the eighty secondary marks, his body shining, arrayed with light that extended a fathom, radiance in excess of a thousand suns, like a living mountain of jewels, handsome in his entirety. And on seeing him, he threw the lotus above the Blessed One. And just where it had been thrown, above the Blessed One, it became as big as a cartwheel and followed the Blessed One wherever he went, stopping when he stopped. On account of this, the caravan leader was predicted to *pratyekabodhi* by the fully awakened Buddha Vipaśyin. His mind thrilled, pleased and delighted, he went back to his house. Now at that time his wife was giving birth, and crying out loudly. He asked the maidservant, "What is happening?" and she explained. The caravan leader was agitated and undertook to make a vow: "May I never in the cycle of rebirths come forth from a mother's womb!"'

The Blessed One said, 'What do you think, monks? The person who at that time and on that occasion was the caravan leader, that was this *pratyekabuddha* Daśaśiras. Through those roots of virtue, through twenty-one aeons he never arose from a mother's womb, and later attained this magnificent state. Therefore, monks, you should train in this way: "Let us pay homage towards *buddhas*, *pratyekabuddhas* and disciples." In this way, monks, you should train.'

This was said by the Blessed One, and the monks were delighted and praised the Blessed One's speech.

25. Sūkṣmatva

The Buddha, the Blessed One, was honoured, revered, respected and worshipped by kings, ministers, the wealthy, the townsfolk, merchants, caravan leaders, gods, *nāgas*, *yakṣas*, antigods, heavenly birds, *kinnaras* and great snakes. That Buddha, the Blessed One, who was venerated as such by gods, *nāgas*, *yakṣas*, antigods, heavenly birds, *kinnaras* and great snakes, who was famous and possessed of great merit, and who was provided with the requisites – robes, bowls, bedding, seats, and medicine to cure the sick – was staying with his community of disciples in Anāthapiṇḍada's park, the Jeta Grove in Śrāvastī.

At that time in Śrāvastī there was a certain merchant. He was rich, of great wealth and property, with plenty of goods and implements, many attendants and possessions, and many friends, courtiers, relations and kin. And that householder was devout and good, of virtuous disposition, dedicated to the good of others as well as his own benefit, compassionate, great-hearted, and devoted to the *dharma*. Then it occurred to him, 'These possessions have the same nature as the moon in water. They are like a ray of light, impermanent, not fixed, of no comfort, of changeable nature, in common with the five mighty punishments.[23] I should take the essence from these possessions that have no essence!'[24] He invited the Blessed One, along with his community of monks, for a meal. He had his house made free from gravel, pebbles and small stones, sprinkled it with sandal-water, and made it fragrant with various scented pieces of wood and sweet-smelling incense. Flower-seats were laid out, cups of sweet sugar cane juice and various foods were made ready, and a messenger announced to the Blessed One that it was time: 'It is the moment, sir. The food is prepared, so the Blessed One should know that it is now time.'

Then the Blessed One, in the morning, took his robe and bowl and, surrounded by a group of monks and attended by the monastic community, approached the place of that householder's dwelling. Having approached, he sat on a seat that had been prepared, in front of the community of monks. Then that householder, knowing the community of monks with the Buddha at their head were comfortably seated, served them with his own hands, waiting on them with pure and excellent food. Having served and waited on them with his own hands, seeing that the Blessed One had eaten, his hands were washed and the bowl removed, he took a lower seat and sat before the Blessed One in order to hear the *dharma*. Then the Blessed One taught, inspired and incited the householder with a *dharma* talk, and having taught, inspired and incited with a *dharma* talk of many kinds, he became silent. And that householder acquired faith, fell at his feet and fostered an intention.

Then the Blessed One smiled . . . [as story 22].

The Blessed One said, 'It is like this, Ānanda. It is like this. It is not without cause or without reason, Ānanda, that *tathāgata*s who are *arhat*s and perfectly and fully awakened display a smile. Did you see, Ānanda, the way this merchant paid me honour in this way?' 'Yes, sir.' 'This merchant, Ānanda, through this root of virtue, the arising of this thought, and this properly given gift, will become a *pratyeka-buddha* called Sūkṣmatva (Insignificance). This is the gift of one who has a faithful thought towards me. Therefore, monks, you should train in this way: "Let us pay homage towards *buddhas*, *pratyeka-buddhas* and disciples." In this way, monks, you should train.'

This was said by the Blessed One, and the monks were delighted and praised the Blessed One's speech.

26. Śītaprabha

The Buddha, the Blessed One, was honoured, revered, respected and worshipped by kings, ministers, the wealthy, the townsfolk, merchants, caravan leaders, gods, *nāgas*, *yakṣas*, antigods, heavenly birds, *kinnaras* and great snakes. That Buddha, the Blessed One, who was venerated as such by gods, *nāgas*, *yakṣas*, antigods, heavenly birds, *kinnaras* and great snakes, who was famous and possessed of great merit, and who was provided with the requisites — robes, bowls, bedding, seats, and medicine to cure the sick — was staying with his community of disciples in Anāthapiṇḍada's park, the Jeta Grove in Śrāvastī.

In Śrāvastī there was a certain householder. He was rich, of great wealth and property, and extensive, wide holdings. He possessed the wealth of Vaiśravaṇa, rivaling Vaiśravaṇa in wealth. And he was devout and good, of virtuous disposition, dedicated to the good of others as well as his own benefit, compassionate, great-hearted, and devoted to the *dharma*. Then this occurred to him: 'These possessions have the same nature as the moon in water. They are impermanent and unfixed like an elephant's ear,[25] changeable in nature and of no comfort, in common with the five mighty punishments. I should take the essence from these possessions that have no essence!' Then when summer time came around he invited the Blessed One, along with his community of monks, for a meal. He had his house made free from gravel, pebbles and small stones, sprinkled it with sandal-water, and made it fragrant with various scented pieces of wood and sweet-smelling incense. Flower-seats were laid out, and cups of sweet sugar cane juice and various foods were made ready. A messenger announced to the Blessed One that it was time: 'It is the moment, sir. The food is prepared, so the Blessed One should know that it is now time.'

Then the Blessed One, in the morning, took his robe and bowl and, surrounded by a group of monks and attended by the monastic community, approached the place of that householder's dwelling. Having approached, he sat on a seat that had been prepared, in front of the community of monks. Then that householder, knowing the community of monks with the Buddha at their head were comfortably seated, served them with his own hands, waiting on them with pure and excellent food. Having served and waited on them with his own hands, seeing that the Blessed One had eaten, his hands were washed and the bowl removed, he took a lower seat and sat before the Blessed One in order to hear the *dharma*. Then the Blessed One taught, inspired, incited and delighted that householder with a *dharma* talk, and having taught, inspired, incited and delighted him with a *dharma* talk of many kinds, he became silent. And that householder acquired faith, fell at his feet and fostered an intention.

Then the Blessed One smiled . . . [as story 22].

The Blessed One said, 'It is like this, Ānanda. It is like this. It is not without cause or without reason, Ānanda, that *tathāgata*s who are *arhat*s and perfectly and fully awakened display a smile. Did you see, Ānanda, the way this householder paid me honour in this way?' 'Yes, sir.' 'This householder, Ānanda, through this root of virtue, the arising of this thought, and this properly given gift, will become a *pratyekabuddha* called Śītaprabha (Cool Light). This is the gift of one who has a faithful thought towards me. Therefore, monks, you should train in this way: "Let us pay homage towards *buddhas*, *pratyekabuddha*s and disciples." In this way, monks, you should train.'

This was said by the Blessed One, and the monks were delighted and praised the Blessed One's speech.

27. The Boatmen (*Nāvikā*)

The Buddha, the Blessed One, was honoured, revered, respected and worshipped by kings, ministers, the wealthy, the townsfolk, merchants, caravan leaders, gods, *nāgas*, *yakṣas*, antigods, heavenly birds, *kinnaras* and great snakes. That Buddha, the Blessed One, who was venerated as such by gods, *nāgas*, *yakṣas*, antigods, heavenly birds, *kinnaras* and great snakes, who was famous and possessed of great merit, and who was provided with the requisites – robes, bowls, bedding, seats, and medicine to cure the sick – wandered together with his community of disciples among the Magadhan people, and arrived at the bank of the Ganges.

Then the Blessed One, surrounded by a group of monks and attended by his monastic community, went to where there were some boatmen. Having approached, he said this to the boatmen: 'Can you help me to cross this river?' The boatmen said, 'You must pay a ferry-fee.' The Blessed One said to those boatmen, 'Sirs, I have also been a boatman. I carried across Nanda, who had fallen in the river of passion; Aṅgulimāla, who had fallen in the foaming sea of hatred; the proud young Mānastabdha, who had fallen into the ocean of pride; and Urubilva-Kāśyapa, who had fallen into the flood of delusion. And I never asked for a ferry-fee! Yet, asked, you do not agree to transport me across.'

One of the boatmen heard the Blessed One's words furnished with the eight qualities, saw his perfect form, and became faithful. He said, 'I will transport the Blessed One and his community of disciples across!' The monks mounted the boat, but the Blessed One, through his power, went ahead from the near shore of the boatman and stood on the further shore. Then the boatman, seeing that miraculous display of power, was humbled and fell at his feet.

Then the Blessed One gave a *dharma* teaching of such a kind that penetrated the four noble truths, hearing which that boatman split apart with the thunderbolt of knowledge the mountain of wrong views about individuality that rises up with twenty peaks, and realized the fruit of stream-entry. Having seen the truth, he uttered three joyous utterances: 'Reverend sir, what the Blessed One has done for us is something not done by our mother, nor by our father, nor by the king, nor by the gods, nor by our beloved kinsmen, nor by those who formerly passed away, nor by ascetics or brahmins. Dried up are the oceans of blood and tears! Traversed are the mountains of bones! The doors to the evil states are closed, and open are the doors to heaven and liberation, for we are certainly established among gods and humans.' And he said:

'Through your power, the hideous path to hell,
paved with so many torments, is closed;
Open is the meritorious path to heaven,
and I have obtained the path to *nirvāṇa*.

And with your help I have achieved the removal of hatred;
Today my purified eye is bright;
I have obtained peace at the feet of the beloved of the
nobles,
as one who has crossed beyond the ocean of suffering.

O Indra among heroes, worshipped by men and gods:
Birth, ageing, death and sickness are over!
One whom it is so difficult to see even in a hundred
thousand births:
O sage, seeing you today has been fruitful!'

Then a second boatman felt very remorseful, and throwing himself down at the feet of the Blessed One he confessed his transgression. And he provided alms for the Blessed One and his community of disciples.

Then the Blessed One smiled . . . [as story 22].

The Blessed One said, 'It is like this, Ānanda. It is like this. It is not without cause or without reason, Ānanda, that *tathāgata*s who are *arhat*s and perfectly and fully awakened display a smile. Did you see, Ānanda, the way this boatman developed a faithful mind in my presence?' 'Yes, sir.' 'This boatman, Ānanda, through this root of virtue, the arising of this thought, and this properly given gift, at a future time will become a *pratyekabuddha* called Saṃsārottaraṇa (Traverser of the Realm of Rebirth). This is the gift of one who has a faithful thought towards me. Therefore, monks, you should train in this way: "Let us pay homage towards *buddhas*, *pratyekabuddhas* and disciples." In this way, monks, you should train.'

This was said by the Blessed One, and the monks were delighted and praised the Blessed One's speech.

28. Gandhamādana

The Buddha, the Blessed One, was honoured, revered, respected and worshipped by kings, ministers, the wealthy, the townsfolk, merchants, caravan leaders, gods, *nāgas*, *yakṣas*, antigods, heavenly birds, *kinnaras* and great snakes. That Buddha, the Blessed One, who was venerated as such by gods, *nāgas*, *yakṣas*, antigods, heavenly birds, *kinnaras* and great snakes, who was famous and possessed of great merit, and who was provided with the requisites – robes, bowls, bedding, seats, and medicine to cure the sick – was staying with his community of disciples near Rājagṛha, in Kalandakanivāpa in the Veṇu Grove.

There was a custom in the Middle Country: in general, the people who lived in the Middle Country anointed their bodies with various unguents. There was a certain son of a householder, and his daughter – who was devout and good, of virtuous disposition – was grinding red sandal-paste. And in the morning the Blessed One dressed himself, took his robe and bowl and, surrounded by a group of monks and attended by the monastic community, entered Rājagṛha for alms.

And that girl saw the Buddha, the Blessed One, adorned with the thirty-two marks of a great man and the eighty secondary marks, his body shining, arrayed with light that extended a fathom, radiance in excess of a thousand suns, like a living mountain of jewels, handsome in his entirety. And having seen him, that girl experienced great faith. Then, this occurred to that faithful person: 'What use to me is a life such as this, in which, having encountered a field [of merit] of this kind, I am unable to perform a service for the Blessed One, because I am held back by poverty?'

Then, not valuing her own life, she smeared both her hands with red sandal-paste, and when she placed her bracelets at the feet of the Blessed One, through the Blessed One's power the whole city of Rājagṛha was filled with the scent of sandal. Then the girl, having seen that miracle, became faithful and fell at the Blessed One's feet. She fostered this intention: 'By this root of virtue may I realize *pratyekabodhi*!'

Then the Blessed One smiled . . . [as story 22].

The Blessed One said, 'It is like this, Ānanda. It is like this. It is not without cause or without reason, Ānanda, that *tathāgata*s who are *arhat*s and perfectly and fully awakened display a smile. Did you see, Ānanda, the way this girl paid me honour in this way?' 'Yes, sir.' 'This girl, Ānanda, through this root of virtue, the arising of this thought, and this properly given gift, will become a *pratyekabuddha* called Gandhamādana (Delighful Fragrance). This is the gift of one who has a faithful thought towards me. Therefore, monks, you should train in this way: "Let us pay homage towards *buddha*s, *pratyekabuddha*s and disciples." In this way, monks, you should train.'

This was said by the Blessed One, and the monks were delighted and praised the Blessed One's speech.

29. Nirmala

The Buddha, the Blessed One, was honoured, revered, respected and worshipped by kings, ministers, the wealthy, the townsfolk, merchants, caravan leaders, gods, *nāga*s, *yakṣa*s, antigods, heavenly birds, *kinnara*s and great snakes. That Buddha, the Blessed One, who was venerated as such by gods, *nāga*s, *yakṣa*s, antigods, heavenly birds, *kinnara*s and great snakes, who was famous and possessed of great merit, and who was provided with the requisites – robes, bowls, bedding, seats, and medicine to cure the sick – was staying with his community of disciples in Anāthapiṇḍada's park, the Jeta Grove in Śrāvastī.

There was a certain gardener in Śrāvastī, and taking wood pieces for tooth-cleaning he entered Śrāvastī. A soothsayer stopped at the gate and said, 'The one who uses this tooth-cleaner will enjoy food of one hundred flavours.' The gardener heard these words, and having heard this he thought, 'To whom should I give this tooth-cleaning stick, which will bring me great honour?' Then this occurred to him: 'This Buddha, the Blessed One, is living in the world and universe, and he is a field of merit that produces great fruit. Surely I should give it to this Buddha, the Blessed One.'

Then that gardener took the tooth-cleaning stick and went to where the Blessed One was. Having approached he honoured the Blessed One's feet with his head and sat to one side. Seated to one side the gardener said this to the Blessed One: 'Blessed One, grant me the favour of receiving this tooth-cleaning stick in my presence.' Then the Blessed One, in order to benefit the gardener, stretched out his golden-coloured arm like an elephant's trunk and took it. Having taken it he used it, and having used it he discarded in front of the gardener. Discarded, that tooth-cleaning stick became fixed in the ground, and where it was buried a great circular banyan tree immediately sprung forth – full-grown, with trunk, leaves, flowers and fruits. Seated in its shade, the Blessed One gave a *dharma* teaching for the many gods and humans. Then the householder Anāthapiṇḍada served the Blessed One with food of a hundred flavours. And that gardener, his mind overcome as a result of that miracle and that service of the Blessed One, fell at his feet like a tree felled at the roots, and undertook to make a fervent aspiration: 'By this wholesome root, may I realize *pratyekabodhi*!'

Then the Blessed One smiled . . . [as story 22].

The Blessed One said, 'It is like this, Ānanda. It is like this. It is not without cause or without reason, Ānanda, that *tathāgatas* who are *arhats* and perfectly and fully awakened display a smile. Did you see,

Ānanda, the way this gardener paid me honour in this way?' 'Yes, sir.' 'This gardener, Ānanda, through this root of virtue, the arising of this thought, and this properly given gift, will not fall into misfortune for thirteen aeons, and in his last life — his last stage, his last bodily existence, his last incarnation — he will become a *pratyekabuddha* called Nirmala (Spotless). This is the gift of one who has a faithful thought towards me. In this way, monks, you should train: "We will honour, revere, respect and worship the teacher. And having honoured, revered, respected and worshipped the teacher, we will live in reliance on him." In this way, monks, you should train.'

This was said by the Blessed One, and the monks were delighted and praised the Blessed One's speech.

30. Valgusvarā

The Buddha, the Blessed One, was honoured, revered, respected and worshipped by kings, ministers, the wealthy, the townsfolk, merchants, caravan leaders, gods, *nāgas*, *yakṣas*, antigods, heavenly birds, *kinnaras* and great snakes. That Buddha, the Blessed One, who was venerated as such by gods, *nāgas*, *yakṣas*, antigods, heavenly birds, *kinnaras* and great snakes, who was famous and possessed of great merit, and who was provided with the requisites — robes, bowls, bedding, seats, and medicine to cure the sick — was staying with his community of disciples in Anāthapiṇḍada's park, the Jeta Grove in Śrāvastī.

Then in the morning the Blessed One dressed himself, and taking his robe and bowl he entered Śrāvastī for alms. A large group of friends, overcome with intoxicating drink, were heading out from Śrāvastī, wearing magnificent clothes and furnished with necklaces of the finest flowers, with lotuses blue, red and white, and other water plants. They were singing and dancing, with various instruments — lutes, tabors and cymbals — playing.

Then the Blessed One entered Śrāvastī for alms. And those friends saw the Buddha, the Blessed One, adorned with the thirty-two marks of a great man and the eighty secondary marks, his body shining, arrayed with light that extended a fathom, radiance in excess of a thousand suns, like a living mountain of jewels, handsome in his entirety. And on seeing him, those who were drunk were no longer so. No longer intoxicated, their minds were turned to faith, and they honoured the Blessed One with dance, song and music, and threw blue lotuses over the Blessed One. And, thrown in this way, they stayed above the Blessed One like a blue peaked-roof, or a blue parasol, or a blue pavilion. And when the Blessed One went, it followed, and when he stayed still it remained. And the Blessed One sent forth blue light, such that Śrāvastī was filled with light resembling sapphire jewels.

Then the group of companions, having acquired faith, fostered this intention: 'By this our virtuous root may we realize *pratyekabodhi*!'

Then the Blessed One smiled . . . [as story 22].

The Blessed One said, 'It is like this, Ānanda. It is like this. It is not without cause or without reason, Ānanda, that *tathāgata*s who are *arhat*s and perfectly and fully awakened display a smile. Did you see, Ānanda, the way this group of companions paid me honour in this way?' 'Yes, sir.' 'This group, Ānanda, through this root of virtue, the arising of this thought, and this properly given gift, will not fall into misfortune for twenty intermediate aeons, and in their last lives – their last stages, their last bodily existences, their last incarnations – they will become *pratyekabuddha*s called Valgusvarā (Lovely Voices). This is the gift of one who has a faithful thought towards me. Therefore, monks, you should train in this way: "Let us pay homage towards *buddha*s, *pratyekabuddha*s and disciples." In this way, monks, you should train.'

This was said by the Blessed One, and the monks were delighted and praised the Blessed One's speech.

Fourth Decade

(Stories 31–40)

31. Padmaka

The Buddha, the Blessed One, was honoured, revered, respected and worshipped by kings, ministers, the wealthy, the townsfolk, merchants, caravan leaders, gods, *nāgas*, *yakṣas*, antigods, heavenly birds, *kinnaras* and great snakes. That Buddha, the Blessed One, who was venerated as such by gods, *nāgas*, *yakṣas*, antigods, heavenly birds, *kinnaras* and great snakes, who was famous and possessed of great merit, and who was provided with the requisites – robes, bowls, bedding, seats, and medicine to cure the sick – was staying with his community of disciples in Anāthapiṇḍada's park, the Jeta Grove in Śrāvastī.

In the autumn the monks were troubled by illness, such that they became pale and jaundiced. Their bodies were thin and their limbs weak. The Blessed One, however, was strong and free from illness, unafflicted, with untroubled limbs. Seeing this, the monks asked the

Blessed One, 'See, Blessed One, these monks are afflicted with an autumnal illness. They are pale and jaundiced, their bodies are thin, and their limbs weak. But the Blessed One is unafflicted, his limbs untroubled. He is by nature strong and free from illness, and possessed of regular digestion.'

The Blessed One said, 'O monks, actions that the Tathāgata performed and accumulated in other previous births have come to fullness and their conditions have matured. Their flood, being at hand, was unavoidable. These actions have been done and accumulated by me, so who else would experience their fruition? Monks, actions that have been done and accumulated do not bear fruit outside, neither in the earth element, nor in the water element, nor in the fire element, nor in the wind element. Rather, deeds done, whether pure or impure, ripen when the aggregates, the physical elements and the sense bases have arisen.

> Actions never come to naught
> even through hundreds of millions of aeons.
> Having reached fullness and at the proper time,
> they bear fruit without fail for embodied beings.

'Formerly, monks, in a past time, a king called Padmaka ruled in the city of Vārāṇasī, which was prosperous and flourishing, peaceful and abundantly supplied, and crowded with many people. Strife, quarrels, riots and tumult had ceased, thieves and disease had departed, and it had plenty of rice, sugar cane, cows and buffaloes. He protected it as dearly as an only son, and it was completely free from troubles. And that king was devout and good, of virtuous disposition, dedicated to the good of others as well as his own benefit, compassionate, great-hearted, devoted to the *dharma*, and affectionate towards the people. He was a giver of great gifts, being generous with everything, renouncing everything, and engaged in extensive donation.

'At that time a disease arose in Vārāṇasī because of a disturbance in the elements or a quirk of fate.[26] Most of the people became pale and sick. Seeing them, the king felt compassionate, and reflected,

"I must be a protector and medicine for these people." So the king assembled doctors who lived in various places, and having observed the motivations, dispositions and propensities of those beings[27] he undertook himself to bring together all the herbs and medicines. But while those beings were being treated, a lot of time elapsed, and although he had amassed doctors, medicines, herbs and attendants it was impossible to cure them.

'The king called together all the doctors and respectfully questioned them again: "Why is my treatment no good?" The doctors deliberated and then spoke with their united understanding about the qualities and faults: "Your majesty, this has the marks of being caused by a disturbance in the elements or a quirk of fate. As such, your majesty, there is but one remedy: the fish named *rohita*. If you were to obtain that, you would be able to cure them." The king began to search for a *rohita* fish, but even when his many spies searched they did not find it, and this they announced to the king.

'On one occasion the king set out along a road outside, and the sick people stood assembled together and said to the king: "Save us from our illness, Great King! Grant us life!" Hearing these powerful words spoken by those who were fading away and sinking into wretchedness and despair, the king's heart was shaken by compassion. With his face clouded over with tears, he reflected, "What would I want with this sort of life, or sovereignty and supreme lordship of this kind? I am a person unable to bring peace to others who are suffering." Having reflected in this way, the king made a great gift of his goods, established the eldest prince in the sovereignty and supreme lordship, asked pardon of his kinsmen and also of the citizens and courtiers, comforted the afflicted, and undertook the eightfold observance. He climbed up to the terrace at the top of the palace and scattered perfume, flowers, fragrances, garlands and unguents. Facing east, he undertook a vow: "By this truth, this true utterance — Having seen these beings tormented by illness and experiencing a terrible plight, I am voluntarily abandoning my own life![28] — by this truth, by this declaration of truth, may I arise as a great *rohita* fish in this sandy river." Having said this, he threw himself off the palace roof terrace.

'At the moment he fell he met his end and arose as a great *rohita* fish in the sandy river. And the gods uttered a cry in all the kingdom: "A great *rohita* fish has arisen in the sandy river as ambrosial medicine for those who have been long afflicted by this great sickness!" On hearing this, a great body of people came out bearing knives and bringing baskets, and began to carve him up with various sharp implements, even as he lived. And the Bodhisattva, though his body was being torn apart, suffused them all with friendliness and tearfully – with face full of tears – he thought: "I have gained something advantageous, namely that these beings will become happy through my own meat and blood." Through that undertaking he satiated those beings with his own flesh and blood for twelve years, and did not turn away from the thought of unsurpassed perfect and full awakening.

'When the illness of these beings was calmed, the *rohita* fish uttered this sound: "Listen, good beings. I am that king Padmaka. Through sacrificing my own life for your benefit, I arose with a body of this kind. You should render your minds faithful towards me. When I have attained unsurpassed perfect and full awakening, then I will liberate you from a terrible sickness and establish you in the perfect condition of *nirvāṇa*." Hearing that, the people became faithful, and the king, courtiers and citizens worshipped him with flowers, perfumes, garlands and unguents. They made this resolve: "O doer of an exceedingly difficult deed, when you have attained unsurpassed perfect and full awakening, let us become your disciples!"'

The Blessed One said, 'What do you think, monks? He who was the king named Padmaka at that time, on that occasion, that was me. And on account of making that kind of sacrifice, I have experienced boundless happiness in the cycle of rebirths and now I have attained unsurpassed perfect and full awakening. In addition, I am possessed of regular digestion. I digest whatever I eat, drink, consume or taste with the same pleasure. I have little pain, and illness for me is a thing of the past.[29] In this way, monks, you should train: "We will cultivate compassion towards all beings." In this way, monks, you should train.'

This was said by the Blessed One, and the monks were delighted and praised the Blessed One's speech.

32. The Morsel (*Kavaḍa*)

The Buddha, the Blessed One, was honoured, revered, respected and worshipped by kings, ministers, the wealthy, the townsfolk, merchants, caravan leaders, gods, *nāgas*, *yakṣas*, antigods, heavenly birds, *kinnaras* and great snakes. That Buddha, the Blessed One, who was venerated as such by gods, *nāgas*, *yakṣas*, antigods, heavenly birds, *kinnaras* and great snakes, who was famous and possessed of great merit, and who was provided with the requisites – robes, bowls, bedding, seats, and medicine to cure the sick – was staying with his community of disciples in Anāthapiṇḍada's park, the Jeta Grove in Śrāvastī.

There the Blessed One addressed the monks: 'O monks, if beings knew the fruits of generosity and the ripe fruits of sharing gifts,[30] as I know the fruits of generosity and the ripe fruits of sharing gifts, then they would not enjoy their last mouthful of water or morsel of food without first having given it and shared it. And if they were to have a worthy recipient, selfishness would not arise, overcome their minds or remain. But when beings do not know the fruits of generosity and the ripe fruits of sharing gifts, as I know the fruits of generosity and the ripe fruits of sharing gifts, then they eat without giving or sharing, with meanness[31] of mind, and selfish thoughts arise, overcome their minds and remain in them.'

The Blessed One spoke thus, and having spoken in this way the teacher and well-farer further said:

> 'For if beings knew what has been said by the Great Sage,
> about the fruits of generosity that are greatly beneficial,
> They would not eat without first giving, would not become
> mean,
> and their minds would never become grasping.

But those fools, obscured by delusion, who do not know,
those beings who would eat with selfish minds,
meanness arises and overcomes their minds and is
established there.'

When the Blessed One had spoken this *sūtra*, the monks became doubtful and asked the Blessed One, the Buddha, who cuts through all doubt: 'It is a marvel, sir, that the Blessed One should explain the quality of generosity, and the ripe fruits of sharing gifts.' The Blessed One said, 'What is the marvel in this, monks, that the Tathāgata should explain the quality of generosity and the ripe fruits of sharing gifts? In a past time I gave up my own last mouthful because of a beggar who had arrived in my doorway. Listen, and concentrate your minds properly and well. I will explain:

'Formerly, monks, in times past, a king named Brahmadatta ruled his kingdom. It was prosperous and flourishing, peaceful and abundantly supplied, and crowded with many people. Strife, quarrels, riots and tumult had ceased, thieves and disease had departed, and it had plenty of rice, sugar cane, cows and buffaloes. He protected it as dearly as an only son. And that king was devout and good, of virtuous disposition, dedicated to the good of others as well as his own benefit, compassionate, great-hearted, devoted to the *dharma*, and affectionate towards the people. He was a giver of great gifts, being generous with everything, renouncing everything, and engaged in extensive donation.

'After a time, a great famine came about, resembling the famine that occurs between the aeons.[32] The people became anxious and afraid at this unseasonable famine, and their necks and cheeks were emaciated with hunger such that their bodies resembled hungry ghosts.[33] They came together as a group and visited the king. Having greeted him with "Victory!" and "Long life!", they said, "Your majesty, protect us from the danger of this famine! Grant us life!"

'The king addressed his steward: "You, man, is there food and water in the storeroom such that there is enough for us and for all of these people?" Hearing this, the steward said, "Your majesty, having investigated the grain I will tell you." Then, with men skilled in counting he made his calculation and announced: "There is for a certain time one morsel each day for all the inhabitants of the kingdom and two morsels for the king." Then the king called the people together and said, "Good people, having come here each day, you can eat in the palace and then go." So each day they came, and each one individually ate a single morsel and then went where they pleased.

'Now there was a certain brahmin who was not part of those calculations, and having heard about it from the others he said to the king, "Your majesty, I heard about the calculations as I was travelling the country. A morsel should be given to me too!" The king gave one of his own two morsels to the brahmin, and proceeded to eat a single morsel like the people.

'It happened that Śakra, king of the gods, saw and knew what was going on below. It occurred to him, "Surely it is a very difficult thing to do, what the king of Vārāṇasī has done. What if I were to investigate this?" So Śakra the king of the gods made himself look like a brahmin and approached the king at his mealtime. After greeting him with "Victory!" and "Long life!", he said, "I am starving. Favour me with your own morsel." The king resolved out of compassion to give up his own life, and gave his own morsel to the brahmin, thus having no food left. Because of his resolve he did this with six food portions, and at the sight of the many people eating, he was filled with extraordinary joy.

'Then Śakra the king of the gods, having seen the king's resolve to carry out something so incredibly difficult, made his brahmin disguise disappear and stood there in his own form. He gladdened the king, saying, "Very good! Very good great king! We are humbled by your lordship's resolve that was so difficult to accomplish. The people have a protector with a king of this kind! Do not grieve, but sow all your seeds in the country. On the seventh day I will let loose the rains of the Great Indra variety, such that all the grain will burst forth." The king had that done, and Śakra let loose the rains of Great Indra such that the famine came to an end and a time of plenty arrived.'

The Blessed One said: 'What do you think, monks? He who at that time and on that occasion was the king named Brahmadatta, that was me. It was I that gave gifts of this type, during a famine of this kind, by letting go of my own life. Therefore in this way, monks, you should train: "We will give such gifts and make merit." In this way, monks, you should train.'

This was said by the Blessed One, and the monks were delighted and praised the Blessed One's speech.

33. Dharmapāla

The Buddha, the Blessed One, was honoured, revered, respected and worshipped by kings, ministers, the wealthy, the townsfolk, merchants, caravan leaders, gods, *nāgas*, *yakṣas*, antigods, heavenly birds, *kinnaras* and great snakes. That Buddha, the Blessed One, who was venerated as such by gods, *nāgas*, *yakṣas*, antigods, heavenly birds, *kinnaras* and great snakes, who was famous and possessed of great merit, and who was provided with the requisites – robes, bowls, bedding, seats, and medicine to cure the sick – was staying with his community of disciples in Rājagṛha in Kalandakanivāpa in the Veṇu Grove.

Now the deluded man Devadatta let loose the elephant Dhanapālaka in order to kill the Blessed One, and he filled a well with poisoned powder, and he sent forth assassins. He was an attacker, an adversary and an enemy to the Blessed One for a long time. Yet the Blessed One had friendly thoughts towards him, thought of his welfare and maintained a compassionate mind. The monks questioned the Blessed One, 'See, Blessed One, how this Devadatta strives to kill the Blessed One, and yet the Blessed One has friendly thoughts towards him, thinks of his welfare and maintains a compassionate mind.'

The Blessed One said, 'O monks, what is the marvel in this now, when the Tathāgata has eradicated attachment, hatred and delusion, is free from birth, ageing, sickness, death, grief, lamentation, suffering, melancholy and mental anguish, and is all-knowing, knowledgeable in all ways, master of all that is to be known? In times past, when I was affected by attachment, hatred and delusion and just a little child, my mind was not corrupted in the presence of someone who was determined to kill me. Listen, and concentrate your minds properly and well. I will explain:

'Formerly, monks, in times past, a king named Brahmadatta ruled his kingdom in the city of Vārāṇasī. It was prosperous and flourishing, peaceful and abundantly supplied, and crowded with many people. Strife, quarrels, riots and tumult had ceased, thieves and disease had departed, and it had plenty of rice, sugar cane, cows and buffaloes. He protected it as dearly as an only son, and it was completely free from troubles. And that king was devout and good, of virtuous disposition, dedicated to the good of others as well as his own benefit, compassionate, great-hearted, devoted to the *dharma*, and affectionate towards the people. He was a giver of great gifts, being generous with everything, renouncing everything, and engaged in extensive donation.

'Now that king had a cruel, passionate and impetuous queen named Durmatī (Evil-minded), and he had a single son named Dharmapāla (Protector of the Dharma), who was born of Durmatī. That Dharmapāla was kind, devout and good, of virtuous disposition, dedicated to the good of others as well as his own benefit, compassionate, great-hearted, devoted to the *dharma*, and affectionate towards the people. The sight of him was dear, pleasing, desirable and charming to all of the brahmins and householders of Vārāṇasī. And having approached a teacher, he learnt his letters along with the other children.

'Some time later, in springtime, the king, along with his queen and his retinue of women, went out to a park in a woodland that was filled with trees in full bloom, and that resounded with the cries of geese, cranes, peacocks, parrots, mynahs, cuckoos and pheasants. There in his park the king amused himself with the women of his inner quarters, and Queen Durmatī was filled with jealousy and anger, and became furious. The king offered her a share of leftover drink, but she, angry, dismissed the king's gift: "Let me drink the blood of your son, if I am to drink a portion of your drink!" They say that someone who is absolutely devoted to sense pleasures does not think at all about the evil deed that is to be done. Thus, although King Brahmadatta was righteous, and although he was being soothed by the women of the inner quarters, because there was no end to his lust and passion he burnt with a fiery anger. His anger swelled, he gave the order: "Go, cut Dharmapāla's throat and bring his blood to drink!"

'Then Prince Dharmapāla, who was in the children's hall, heard about this and began to cry. He said, "Alas for the community of beings in the cycle of rebirths, that under the power of anger they would sacrifice a child who has come from their own body!" Then Dharmapāla, adorned in all his ornaments, fell at the feet of his father and said, "Good father, be gracious. I am blameless and should not be sacrificed. And all fathers cherish[34] their sons." The king replied, "Son, if your mother will relent, I too will do so." So Dharmapāla instead approached his mother, and threw himself crying at her feet. With hands joined in respect he said, "Mother, relent! Don't deprive me of my life!" But she was not pleased with this wretched and pitiable speech and did not relent. The executioners cut Prince Dharmapāla's throat with a sharp sword and Queen Durmatī drank his blood. Durmatī did not repent, but Prince Dharmapāla died with his mind kindly disposed towards his mother, father and the executioners.'

The Blessed One said, 'What do you think, monks? He who was that prince named Dharmapāla at that time, on that occasion, that was me. And Queen Durmatī, that was Devadatta.[35] Even then, in the hands of the executioner, I had friendly thoughts, and likewise now I have friendly, kind and compassionate thoughts towards one who strives to kill me. In this way you should train, monks: "We will cultivate friendly thoughts towards all beings." In this way, monks, you should train.'

This was said by the Blessed One, and the monks were delighted and praised the Blessed One's speech.

34. Śibi

The Buddha, the Blessed One, was honoured, revered, respected and worshipped by kings, ministers, the wealthy, the townsfolk, merchants, caravan leaders, gods, *nāgas*, *yakṣas*, antigods, heavenly birds, *kinnaras* and great snakes. That Buddha, the Blessed One, who was venerated as such by gods, *nāgas*, *yakṣas*, antigods, heavenly birds, *kinnaras* and great snakes, who was famous and possessed of great merit, and who was provided with the requisites — robes, bowls, bedding, seats, and medicine to cure the sick — was staying with his community of disciples in Anāthapiṇḍada's park, the Jeta Grove in Śrāvastī.

At that time and on that occasion in Śrāvastī there were two gatherings of the monks, one on the first day of the Āṣāḍha rains [June/July], and the second at the full moon of Kārtika [October/November]. There the monks baked their bowls, washed their robes, and sewed together dust-heap rags. One of the monks wanted to sew a robe but was unable to insert the thread into the hole of the needle. He spoke with words that were heavy with grief and lamentation: 'Who in the world wishes for merit?' The Blessed One was taking his walk not far away. The Blessed One, sounding like a kettledrum or as beautiful as a cuckoo — deep, sweet and splendid — stretched out his arm like the trunk of an elephant and said, 'O monk, I in the world wish for merit!' Then that monk, hearing heard the Blessed One's voice that was endowed with the five qualities,[36] became agitated and quickly seized the Blessed One's hand and placed it on his own head. He said, 'Blessed One, this hand of yours has accumulated generosity, good conduct, forbearance, vigour, meditation and wisdom during three incalculable aeons.' And then the Blessed One said, 'I am eager for merit, monk. I have a taste for obtaining merit, monk, such that I am never satiated.'

The monks became doubtful and asked the Blessed One, the Buddha, who cuts through all doubt: 'It is a marvel, sir, that the Blessed One is never satiated when it comes to the accumulation of merit.' The Blessed One said, 'O monks, what is the marvel in this now, when the Tathāgata has eradicated attachment, hatred and delusion, is free from birth, ageing, sickness, death, grief, lamentation, suffering, melancholy and mental anguish, and is all-knowing, knowledgeable in all ways, master of all that is to be known? Even in times past, when I was affected by attachment, hatred and delusion, and was not free from birth, ageing, sickness, death, grief, lamentation, suffering, melancholy and mental anguish, I was not satiated with the accumulation of merit. Listen, and concentrate your mind properly and well, and I will explain:

'Formerly, monks, in times past, a king named Śibi ruled his kingdom in the capital city Śibighoṣā. It was prosperous and flourishing, peaceful and abundantly supplied, and crowded with many people. Strife, quarrels, riots and tumult had ceased, thieves and disease had departed, and it had plenty of rice, sugar cane, cows and buffaloes. He protected it as dearly as an only son, and it was completely free from troubles. That king was devout and good, of virtuous disposition, dedicated to the good of others as well as his own benefit, compassionate, great-hearted, devoted to the *dharma*, and affectionate towards the people. He was a giver of great gifts, being generous with everything, renouncing everything, and engaged in extensive donation. At daybreak he rose, entered the sacrificial arena and bestowed food on those who desired food, and clothes on those in need of clothes. He parted with wealth, grain, gold, money, jewels, pearls, beryl, conches, stone and coral, and he never became satiated with the accumulation of merit. He entered his inner quarters and gave food and covers to the people there, and also to the princes and courtiers, the army, and the city and country folk.

'Then it occurred to King Śibi, "Human beings are satisfied with this, but the small animals remain, and what will satisfy them?" He had given up his whole fortune and lived in a single cloth, but it occurred to him that his own body remained. He thought, "I will give my own body to the small animals." He cut his own body with a sword, presented himself where the gnats and mosquitoes were, and remained there. He refreshed them with his blood, as if they were as dear as his only son.

'Then Śakra the king of the gods became aware of what was going on below. It occurred to him, "Does this King Śibi do this for the benefit of living beings, out of compassion? I should investigate this." He made himself appear as a vulture, coloured black like kohl, approached King Śibi, and began to pluck out an eye with his beak. The king did not tremble, but regarded that vulture with eyes filled with friendliness and said, "Dear child, use my body as you please: I make a gift of it."

'Then Śakra the king of the gods was overcome, and making himself appear as a brahmin he stood before King Śibi and said, "Good, lord of the earth. Give me your pair of eyes." The king responded, "Great brahmin, take as it pleases you. I have no obstacles in this."[37]

'At this Śakra the king of the gods became even more pleased. Putting aside his disguise as a brahmin he stood in his own form and spoke encouragingly to the king: "Very good! Very good, O lord of the earth! Your resolve is firm, your aspiration is unshakeable, and you have attained great compassion towards living beings, such that you are even confident in the face of terrifying experiences. With this resolve it will not be long before you awaken to unsurpassed full and complete buddhahood!"'

The Blessed One said, 'What do you think, monks? He who on that occasion, at that time, was the king called Śibi, that was me. Even at that time I was never satiated with accumulating merit, and how much more so now. In this way, monks, you should train: "We will give gifts; we will make merit." In this way, monks, you should train.'

This was said by the Blessed One, and the monks were delighted and praised the Blessed One's speech.

35. Surūpa

The Buddha, the Blessed One, was honoured, revered, respected and worshipped by kings, ministers, the wealthy, the townsfolk, merchants, caravan leaders, gods, *nāgas*, *yakṣas*, antigods, heavenly birds, *kinnaras* and great snakes. That Buddha, the Blessed One, who was venerated as such by gods, *nāgas*, *yakṣas*, antigods, heavenly birds, *kinnaras* and great snakes, who was famous and possessed of great merit, and who was provided with the requisites — robes, bowls, bedding, seats, and medicine to cure the sick — was staying with his community of disciples in Anāthapiṇḍada's park, the Jeta Grove in Śrāvastī.

When the Blessed One had come out of his meditative seclusion and taught the sweet *dharma* — sweet as honey[38] — to the fourfold assembly, several hundred of those assembled heard the sweet *dharma* from the Blessed One with unwavering faculties.[39] Then the monks became doubtful and asked the Blessed One, the Buddha, who cuts through all doubt: 'See, sir, how these beings have become receptacles for the jewel of the *dharma*, and regard it as worthy of listening to with respect.' The Blessed One said, 'Listen, monks, just as the Tathāgata listened to the *dharma* with respect and comprehended it. Concentrate your mind properly and well, and I will explain:

'Formerly, monks, in times past, in the city of Vārāṇasī, a king named Surūpa (Handsome) ruled. It was prosperous and flourishing, peaceful and abundantly supplied, and crowded with many people. Strife, quarrels, riots and tumult had ceased, thieves and disease had departed, and it had plenty of rice, sugar cane, cows and buffaloes. He protected it as dearly as an only son, and it was completely free from troubles. And that king was devout and good, of virtuous disposition, dedicated to the good of others as well as his own benefit, compassionate, great-hearted, devoted to the *dharma*, and affectionate towards the people. He was a giver of great gifts, being generous with everything, renouncing everything, and engaged in extensive donation. And that king had a queen named Sundarikā (Beauty), and she was handsome, good-looking and pleasant, furnished with all major and minor limbs. And he had a single son named Sundaraka (Good-looking), who was cherished and loved, dear and charming, patient and amenable.

'Now on a certain occasion King Surūpa became desirous of the *dharma*, and having assembled all his courtiers he said, "Lords, seek *dharma* teachings.[40] It is the *dharma* that pleases me." Then those courtiers, having joined their palms in respect, reported to the king, "The *dharma* is hard to obtain, Great King. We have heard, Great King, that *dharma* arises from the arising of *buddhas* in the world." The king fastened a golden casket on top of a flagpole and made a proclamation with bells through the whole realm: "I will give this golden casket to whoever will speak the *dharma* to me, and I will pay him great honour!" A great deal of time went by, and no teacher of the *dharma* could be found. The king was tormented with longing on account of the *dharma*.

'Śakra the king of the gods saw and understood what was going on below. He saw the king distressed on account of the *dharma*, and this occurred to him: "What if I were to test this King Surūpa?" Thus, having made himself into the form of a *yakṣa*, altering his hands, feet and eyes, he said to the king in the midst of his multiple assemblies, "Sir is desirous of the *dharma*. I will speak the *dharma* to you."

'At hearing the word "*dharma*", the king became delighted and joyful, and said to the *yakṣa*, "Speak, *guhyaka*, and I will hear *dharma* teachings."[41] The *guhyaka* replied, "Oh great king, *dharma* teachings manifest only to the happy.[42] I am hungry, so offer me some food." Hearing this, the king addressed his men: "Bring different kinds of food and drink for him!" The *yakṣa* said, "I eat freshly killed flesh and blood. Grant me your only son, Sundara." Having heard that, the king became extremely dejected: "After a long time,[43] today I get to hear the *dharma*, but at a price it is not worth." But Prince Sundara heard this and, falling at his father's feet, he begged the king: "Excuse me, your majesty. Your majesty's wish should be fulfilled.[44] Give me as food to the *guhyaka*." So the king, for the sake of the *dharma*, gave his only son, who was cherished and loved, dear and charming, patient and amenable, to the *yakṣa*.

'Then the *yakṣa*, through his supernormal power, made it appear to the king and his assembly that he was tearing apart his major and minor limbs one by one, eating them and drinking his blood.[45] Having seen that, the king, desiring the *dharma*, did not grieve. The *guhyaka* said to the king, "I am not satiated, earthly king. Give me more!" Then the king gave him his beloved wife, and he appeared to eat her in the same way. He spoke to the king further: "Oh earthly king, today I do not get enough to satisfy me." Then the king said to the *yakṣa*, "Dear one, I have given my only son and my beloved wife. Do you ask for more?" The *guhyaka* replied, "Give me your own body! This will bring me satisfaction." The king said, "If I give you my own body, how will I then be able to hear the *dharma*? Won't you speak the *dharma* to me first? I will give up my own body after I have gained the *dharma*." Then the *guhyaka*, having gained this promise from the king, taught the *dharma* before that assembly of several hundred:

> "Grief is born from what is dear.
> Fear is born from what is dear.
> For those who are free from what is dear,
> there is no grief, and how could there be fear?"

'Upon hearing this verse, the king was delighted of mind, his senses joyful and glad. He said to the *yakṣa*, "*Guhyaka*, here is my body. Do with it as you wish."

'Then Śakra the king of the gods knew that the king was as unshakeable as Mount Meru with regard to unsurpassed perfect and full awakening. He set aside his *yakṣa* form and stood in his own form. With his eyes opened by faith, he took the son in one hand and the wife in the other, and said in order to encourage the king, "Very good! Excellent, good man! You are firm in your preparation. With this resolve it will not be long before you awaken to unsurpassed perfect and full awakening. And you are reunited with the people you love."[46] Then the king said this to Śakra the king of the gods:

"Very good, very good Kauśika! My desire for the *dharma* has been fulfilled!"'

The Blessed One said, 'What do you think, monks? He who, at that time and on that occasion, was the king called Surūpa, that was me. Ānanda was Prince Sundara, and this Sundarikā was Yaśodharā. Even then, monks, I gave up cherished belongings for the sake of the *dharma*, and even gave up my own life, how much more so now. In this way you should train, monks: "We will revere, pay respects to, honour and worship the *dharma*. Having revered, paid respects to, honoured and worshipped the *dharma* we will live in reliance on it." In this way, monks, you should train.

This was said by the Blessed One, and the monks were delighted and praised the Blessed One's speech.

36. Maitrakanyaka

The Buddha, the Blessed One, was honoured, revered, respected and worshipped by kings, ministers, the wealthy, the townsfolk, merchants, caravan leaders, gods, *nāgas*, *yakṣas*, antigods, heavenly birds, *kinnaras* and great snakes. That Buddha, the Blessed One, who was venerated as such by gods, *nāgas*, *yakṣas*, antigods, heavenly birds, *kinnaras* and great snakes, who was famous and possessed of great merit, and who was provided with the requisites — robes, bowls, bedding, seats, and medicine to cure the sick — was staying with his community of disciples in Anāthapiṇḍada's park, the Jeta Grove in Śrāvastī.

There the Blessed One addressed the monks: 'O monks, those families in which the mother and father are properly honoured, properly worshipped and properly looked after with joy are "with Brahmā". And what is the reason for that? Because, in accordance with the *dharma*, for the son of the family the mother and father have become Brahmā gods. Those families in which the mother and father are properly honoured, properly worshipped and properly looked after with joy are "with a teacher". And what is the reason for that? Because, in accordance with the *dharma*, for the son of the family the mother and father are teachers. Those families in which the mother and father are properly honoured, properly worshipped and properly looked after with joy are "worthy of sacrifice".[47] And what is the reason for that? Because, in accordance with the *dharma*, for the son of the family the mother and father are worthy of sacrifice. Those families in which the mother and father are properly honoured, properly worshipped and properly looked after with joy are "with Agni". And what is the reason for that? Because, in accordance with the *dharma*, for the son of the family the mother and father are Agni. Those families in which the mother and father are properly honoured, properly worshipped and properly looked after with joy are "with the gods". And what is the reason for that? Because, in accordance with the *dharma*, for the son of the family the mother and father are gods.' Thus spoke the Blessed One. Having said this the well-farer, the teacher, also spoke the following:

> 'For a mother and father are Brahmā, and one's first teacher;
> To a son they are worthy of sacrifice; they are Agni, and the
> gods.
>
> Therefore the wise should revere and honour them,
> by massaging, bathing and cleaning their feet,
> or with food and drink, clothes, beds and seats.
>
> That wise man who attends on his mother and father,
> becomes irreproachable, and after death enjoys heaven.'

When the Blessed One had spoken this *sūtra*, the monks became doubtful, and questioned the Blessed One, the Buddha, who cuts through all doubt: 'It is a marvel, sir, that the Blessed One should speak in praise of attending on one's venerable mother and father!' The Blessed One replied, 'O monks, what is the marvel in this now, if the Tathāgata, who has eradicated attachment, hatred and delusion, who is free from birth, ageing, sickness, death, grief, lamentation, suffering, melancholy and mental anguish, and is all-knowing, knowledgeable in all ways, master of all that is to be known, should speak in praise of attending on one's venerable mother and father? In times past, when I was affected by attachment, hatred and delusion, and was not free from birth, ageing, sickness, death, grief, lamentation, suffering, melancholy and mental anguish, having done my mother a small injury I experienced powerful suffering. Listen, monks. Focus your minds properly and well, and I will explain:

'Formerly, monks, in times past, there was in this city of Vārāṇasī a caravan leader called Mitra (Friend). He was rich, of great wealth and property, and extensive, wide holdings. He possessed the wealth of Vaiśravaṇa, rivaling Vaiśravaṇa in wealth. He took a wife from a suitable family, and he played with her and made love to her and amused himself. But the sons that were born as a result of his playing and love-making and enjoyment died.[48] Resting his cheek in his hand, he remained lost in thought: "I have a house full of riches, but I have no son or daughter. After my death, having declared me sonless the king will appropriate all my property." His friend advised, "If a son is born to you, you should give him a girl's name, and then he will be long-lived."

'He, sonless and desiring a son, entreated Śiva, Varuṇa, Kubera, Śakra, Brahmā and so on, and various other gods, the gods of the grove, the gods of the forest, the gods of four-way crossroads, the gods of three-way crossroads and the gods who receive oblations. He also implored his lineage gods, the gods who shared his nature, and his tutelary gods. For there is this saying in the world: that sons and daughters are born because of entreaties. But this is not so, for if it were the case then each person would have a thousand sons just like a wheel-turning king. Rather, sons and daughters are born from the coming-together of three favourable conditions. Which three? The mother and father unite in love-making, the mother is healthy and in her fertile period, and a *gandharva* is present. Sons and daughters are born from the coming-together of these three favourable conditions. But he continued to make entreaties, and a certain being came out from a certain group of beings and descended into his wife's womb.

'There are five particular characteristics of any wise woman. What are the five? She knows when a man is enamoured and when he is indifferent. She knows the right time, for she knows when she is in her fertile period. She knows when she has conceived, and she knows who has impregnated her. She knows when it is a boy and when it is a girl, for if it is a boy it lies on the right side of her womb and stays there, and if it is a girl it lies on the left side of her womb and stays there.

'She was thrilled and delighted and addressed her husband, "You are fortunate, noble lord! I have become pregnant. And because it lies on the right side of my womb it will certainly be a boy!" He too was thrilled and delighted, and he puffed out his chest and stretched out his right arm, and uttered this joyous speech: "O that I might see the face of a son, desired for a long time! May he not be born unworthy of me! May he do his duty! Having been supported by me, may he be my support! May he claim his inheritance, and may my family lineage last a long time! And when we are gone, may he give gifts large or small and make merit, saying, 'May this follow these two, wherever they have gone or arisen' and thereby dedicate it in our names!"

'Knowing that she was pregnant, he kept her on the upper storey of a lofty palace, unrestrained, with everything necessary for the cold when it was cold, and everything necessary for the heat when it was hot. She was provided with food as prescribed by the doctors, neither too bitter nor too sour, neither too salty nor too sweet, neither too sharp nor too astringent, with food that was free from bitterness, sourness, saltiness, sweetness, sharpness and astringence. She was adorned with strings of pearls, and like a celestial nymph roving the Nandana Grove she moved from bed to bed and from seat to seat without descending to the ground below. And she did not hear any unpleasant sound while her foetus was maturing.

'After eight or nine months had passed she gave birth. A boy was born who was well formed, beautiful, pleasing, brilliant, golden-coloured, with a parasol-shaped head, pendulous arms, a broad forehead, a loud voice, eyebrows that joined, a prominent nose, and furnished with all the major and subsidiary limbs. When he was born they celebrated his birth-festival and fixed the naming ceremony: "What should be this boy's name?" His kinsmen said, "This boy is the son and daughter of Mitra, so the boy should be called Maitrakanyaka (Daughter of Mitra)."[49]

'The child Maitrakanyaka was given eight nurses: two nurses to carry him, two nurses to feed him, two nurses to clean him, and two nurses to play with him. He was raised by the eight nurses and nourished with milk, curds, fresh butter, clarified butter, the residue of the clarified butter and other foods of excellent, beneficial characteristics, so he grew quickly like a lotus in a pool.

'His father crossed the great ocean and there met his death. When Maitrakanyaka was grown up, he said to his mother, "Mother, what work was my father's livelihood? Following him, I too would like to work at that." His mother replied, "Son, your father was an agriculture tradesman.[50] If you desire to, you too should be an agriculture tradesman." She thought, "If I tell him that he was a merchant on the great ocean, then he too at some stage will go out on the great ocean and meet his death there."

'So he established an agricultural trade shop, and on the first day he made four coins, and he gave them to his mother, saying, "Mother, bestow these on ascetics, brahmins, poor men and beggars." And she further said, "Your father was a perfume-seller." So he gave up being an agricultural tradesman and established a perfume shop, and he made eight coins. These too he gave to his mother, and then she said, "Your father was a goldsmith." So he gave up that shop and set up a goldsmith shop. In the first day he made sixteen coins and gave them to his mother. On the second day he made thirty-two coins and presented these also to his mother. But the goldsmiths became jealous and, knowing all the appointed trades, they said, "Maitrakanyaka, why are you pursuing an inappropriate livelihood? Your father was a merchant on the great ocean. Who directed you into this wrong trade?"

'Prompted by what the goldsmiths said, he went to his mother and said, "Mother, I have heard it said that our father was a merchant on the great ocean. Grant permission:[51] I too will go out on the great ocean!" His mother replied, "This is true, son. But you are young and my only son. Don't abandon me and go out on the great ocean!" But he, insulted by those jealous-minded bad friends, did not give up. He disobeyed his mother's words and had a bell sounded in the city of Vārāṇasī: "Listen, good men, citizens of Vārāṇasī! The merchant Maitrakanyaka, a caravan leader, is going out into the great ocean! Whoever among you is courageous enough to go out on the great ocean with Maitrakanyaka the caravan leader, without taxes, customs fees and ferry money, they should assemble their wares for taking on the great ocean."

'He carried out the auspicious ceremonies, portentous rites and benedictions, and then with a retinue of five hundred merchants and with carts, carriers, bags and baskets, buffaloes, cows and donkeys, he assembled his wares for going on the great ocean and set out. His mother, her heart agitated with love, her face clouded over with tears, clutched at his feet: "Son, don't abandon me and go out on the great ocean!" But though he was pleased by these words that were heavy with distress and lamentation, he made his resolve. He struck his mother on the head with his foot and departed with his caravan. His mother said, "O my son, may this deed not ripen for you!"

'In due course, passing through villages, towns, districts, capitals and cities, he reached the shore of the ocean. He obtained a vessel for five hundred pieces of silver, and taking the five types of crew[52] — the conveyer, sailor, fisherman and helmsman — he made three proclamations and set off onto the sea.

'But as the boat was going along, it unluckily fell into trouble on account of a *makara* fish, and Maitrakanyaka, clinging to a plank of wood, reached dry land. He walked about on that land until he saw, not far off, a city named Ramaṇaka (Charming). He approached it, and there four celestial nymphs appeared, beautiful, good-looking and charming. They said, "Come, Maitrakanyaka, you are welcome. Here is our food-house and drink-house, our clothes-house and our sleeping-house, abounding in various kinds of gems, pearls, beryl, conch-shells, crystal, coral, gold and silver. Come, and we will enjoy ourselves." He experienced pleasure with them for several years, just like a being who has made merit and done good deeds. They prohibited him from going along the path south, but being forbidden from the southern road only made him want to go there more.

'In due course he went along that path to the south and saw a city called Sadāmatta (Constant Revelry). He arrived at the gate, and eight celestial nymphs came out, who were even more beautiful, more good-looking and more charming. They said, "Come, Maitrakanyaka, you are welcome. Here is our food-house and drink-house, our clothes-house and our sleeping-house, abounding in various kinds of gems, pearls, beryl, conch-shells, crystal, coral, gold and silver. Come, and we will enjoy ourselves." He experienced pleasure with them for several years, just like a being who has made merit and done good deeds. They prohibited him from going along the path south, but being forbidden from the southern road only made him want to go there more.

'Again he went along that path to the south and saw a city called Nandana (Beautiful). He arrived at the gate, and sixteen celestial nymphs came out, who were even more beautiful, more good-looking and more charming. They said, "Come, Maitrakanyaka, you are welcome. Here is our food-house and drink-house, our clothes-house and our sleeping-house, abounding in various kinds of gems, pearls, beryl, conch-shells, crystal, coral, gold and silver. Come, and we will enjoy ourselves." He experienced pleasure with them for several years, just like a being who has made merit and done good deeds. They too prohibited him from going along the path south, but being forbidden from the southern road only made him want to go there more.

'So once again he went along that path to the south and saw a palace called Brahmottara (Highest Brahmā). He arrived at the gate, and thirty-two celestial nymphs came out, who were even more beautiful, more good-looking and more charming. They said, "Come, Maitrakanyaka, you are welcome. Here is our food-house and drink-house, our clothes-house and our sleeping-house, abounding in various kinds of gems, pearls, beryl, conch-shells, crystal, coral, gold and silver. Come, and we will enjoy ourselves." He experienced pleasure with them for several years, just like a being who has made merit and done good deeds. They too prohibited him from going along the path south, but being forbidden from the southern road only made him want to go there more.

'When he went along that path to the south his wishes came to pass, so yet again he went along the path to the south, and he saw a city made of iron. He went in, and the moment that he had entered the gate closed. Then he went into the inner part, and that gate closed. Then he went further inside and there saw a man of great stature. A wheel made of iron turned on his head, blazing and burning, flaming like a single flame. Pus and blood oozed from his head and this was his food.

'Maitrakanyaka asked that man, "O person, who are you?" He replied, "I am someone who injured his mother." And as soon as the man gave this explanation, Maitrakanyaka's action faced him: "I too am someone who injured his mother! I think that I have been drawn here in this way because of that action." Immediately a voice appeared in the sky: "He who was bound is freed! He who was free is bound!" The moment this was said, the wheel vanished from that person's head and appeared on the head of Maitrakanyaka. Then, observing Maitrakanyaka suffering, that person spoke this verse:

> "Having passed through Ramaṇaka, Sadāmatta and
> Nandana,
> and Brahmottara Palace, why did you come here?"

Maitrakanyaka told him:

> "Having passed through Ramaṇaka, Sadāmatta and
> Nāndana,
> and Brahmottara Palace according to my wish, I came here.
> For karma drags one a long way; karma continues a long
> time;
> Karma drags one to a place where the karma ripens.
> Because of the ripening of karma the wheel is borne on my
> head,
> blazing and flaming, oppressing my life-breath."

The person said:

"With wicked thoughts you mistreated your mother,
striking her on the head with your foot. This is the fruit of
that action."

Maitrakanyaka said:

"For how many thousands of years will this wheel turn on
my head,'
blazing and flaming, oppressing my life-breath?"

The person declared:

"For sixty-thousand years and sixty-hundred years
this wheel of blazing iron will revolve on your head."

Maitrakanyaka said, "O person, will anyone else also come here?" The man replied, "Someone who has done this kind of deed." Then Maitrakanyaka, experiencing painful feelings, generated compassion towards these beings and said to the man, "I wish, O man, for the sake of all beings, to bear this wheel upon my head. Let not anyone else who has done this kind of deed come here!" The moment he said this, the wheel flew up from Maitrakanyaka the Bodhisattva's head to a height of seven palm trees and stayed there in the sky. And having met his time, he arose among the gods in the Tuṣita heaven.'[53]

The Blessed One said, 'What do you think, monks? He who at that time and on that occasion was Maitrakanyaka, that was me. I did business and presented the coins to my mother, and through the ripening of that act of mine I experienced much pleasure in the four great cities. But I slightly injured my mother, and because of the ripening of that act I experienced the suffering of this kind. Therefore, monks, you should train in this way: "We will honour our mother and father and not do them injury. Let there be no faults here like those of Maitrakanyaka or of that other man, but only let there be these qualities of the sons of the gods." In this way, monks, you should train. For what reason? Because, monks, a son's parents do difficult things, nourishing and supporting him, cherishing him and giving him milk, showing him the wonderful Jambūdvīpa continent. A son who would carry his mother on one shoulder and his father on the other for a full one hundred years, or who would give them the gems, pearls, beryl, conch-shells, crystal, coral, silver, gold, emeralds, cat's-eye gems, rubies and right-spiralling conches on this great earth, or establish them in this way to lordship and sovereignty, even that son would still not have served or benefitted his mother and father enough. But someone who introduces his mother and father who are without faith to the riches of faith, educates them in it, bestows it upon them and establishes them in it; or if they are without virtue, introduces virtue to them, educates them in it, bestows it upon them and establishes them in it; or in the riches of generosity if they are mean, or in the riches of wisdom if they are lacking wisdom; that son would have served and benefitted his mother and father enough.'

This was said by the Blessed One, and the monks were delighted and praised the Blessed One's speech.

37. The Hare (*Śaśa*)

The Buddha, the Blessed One, was honoured, revered, respected and worshipped by kings, ministers, the wealthy, the townsfolk, merchants, caravan leaders, gods, *nāgas*, *yakṣas*, antigods, heavenly birds, *kinnaras* and great snakes. That Buddha, the Blessed One, who was venerated as such by gods, *nāgas*, *yakṣas*, antigods, heavenly birds, *kinnaras* and great snakes, who was famous and possessed of great merit, and who was provided with the requisites – robes, bowls, bedding, seats, and medicine to cure the sick – was staying with his community of disciples in Anāthapiṇḍada's park, the Jeta Grove in Śrāvastī.

In Śrāvastī there was a certain guildsman, who was rich, of great wealth and property, and extensive, wide holdings. He possessed the wealth of Vaiśravaṇa, rivaling Vaiśravaṇa in wealth. He took a wife from a suitable family, and together with her he played, enjoyed himself and made love. After some time of playing, love-making and enjoyment, it happened that a being entered his wife. After eight or nine months she gave birth, and a little boy was born. He grew up to be big and strong. His father lost all his wealth, and his possessions wasted away, and having numerous friends, relations and kinsmen, he sent his son to them from time to time. He was indulged by those relations so that he became very affectionate towards them.

On a certain occasion he set out for the Jeta Grove, and there he saw the Buddha, the Blessed One, adorned with the thirty-two marks of a great man and the eighty secondary marks, his body shining, arrayed with light that extended a fathom, radiance in excess of a thousand suns, like a living mountain of jewels, handsome in his entirety. He developed faith and honoured the feet of the Blessed One, and sat before him ready to hear the *dharma*. The Blessed One gave a *dharma* talk that created disgust with the cycle of rebirths, and hearing this he became one who sees the faults in the cycle of rebirths and the qualities in *nirvāṇa*. Having sought permission from his parents, he went forth in the dispensation of the Blessed One. But although he renounced in this way, he dwelled among his relations. Then the Blessed One restrained him from contact with householders and directed him to the forest, but that did not please him.

Three times the Blessed One restrained him from contact with the householders: 'Dear one, there are many faults and offences in associating with householders. There are forms that are perceived by the eyes as lovely, desirable, beloved, dear, agreeable, conducive to pleasure and delightful; sounds perceived by the ear; smells perceived by the nose; flavours perceived by the tongue; contacts perceived by the body; and phenomena perceived by the mind as lovely, desirable, beloved, dear, agreeable, conducive to pleasure and delightful, but which are really like thorns.' And he praised in many ways the qualities of the forest, in which, for one established there, virtuous qualities increase.

At last that son of a good family came to the Blessed One, his skilful friend, and took up residence in the forest. And by applying himself, striving and exerting, he understood that this fivefold wheel of rebirth is in constant motion. Having rejected all conditioned things as being characterized by decay, decline, destruction and ruin, through destroying all the defilements he achieved the state of arhatship. Having become an *arhat*, he was dispassionate towards the triple world. He considered a clod of earth the same as gold, and empty space the same as the palm of his hand, indifferent alike to an axe and sandal-paste. Having attained the knowledges, supernormal knowledges and special knowledges, he turned away from honours, desires, possessions and continued existence. He became worthy of worship, respect and veneration by the gods including Indra and Upendra. He recalled his former lives and saw the incredibly difficult feats of the Blessed One. He approached the Blessed One and respectfully praised and honoured him.

The monks became doubtful, and questioned the Blessed One, the Buddha, who cuts through all doubt: 'See, sir, how this son of a good family was three times restrained by the Blessed One from interaction with householders and directed to the forest, and there was established in arhatship.' The Blessed One said, 'O monks, what is the marvel in this now, if this son of a good family was three times restrained from interaction with householders and directed to the forest, and was there established in arhatship through me, when I have eradicated attachment, hatred and delusion, am free from birth, ageing, sickness, death, grief, lamentation, suffering, melancholy and mental anguish, and am all-knowing, knowledgeable in all ways, master of all that is to be known? In times past, when I was affected by attachment, hatred and delusion, and was not free from birth, ageing, sickness, death, grief, lamentation, suffering, melancholy and mental anguish, this son of a noble family was restrained from contact with householders and directed to the forest because of me sacrificing my own life. Listen, monks. Focus your minds properly and well, and I will explain:

'Formerly, monks, in times past, in a certain mountain cave that was furnished with springs, flowers and fruits, lived a sage engaged in severe austerities. He consumed fruits, roots and water, wore deerskin and bark-cloth, and conducted fire sacrifices. And this sage was friends with a hare that had a human voice. Three times every day he came near to that sage, and having approached, he offered salutation, and then carried on a conversation with a variety of talk. The two of them continued in strong affection, like a father and son, until after some time a great drought came to pass, such that the rivers and wells had little water, and the trees were empty of flowers and fruits. Then that sage in his hermitage was unhappy due to the lack of food. He began to throw off his deerskin and bark-cloth.

'Then, seeing what was happening, the hare asked him, "Great sage, where are you going?" The sage replied, "I am going to a village. There I will subsist on cooked food." Hearing the sage's words, he became upset, considering himself like one separated from his mother and father. Falling at the sage's feet he said, "Don't abandon me! Household-dwelling is fraught with many faults, while forest-dwelling abounds in good qualities!" But despite speaking like this many times, he could not dissuade him. So then the hare said, "If you are determined to go, then please wait for just one day. Tomorrow you may go as you please." Then this occurred to the sage: "Surely he wishes to offer me some food, for these beings who are in the form of animals keep a hoard." So he consented.

'Then when the daily observances were done and it was time for food, the hare approached and circumambulated that sage and then began to ask pardon: "Forgive me, great sage, if I — arisen in an animal form and deprived of reason and comprehension — have committed any fault towards you." Having said this, he suddenly sprang forth and landed in the fire. The sage was shocked, and with his face clouded with tears he pulled him to his chest as if he was his dear only son and said, "Dear one, what is this you are doing?" The hare replied, "Great sage, out of love for the forest you can subsist for a day and a night on my own meat." And:

> "There is nothing in the forest for this full-grown hare:
> no beans, no sesame, no rice.
> But you should today make use of this, my body,
> consecrated in the fire, and live in the forest of austerities."

'Then the sage, having heard the hare's words, experienced profound shock and said, "If this is so, out of affection for you I will willingly give up my life right here, and not go down to the vicinity of the village!" Hearing these words, the hare was delighted, and with his face upturned he gazed at the sky and made this entreaty. He said:

> "Having come to the forest my heart delights in solitude!
> By this statement of truth may the god rain down the rains
> of Great Indra!"

'The moment he said this, through the power of the Bodhisattva the abode of Great Indra shook, and the gods became aware of what was going on below, saying "What has happened?" It is said that they saw because of the power of the Bodhisattva. Because of Śakra the king of the gods, the rains of Great Indra rained down, so that the hermitage was once again filled with an abundance of grass, shrubs, herbs, flowers and fruits.

'Then that sage approached the hare as a spiritual friend, and living there he realized the five supernormal knowledges. The sage said to the hare, "Friend hare, what result do you wish for, from this very difficult undertaking and your cultivation of compassion?" He said, "To be a *buddha* in this dark world that is leaderless and lacking a guide, to carry across those beings who have not crossed over, liberate those who are not liberated, console those in need of consolation, bring to complete *nirvāṇa* those who have not entered complete *nirvāṇa*." Then that sage, having heard these words, said to the hare, "When you become a *buddha*, may you take notice of me again." The hare said, "Let it be so."'[54]

The Blessed One said, 'What do you think, monks? He who was at that time and on that occasion the hare, that was me, and that sage was this son of a good family. In this way, monks, you should train: "We will dwell as good friends, good companions, good associates, not evil friends, evil companions, evil associates." In this way, monks, you should train.'

Then Venerable Ānanda said to the Blessed One, 'Sir, when I am here alone and solitary in retreat, this thought arises in my mind, that this is half of the religious life,[55] namely good friendship, good companionship and good associations, and not evil friendship, evil companionship and evil associations.' The Blessed One said, 'You should not say this, Ānanda, that this is half of the religious life, namely good friendship, good companionship and good associations, and avoiding evil friendship, evil companionship and evil associations. Ānanda, this is the entire, complete, whole, pure, accomplished religious life, namely good friendship, good companionship and good associations, and avoiding evil friendship, evil companionship and evil associations. What is the reason for this? Because, Ānanda, beings who are subject to the experience of rebirth come to me as their spiritual friend and are liberated from the experience of rebirth, and those beings who experience ageing, sickness, grief, death, lamentation, suffering, melancholy and mental anguish are freed from mental anguish. In this manner, Ānanda, it should be understood, that this is the entire, complete, whole, pure, accomplished religious life, namely good friendship, good companionship and good associations, and avoiding evil friendship, evil companionship and evil associations. In this way, monks, you should train.'[56]

This was said by the Blessed One, and the monks were delighted and praised the Blessed One's speech.

38. The Dharma-seeker (*Dharmagaveṣī*)

The Buddha, the Blessed One, was honoured, revered, respected and worshipped by kings, ministers, the wealthy, the townsfolk, merchants, caravan leaders, gods, *nāgas*, *yakṣas*, antigods, heavenly birds, *kinnaras* and great snakes. That Buddha, the Blessed One, who was venerated as such by gods, *nāgas*, *yakṣas*, antigods, heavenly birds, *kinnaras* and great snakes, who was famous and possessed of great merit, and who was provided with the requisites — robes, bowls, bedding, seats, and medicine to cure the sick — was staying with his community of disciples in Anāthapiṇḍada's park, the Jeta Grove in Śrāvastī.

It was the householder Anāthapiṇḍada's habit that, having risen at dawn and approached in order to see the Blessed One, he cleaned the Jeta Grove. But one time the householder Anāthapiṇḍada was delayed, and the Blessed One, in order to show a meritorious path to those beings who desired merit, took up the broom and began to clean the Jeta Grove himself. Having seen the Blessed One doing this, the great disciples — Śāradvatīputra, Maudgalyāyana, Kāśyapa, Nanda, Revata and so on — also began to clean. Then, having cleaned the Jeta Grove along with his disciples, he entered the meeting hall and sat in front of the community of monks on the seat that had been prepared. Having sat down, the Blessed One addressed the monks: 'There are these five benefits, monks, in cleaning. What five? One purifies one's own mind, one purifies another's mind, one becomes pleasing to the gods,[57] one accumulates suitable roots of virtue, and at the break-up of the body one arises in a good destiny, a heaven realm, among the gods. These are the five benefits of cleaning.'

Then the four assemblies, having heard the five benefits of cleaning in the presence of the Blessed One, became faithful, their minds pleased, joyful and happy, and getting up from their seats they raised their hands respectfully towards the Blessed One. They said this to the Blessed One: 'Blessed One, as the Blessed One's servants we wish to always clean the whole Jeta Grove. Grant us this favour.' The Blessed One consented to them through his silence, and so the four assemblies, knowing that the Blessed One had consented, took up brooms and began to sweep the whole of the Jeta Grove. And when they had swept the whole of the Jeta Grove as far as the grove road, they sat a little way from the Blessed One in order to hear a *dharma* teaching, and listened with respect.

The householder Anāthapiṇḍada returned to that region, and he heard that the Blessed One himself, along with his great disciples, had cleaned the Jeta Grove. Having heard the Blessed One's teaching on the five benefits of cleaning, he was full of regret and reflected:

'Oh why have I done this? I have thrown away my intention to clean this monastery of the Blessed One:

a field of merit in which a seed planted today produces fruit today also, endless fruit produced even from a small seed;
an extremely pleasant ground where all the disciples live together in the presence of the Tathāgata;
a place of happiness for all the gods, antigods, humans, *gandharvas*, divine birds, *kinnaras* and great snakes;
where there is no place for all the malicious beings, *bhūtas*, hungry ghosts, *piśācas*, *yakṣas*, *rākṣasas* and hell-beings;
an abode that has no place for Māra or any of Māra's assembly, whether they are deities or humans;
a place characterized by the destruction of oppression;
where the occurrence of greed, hatred, delusion, selfishness, envy, pride and wickedness among beings is unknown;
unfrequented by those of evil conduct and unattractive to those under the influence of bad friends;
a place that is neither seen nor thought of by those who are faithless or devoid of *dharma* and liberality, and which does not cross the mind of those of bad conduct and inappropriate living;
a refuge that is not obtained by those lacking in compassion, the angry, or harsh-speakers, and which is far away for those who are apathetic or of little vigour, or who are restless and give up on their undertakings;
a place of darkness for those lacking in meditative attainments and whose memories are obscured, and for those who live according to a wrong view, and those who are established on a wrong path;
a place not arrived at or obtained by those who have wrong understanding or other faulty opinions and knowledge;
but extremely pleasing to the generous and a place of great delight for those intent on moral conduct;

approached respectfully and obtained by those living with
patience;
arrived at and gained by those who are always vigorous in
their undertakings;
a place for those who love meditation to abide;
a field never lacking in understanding and clarity for those
who maintain wisdom.

'It is in this type of monastery, that is under the mastery of the Buddha, that I have thrown away my intention to clean! But I will never do this again!' Having resolved on that, he wondered, 'How can I approach Blessed One, when he, along with his great disciples, did the cleaning himself?' So Anāthapiṇḍada stood there, visibly embarrassed, his heart afflicted by shame.

Blessed ones, *buddhas*, know yet ask questions. And so he asked the monks, 'What is going on?' The monks replied, 'Sir, Anāthapiṇḍada, embarrassed in mind and body and with his heart afflicted by shame, does not wish to approach, to even place a foot down here, in the vicinity of the Blessed One, precisely because the Blessed One, together with his great disciples, cleaned the Jeta Grove himself.' Then the Blessed One said, 'The householder should be brought here to hear[58] the words of the Buddha. Why? Because blessed ones, *buddhas*, regard the true *dharma* as venerable, for the *dharma* is venerable to *arhats*.'

Then Anāthapiṇḍada, at the singing of this verse, approached the place where the Blessed One was. Having approached, he worshipped the feet of the Blessed One and sat down before him, a little way apart, in order to hear a *dharma* talk. Then the Blessed One taught, inspired, incited and pleased him with a *dharma* talk. In many ways the Blessed One proceeded to teach, inspire, incite and please him with a *dharma* talk.

Then the monks became doubtful and questioned the Blessed One, the Buddha, who cuts through all doubt: 'It is a marvel, sir, that the Blessed One, being respectful of and reverential towards the *dharma*, should speak in praise of the *dharma* like this. See, sir, how these beings have become vessels for the jewel of the *dharma*, such that they have reverently set about cleaning all of the Jeta Grove, and they regard the *dharma* as worthy of hearing.' The Blessed One said, 'What is the marvel in this now, monks, if the Tathāgata, who has destroyed greed, hatred and delusion, and is completely free from birth, ageing, sickness, death, grief, lamentation, suffering, melancholy and mental anguish, should be respectful of and reverential towards the *dharma* and speak in praise of the *dharma*. For in times past, when I was affected by greed, hatred and delusion, and was not free from birth, ageing, sickness, death, grief, lamentation, suffering, melancholy and mental anguish, sacrificed even my own life for the sake of the *dharma*. Listen, focus your minds properly and well, and I will explain:

'Formerly, monks, in times past, a king named Brahmadatta ruled his kingdom in the city of Vārāṇasī. It was prosperous and flourishing, peaceful and abundantly supplied, and crowded with many people. Strife, quarrels, riots and tumult had ceased, thieves and disease had departed, and it had plenty of rice, sugar cane, cows and buffaloes. He protected it as dearly as an only son. And that king was devout and good, of virtuous disposition, dedicated to the good of others as well as his own benefit, compassionate, great-hearted, devoted to the *dharma*, and affectionate towards the people. He was a giver of great gifts, being generous with everything, renouncing everything, and engaged in extensive donation.

'On a certain occasion he played with his wife, made love to her and amused himself with her. And after some time, from that play and love-making and amusement, that queen became pregnant. She had a pregnancy craving:[59] "I would listen to a good speech!" She told the king, and the king summoned soothsayers and questioned them. They said, "Your majesty, this is an indication of the being within."

'So the king, in order to get a good speaker, had a golden casket travel through villages, cities, towns, districts and the capital, but no good speaker could be found. Meanwhile, after nine months had passed she gave birth. A boy was born who was well formed, beautiful, pleasing, brilliant, golden-coloured, with a parasol-shaped head, pendulous arms, a broad forehead, a loud voice, eyebrows that joined, a prominent nose, and furnished with all the major and subsidiary limbs. When he was born they celebrated his birth-festival and fixed the naming ceremony: "What should be this boy's name?" The courtiers said, "Because this boy desired good speech even before his birth, the boy's name should be Subhāṣitagaveṣī (Desirous of Good Speech)."[60] And so he was named Subhāṣitagaveṣī.

'The child Subhāṣitagaveṣī was given eight nurses: two nurses to carry him, two nurses to feed him, two nurses to clean him and two nurses to play with him. He was raised by the eight nurses and nourished with milk, curds, fresh butter, clarified butter, the residue of the clarified butter and other foods of excellent, beneficial characteristics, so he grew quickly like a lotus in a pool. And when in due course he had grown up, even then he desired good speech and did not get it.

'When his father passed away, he was established in the kingship. He commanded his courtiers: "Chiefs, my purpose is good speech. I desire good speech." Those courtiers paraded the golden casket through the whole of Jambūdvīpa for the sake of good speech, but they did not find good speech. They reported this to the king. The king was tormented with longing on account of wishing to hear good speech.

'It happened that Śakra, king of the gods, saw and understood what was going on below. He saw the king frustrated in his efforts to hear good speech, and it occurred to him, "What if I were to test this king?" So Śakra the king of the gods took on the form of a *guhyaka*, altering his hands, feet and eyes, and spoke this verse before the king:

> "One should live the *dharma*, behaving well; one should not
> behave badly.
> One who lives according to the *dharma* is happy in this world
> and the next."

'Then the king, gazing at him with eyes wide in amazement, said to the *guhyaka*, "Speak, speak to me, *guhyaka*! I would hear these verses!" Then the *guhyaka* said to the king, "If I am to speak thus, you should do something for me, just as I am going to do as you command." The king said, "What do you command?" The *guhyaka* replied, "If, having burned a fire in a pit with acacia wood for seven days and nights, you cast yourself in there, then I will speak another verse for you." Hearing that, the king was delighted and said to that *guhyaka*, "Let it be so." Then the king, having made this promise to the *guhyaka*, had it proclaimed with gongs throughout his realm: "In seven days the king, in order to hear good speech, will cast himself into a fire pit. Whoever wishes to see wonders should come!"

'Then several hundred thousand beings assembled, and several hundred thousand deities assembled in the sky, and having approached because of the pure resolve of the Bodhisattva, they remained there to see the marvel.[61] Then the *guhyaka* flew up into the sky and said to the Bodhisattva, "Great king, you should do what you agreed." The king consecrated his eldest son in the kingship, asked pardon of his courtiers and the city and country folk, and comforted the people in general. Having come close to that fire pit, he spoke this verse:

> "This pit of coals, terrifying like the red blazing sun,
> I hasten towards for the sake of *dharma*, without hesitation
> or fear for my life.
> And this fiery pit will become, through the power of my
> virtuous merit,
> a cool lotus pool filled with lotuses, its water perfumed with
> sandal-paste."

'Having said this, the Bodhisattva fell into the fire pit, and at the moment that he fell into it, the fire pit appeared as a lotus pool. Then Śakra the king of the gods, seeing this great miracle, that marvel that humbled gods and men, cast off his appearance as a *yakṣa* and, standing in his own form, spoke the verse:

> "One should live the *dharma*, behaving well; one should not
> behave badly.

> One who lives according to the *dharma* is happy in this world
> and the next."

'Then the Bodhisattva took up that verse and had it written on a golden plate and circulated through the villages, cities, towns, countries and capital cities in the whole of Jambudvīpa.'

The Blessed One said, 'What do you think, monks? He who at that time and on that occasion was the king, that was me. Even then for the sake of hearing good speech I gave up my own life, how much more so now. In this way you should train, monks: "We will honour, praise, respect and worship the *dharma*, and having honoured, praised, respected and worshipped the *dharma* we will live in reliance on it." In this way, monks, you should train.'

This was said by the Blessed One, and the monks were delighted and praised the Blessed One's speech.

39. Anāthapiṇḍada

The Buddha, the Blessed One, was honoured, revered, respected and worshipped by kings, ministers, the wealthy, the townsfolk, merchants, caravan leaders, gods, *nāgas*, *yakṣas*, antigods, heavenly birds, *kinnaras* and great snakes. That Buddha, the Blessed One, who was venerated as such by gods, *nāgas*, *yakṣas*, antigods, heavenly birds, *kinnaras* and great snakes, who was famous and possessed of great merit, and who was provided with the requisites – robes, bowls, bedding, seats, and medicine to cure the sick – was staying with his community of disciples in Anāthapiṇḍada's park, the Jeta Grove in Śrāvastī.

Now the Blessed One in the morning got dressed, and taking his robe and bowl entered Śrāvastī for alms, and wandering in due course he went down the royal road. And there on the royal road a certain brahmin approached, and he saw the Buddha, the Blessed One, adorned with the thirty-two marks of a great man and the eighty secondary marks, his body shining, arrayed with light that extended a fathom, radiance in excess of a thousand suns, like a living mountain of jewels, handsome in his entirety. Having seen him he gazed at him for a long time and then drew a line in the earth and said to the Blessed One, 'O Gautama, you may not cross this line without giving me five hundred pieces of silver.' Then the Blessed One, in order to demonstrate the consequences of actions, and in order to abstain from taking what is not given, remained on that spot like a threshold stone.

Word spread throughout Śrāvastī that apparently the Blessed One had been detained by a brahmin on the royal road asking for five hundred pieces of silver. Then King Prasenajit the Kośalan heard this and, with his entourage of courtiers, went to where the Blessed One was. Having approached, he said this to the Blessed One, 'Go, Blessed One! I will make the payment.' The Blessed One said, 'No, great king, it is not for you to pay: it is for another to pay.' Then Viśākhā the mother of Mṛgāra, the officials Ṛṣidatta and Purāṇa, the gods Śakra and Brahmā and so on, and the four world-guardians beginning with Vaiśravaṇa, took gold and coins and approached the Blessed One. But the Blessed One said to them too, 'It should not be paid by these honourable ones.' Then the householder Anāthapiṇḍada heard about it, and filling baskets with gold and coins and taking an additional five hundred pieces of silver, he approached the Blessed One: 'Blessed One, accept this.' The Blessed One replied, 'Householder, you should pay this. Give it to the brahmin.' And so the householder Anāthapiṇḍada gave the basket of gold to the brahmin.

The monks became doubtful, as did the assembled company and the king, and they questioned the Blessed One, the Buddha, who cuts through all doubt: 'See, Blessed One, how this brahmin detained the Blessed One and Anāthapiṇḍada gave him coins. How did it come about that he could obstruct the Blessed One?' The Blessed One said, 'Do you wish to hear about it, monks?' 'Indeed, sir.' 'Then listen, monks, concentrate your minds properly and well, and I will explain. O monks, the Tathāgata performed and accumulated these actions in other previous births, and they have become inevitable.

Who else would experience their fruition? Monks, deeds done do not bear fruit outside, neither in the earth element, nor in the water element, nor in the fire element, nor in the wind element. Rather, deeds done, whether pure or impure, ripen when the aggregates, the physical elements and the sense bases have arisen.

> Actions never come to naught
> even through hundreds of millions of aeons.
> Having reached fullness and at the proper time,
> they bear fruit without fail for embodied beings.

'Formerly, monks, in times past, a king named Brahmadatta ruled his kingdom in the city of Vārāṇasī. It was prosperous and flourishing, peaceful and abundantly supplied, and crowded with many people. Strife, quarrels, riots and tumult had ceased, thieves and disease had departed, and it had plenty of rice, sugar cane, cows and buffaloes. He protected it as dearly as an only son.

'His eldest son was the crown prince, and on a certain occasion during spring, when the trees were blossoming and it was resounding with the cries of geese, cranes, peacocks, parrots, mynahs, cuckoos and pheasants, he sported and played in a wooded park, with a retinue of courtiers' sons. One of his friends, the son of a courtier, played a game of dice with another man. That courtier's son lost five hundred pieces of silver to the other man, and the king's son provided surety for the debt. [. . .][62]

'Thus during my transmigration I experienced endless misfortunes concerning my wealth, and even now my completely awakened buddhahood is obstructed by him. For thus, monks, entirely black deeds have entirely black fruits, entirely white deeds have entirely white fruits, and mixed deeds have mixed fruits. Therefore, monks, having cast aside black deeds and those that are mixed, one should direct oneself to performing deeds that are wholly white. And one should strive to avoid taking what is not given, such as was his fault. In this way, O monks, you should train.'

This was said by the Blessed One, and the monks were delighted and praised the Blessed One's speech.

40. Subhadra

The Buddha, the Blessed One, was honoured, revered, respected and worshipped by kings, ministers, the wealthy, the townsfolk, merchants, caravan leaders, gods, *nāgas*, *yakṣas*, antigods, heavenly birds, *kinnaras* and great snakes. That Buddha, the Blessed One, who was venerated as such by gods, *nāgas*, *yakṣas*, antigods, heavenly birds, *kinnaras* and great snakes, who was famous and possessed of great merit, and who was provided with the requisites — robes, bowls, bedding, seats, and medicine to cure the sick — was staying with his community of disciples in Kuśinagarī, in the country of the Mallas, in the grove of the twin *śāla* trees.

At the time of his complete *nirvāṇa* the Blessed One addressed Venerable Ānanda: 'Ānanda, prepare a raised couch for the Tathāgata, between the twin *śāla* trees, with its head facing north. Today, in the middle watch of the night, the Tathāgata will become completely extinguished, in the *nirvāṇa* element that is without remainder.'[63] 'Yes, sir,' replied the Venerable Ānanda to the Blessed One, and he prepared a raised couch between the two *śāla* trees with its head facing north, and then approached the Blessed One. Having approached he honoured the Blessed One's feet with his head and stood to one side. Standing to one side, Venerable Ānanda said this to the Blessed One: 'Sir, the raised couch, between the two *śāla* trees and with its head pointing north, is ready for the Tathāgata.' Then the Blessed One approached that couch, and having approached it he lay down on his right side, placing one foot on the other, conscious of the world,[64] mindful and fully aware, and turned his mind to consideration of *nirvāṇa*.

At that time the wandering mendicant[65] Subhadra was living in Kuśinagarī, and he was of advancing years, old and frail.[66] He, being one hundred and twenty years old, was honoured, praised, respected and worshipped by the Mallas who lived in Kuśinagarī, and he was believed to be an *arhat*. The mendicant Subhadra heard that in the middle watch of the night the ascetic Gautama was going to become completely extinguished in the *nirvāṇa* element that is without remainder. He thought, 'I have doubt regarding the *dharmas*, but I still have hope. This Blessed One Gautama has the power to dispel that doubt of mine.' So having heard this he left Kuśinagarī and went to that grove of the twin *śāla* trees.

At that time Venerable Ānanda was walking on the walkway in the open air outside the monastery, and the mendicant Subhadra saw Venerable Ānanda. Having seen him from afar, he approached Venerable Ānanda, and having approached he exchanged various suitably friendly and pleasant greetings with Venerable Ānanda, and then stood to one side. Standing to one side Subhadra the mendicant said to Venerable Ānanda, 'O Ānanda, I heard that today, in the middle watch of the night, the ascetic Gautama is going to become completely extinguished in the *nirvāṇa* element that is without remainder. I have doubt regarding the *dharmas*, but I still have hope. This Blessed One Gautama has the power to dispel that doubt of mine. Ānanda, if it is not troublesome to the Blessed One,[67] I would enter and question him on a certain matter, if you would allow me in for an answer to my question.' Ānanda replied, 'Enough, Subhadra. Do not trouble the Blessed One. The Blessed One is tired of body; the well-farer is exhausted of body.'

A second and a third time the mendicant Subhadra said this to Venerable Ānanda: 'O Ānanda, I heard that today, in the middle watch of the night, the ascetic Gautama is going to become completely extinguished in the *nirvāṇa* element that is without remainder. I have doubt regarding the *dharmas*, but I still have hope. This Blessed One Gautama has the power to dispel that doubt of mine. Ānanda, if it is not troublesome to the Blessed One, I would enter and question him on a certain matter, if you would allow me in for an answer to my question.' But a second and a third time Venerable Ānanda said this to the mendicant Subhadra: 'Enough, Subhadra. Do not trouble the Tathāgata. The Blessed One is tired of body; the well-farer is exhausted of body.'

Then Subhadra the mendicant said to Venerable Ānanda: 'O Ānanda, I have heard in the presence of mendicants of old

— venerable elders,[68] eminent wandering teachers — that *tathāgatas*, *arhats*, perfectly awakened ones, arise in the world as rarely as the *udumbara* flower. And today in the middle watch of the night, the Blessed One Gautama is going to become completely extinguished in the *nirvāṇa* element that is without remainder. I have doubt regarding the *dharmas*, but I still have hope. This Blessed One Gautama has the power to dispel that doubt of mine. Ānanda, if it is not troublesome to the Blessed One, I would enter and question him on a certain matter, if you would allow me in for an answer to my question.' But again Venerable Ānanda said to Subhadra the mendicant: 'Enough, Subhadra. Do not trouble the Tathāgata. The Blessed One is tired of body; the well-farer is exhausted of body.'

Then the Blessed One heard, with his purified divine ear that surpassed human power, Venerable Ānanda's problematic conversation with the mendicant Subhadra. Having heard it, he said to Venerable Ānanda, 'Enough, Ānanda. Do not restrain the mendicant Subhadra. Let him enter and question me as he wishes to. This will be the final conversation I have with mendicants from another sect, and this — namely the mendicant Subhadra — will be the last of the followers I call forth in person by saying "Come, monk!"'

Then the mendicant Subhadra, having been granted permission by the Blessed One, was pleased, happy and delighted, and having become intensely joyful and contented he approached the Blessed One. After approaching, he exchanged various suitably friendly and pleasant greetings with the Blessed One, and then sat to one side. Seated to one side, Subhadra the mendicant said this to the Blessed One: 'O Gautama, there are these various sectarian teachers[69] in the world, namely Pūraṇa Kāśyapa, Māskarī Gośālīputra, Sañjayī Vairūṭīputra, Ajita Keśakambala, Kakuda Kātyāyana and Nirgrantha Jñātaputra.[70] Explain to me each of their teachings.'[71] So at that time the Blessed One spoke these verses:

> 'Subhadra, I was twenty-nine years old,
> when I went forth in search of the good.
> More than fifty years have passed,
> since I went forth, Subhadra.

> Good conduct, meditative practice and wisdom,
> and one-pointedness of mind were cultivated by me,
> and I spoke the way of the noble *dharma*;
> There is no other "ascetic" outside this.'[72]

'Subhadra, in whatever *dharma* and discipline the eightfold path of the noble ones is *not* found, there is found no first ascetic, and nor is a second, third or fourth ascetic found there.[73] But, Subhadra, in a *dharma* and discipline in which the eightfold path of the noble ones *is* found, the first ascetic is found there, and second, third and fourth ascetics are found there. Subhadra, the eightfold path of the noble ones *is* found in this *dharma* and discipline, and here the first ascetic is found, and here the second, here the third, and here the fourth. There are no ascetics or brahmins outside this, and false teachings by ascetics or brahmins are empty. Thus I roar forth with my accomplished lion's roar in this assembly!'

Now, while he was speaking about this way of the *dharma*, the *dharma*-eye that is pure and free from dust arose for the mendicant Subhadra with regard to the *dharmas*. Then the mendicant Subhadra, having seen *dharmas*, obtained *dharmas*, penetrated *dharmas*, crossed over his desires and passed beyond doubt, no longer dependent on others or led by others, fully confident in regard to the *dharmas* taught by the teacher.[74] He got up from his seat, placed his upper robe over his shoulder, and, raising his hands in respect towards Venerable Ānanda, he said to Venerable Ānanda, 'Sir, Ānanda has obtained a great benefit, in that Ānanda has been consecrated as the pupil of a great teacher, by the great teacher, the Blessed One. But we too would obtain that great benefit, we would take the going forth into the well-proclaimed *dharma* and discipline and become ordained as a monk.'

So Venerable Ānanda said to the Blessed One, 'Sir, this mendicant Subhadra wishes to go forth into the well-proclaimed *dharma* and discipline and become ordained as a monk.' The Blessed One addressed the mendicant Subhadra: 'Come, monk. Live the religious life.' And he went forth under that venerable one,[75] and ordained, becoming a monk.

Having gone forth like this, the venerable one roamed about withdrawn and solitary, mindful, zealous and exerting himself. In order to live alone, withdrawn, mindful, zealous and exerting oneself, noble sons remove their hair and beards, clothe themselves in ochre robes and with complete faith go forth from their homes into homelessness. He saw the perfect ideal of unsurpassed religious life, realized and obtained knowledge of the *dharma* himself, and declared: 'Birth is destroyed for me! I have lived the holy life and done what needed to be done. I know I have no further rebirth.' He became possessed of perfect knowledge, venerable, an *arhat*, completely liberated. Then this occurred to the venerable Subhadra who had obtained arhatship and recognized the happiness of liberation: 'It is not proper that I should see the Teacher enter complete *nirvāṇa*. So I will enter complete *nirvāṇa* first.' And so Venerable Subhadra achieved complete *nirvāṇa* first of all, and after him the Blessed One.

When Subhadra was established in arhatship by the Blessed One, who had come to his last resting place, during the time when painful feelings were impeding his *dharmas*, when his *dharmas* were being cut through[76] and his bonds loosening,[77] and when many Mallas of Kuśinagarī were directed to the *dharma*, at that time the monks became doubtful and questioned the Blessed One, the Buddha, who cuts through all doubt: 'It is a marvel, sir, that the Blessed One freed this mendicant Subhadra from the net of the cycle of rebirths and established him in the endless state of *nirvāṇa*, even when his *dharmas* were being cut through and his bonds loosening.' The Blessed One said, 'What is the marvel in this now, monks, when I have made an end of greed, hatred and delusion, and am completely freed from birth, ageing, sickness, death, grief, lamentation, suffering, melancholy and mental anguish, that I have freed the mendicant Subhadra from the net of the cycle of rebirths and established him in the endless state of *nirvāṇa*? In times past, when I experienced greed, hatred and delusion, and was not freed from birth, ageing, sickness, death, grief, lamentation, suffering, melancholy and mental anguish, and was deprived of reason and comprehension having arisen in an animal birth, I saved Subhadra and the Mallas of Kuśinagarī by giving up my own life. Listen, concentrate your minds properly and well, and I will explain:

'Formerly, monks, in times past, in a certain mountain cave lived the head of a herd of deer, surrounded by many thousands of deer. He was wise, learned and astute. Having noticed that herd of deer a hunter made it known to the king, and then went out with the king and his fourfold army and surrounded the whole herd of deer. Then it occurred to the leader of the herd, "If I do not protect them now, this very day they will all come to nothing."

'So that leader of the herd began to examine all sides: "In which direction may this family of deer find refuge?" And he saw in that mountain cave a river going along, and that river had a swift current that could carry away a mountain.[78] And those deer were weak, so the leader of the herd at once entered that river and stood in the middle, and shouted out: "Come, sirs! Jump up from this bank, place your feet on my back and stand firm on the other shore. By this means I foresee you have life; otherwise it is death!" Those deer did so, and because of their hooves falling on his back, his skin was cut, so that he appeared like a heap of flesh, blood and bones. But he did not give up his resolve, remaining compassionate towards those deer.

'When they had all crossed over from his back he began to look: "Let there be nobody else who has not crossed over." He saw a young deer who had not crossed, and so that leader of the deer, though his body was being cut up and he was being freed from bonds,[79] not caring about his own dear life, he crossed to the bank, mounted the young deer on his back, crossed the river and placed him on the shore. Seeing that the herd of deer had crossed, at the moment of his death he made a fervent aspiration: "Just as I have made a gift of my own dear life for these deer and this young deer, and saved them from disaster, in the same way may I in a future time, when I have attained unsurpassed perfect and full awakening, liberate them from the net of the cycle of rebirths."'

The Blessed One said, 'What do you think, monks? He who at that time and on that occasion was the leader of the deer, that was me.

The Mallas of Kuśinagarī were these deer, and this Subhadra was the young deer.'

The monks became doubtful and asked the Blessed One, the Buddha, who cuts through all doubt: 'What actions had Subhadra done in order to be the last personal disciple?' The Blessed One said, 'In other former births, monks, Subhadra performed and accumulated actions.[80] These do not bear fruit outside, neither in the earth element, nor in the water element, nor in the fire element, nor in the wind element. Rather, deeds done, whether pure or impure, ripen when the aggregates, the physical elements and the sense bases have arisen.

> Actions never come to naught
> even through hundreds of millions of aeons.
> Having reached fullness and at the proper time,
> they bear fruit without fail for embodied beings.

'Formerly, monks, in a past time in this Fortunate Aeon, when a human lifespan was twenty thousand years, a fully and perfectly awakened one called Kāśyapa arose in the world. He was perfected in knowledge and conduct, a well-farer, an unsurpassed knower of the world, a tamer of people who should be tamed, a teacher of gods and humans, a *buddha*, a blessed one. He lived near to the city of Vārāṇasī, in the deer-park at Ṛṣipatana. That Blessed One, the perfect and fully awakened Kāśyapa, had a nephew named Aśoka, and, seeking liberation, he went forth in the presence of the Blessed One. Thinking that liberation was in his power, he did not make much effort.

'A long time later, Aśoka spent the rainy season in the country. The Blessed One, the fully awakened Buddha Kāśyapa, having done all the work of a *buddha*, like a fire that had run out of fuel, reached his final resting place, and Aśoka the monk was in secluded meditation[81] under an *aśoka* [tree]. The deity who lived in that *aśoka* tree heard about the complete *nirvāṇa* of the Blessed One, the fully awakened Buddha Kāśyapa, and began to cry. And as she cried, teardrops began to fall onto Aśoka's body. Aśoka turned his face upwards and said to the crying deity, "Why are you crying, deity?" The deity said, "Today, in the middle watch of the night, will be the complete *nirvāṇa* of the Blessed One, the full and perfect Buddha Kāśyapa."

'Having heard the deity's words, Aśoka trembled as if he had been mortally wounded, and began to weep pitifully. Then the deity asked, "Why are you crying?" Aśoka replied, "Because I am separated from my teacher and separated from my kinsman! Kāśyapa the perfectly awakened one is my uncle, and I have been living complacently, without striving. It is far away, and I am just an ordinary man. Because of the lost time, I am not able to attain distinction."

'The deity said, "But if I were to take sir to the Blessed One's presence, would that be possible?" Aśoka replied, "Yes, for my awakening would be matured at the moment of seeing the Blessed One, and I would be able to attain distinction." So the deity, using supernormal power, took Aśoka to the presence of the Blessed One, and at the sight of the Blessed One he became faithful. Then the Blessed One Kāśyapa explained the *dharma* in such a way that on hearing it he realized arhatship. And that venerable Aśoka attained to complete *nirvāṇa* first, and then the Blessed One, the perfectly awakened Kāśyapa.

'Then that deity, seeing that Venerable Aśoka had attained complete *nirvāṇa*, became joyful and thought, "This venerable person has attained distinction, having come here entirely because of me. In the same way may I, in a future time, be among the renouncers of this young man named Uttara, to whom the Blessed One Kāśyapa has explained, 'Young man, you will be a perfectly awakened one, an *arhat*, a *tathāgata* named Śākyamuni, when the lifespan of men is a hundred years!' Among his renouncers, when he has reached his final resting place, may I become the last of his personal disciples, called forth with the words 'Come, monk!' And may I achieve complete *nirvāṇa* before the Blessed One, and then the Blessed One Śākyamuni."'

The Blessed One said, 'What do you think, monks? She who at that time on that occasion was the deity, that was Subhadra. Therefore, monks, you should train in this way: "We will dwell as good friends, good companions, good associates, not evil friends, evil companions, evil associates." In this way, monks, you should train.'

Then Venerable Ānanda said to the Blessed One, 'Sir, when I am here alone and solitary in retreat, this thought arises in my mind, that this is half of the religious life, namely good friendship, good companionship and good associations, and avoiding evil friendship, evil companionship and evil associations.' 'You should not say this, Ānanda, that this is half of the religious life, namely good friendship, good companionship and good associations, and avoiding evil friendship, evil companionship and evil associations. Ānanda, this is the entire, complete, whole, pure, accomplished religious life, namely good friendship, good companionship and good associations, and avoiding evil friendship, evil companionship and evil associations. What is the reason for this? Because, Ānanda, beings who are subject to the experience of rebirth come to me as their spiritual friend and are liberated from the experience of rebirth, and those beings who experience ageing, sickness, grief, death, lamentation, suffering, melancholy and mental anguish are freed from mental anguish. In this manner, Ānanda, it should be understood, that this is the entire, complete, whole, pure, accomplished religious life, namely good friendship, good companionship and good associations, and avoiding evil companionship, evil friendship and evil associations. In this way, Ānanda, you should train.'

This was said by the Blessed One, and the monks were delighted and praised the Blessed One's speech.

Part B Notes

1 The word here translated as ‘full’ is *pūrṇa*, so the miracle is closely related to the name of the protagonist.

2 The inclusion of the predictee’s response to his prediction is unusual in this collection, and interrupts the Buddha’s teaching, which normally continues straight on to the reflections his monks should keep in mind.

3 *karmāntevāsinā*, more literally ‘through dwelling near karma’ or ‘through being a pupil of karma’.

4 This is a very rare occurrence of a woman being predicted to attain buddhahood, though notably she still becomes a male *buddha*. On the exclusion of women from the path to buddhahood in Pāli/Theravāda Buddhism, and its possible link to the *jātaka* genre, see Appleton 2011.

5 It is not clear whether this means the lower floors of the palace or simply the ground beneath the seats and beds. I have tried to maintain the ambiguity, though I am generally swayed by Rotman’s note on a parallel passage in the *Divyāvadāna* (Rotman 2008: 392–3 n94) that since she is being compared with a divinity it would make sense for her feet not to touch the ground, this being one of the features of the gods.

6 See Part A note 16 on page 57 for references to translations of the Chinese and Tibetan, and a brief summary of the story.

7 The ‘teaching on the young’, which is found in the Pāli as *Saṃyutta Nikāya* 3.1. The king casts doubt on the Buddha’s attainment of buddhahood on account of the fact that he seems to be quite young, but the Buddha offers a teaching that persuades him.

8 Speyer (1902: 41) records a gap here, though only because he thinks it unlikely that no description of the war would be given. No meaning appears to be lost.

9 This covers all the realms within *saṃsāra*, those of material form (where beings have bodies) and the more refined higher heavens, where one exists is as pure consciousness or even as neither conscious nor unconscious.

10 Usually when *dharma*s are described as *saṃskṛta* and its opposite, the technical meaning of conditioned and unconditioned phenomena would be meant. However, here, as in AvŚ 40 below, the plural *dharma*s seems still to refer to the meaning ‘teachings’ or ‘truths’.

11 Unlike the other occurrences of this formula, here a ‘properly given gift’ is not mentioned, presumably because the aspirant has not given any gift accompanying his aspiration.

12 According to Speyer’s index, the term *nausaṃkrama*, which only appears in this story of the *Avadānaśataka*, means ‘bridge made up of ships joined together’ (1902: 229). This meaning is supported by the occurrence of both *naukrama* and *nausaṃkrama* in *Divyāvadāna* 3, where they refer to a crossing that parallels a bridge made up of *nāga* hoods. Edgerton (1953:

vol. 2, 313) argues that the term must instead apply to a boat-course or waterway.

13 A deed done (*kṛta*) is not necessarily a deed accumulated (*upacita*), since not all deeds have karmic fruits. See Dhammajoti 2009: 413–16 for a discussion of the Sarvāstivāda position on this.

14 The change of emphasis from 'post' (*stambha*, of the title) to 'palace' (*prāsāda*) is curious here, and suggests the story may be linked to others in which there is similar confusion between a sacrificial post (*yūpa*) and a palace: see the interesting discussion in Granoff 2010.

15 Following Speyer's MS reading *vibhūṣitān* rather than his emendation *vibhūṣikāṃ* or Vaidya's suggested alternative *vibhūtikāṃ*, which he attributes, apparently without basis, to Speyer. See Edgerton's discussion (1953: vol. 2, 495).

16 In Speyer's sources there is some variation between 'hundreds of millions' and simply 'hundreds'. I have followed Speyer's emendation of all occurrences to the former, which undoubtedly communicates the desired message.

17 *sapta svarānādarśayati ekaviṃśati mūrcchanāḥ*. There are seven notes (*svara*) in the scale, which are combined in various patterns to form the basis of melodies, and these combinations are known as *mūrcchanas*.

18 Following Speyer's conjecture (1902: 96n2) and his emendation of *śūnyākāraṇaca* to *śūnyākāreṇaiva*. Feer (1979: 77) is clearly puzzled since he reads 'et cela à plusieurs reprises (?)'.

19 In what is presumably a pun on Buddha Prabodhana's name, the verb is *prabodhayati*.

20 Strictly speaking, one hundred *padas*, which are usually quarter-verses.

21 There is a gap in the MS here, as recorded in Speyer 1902: 113. Feer (1979: 87) fills the gaps from the Tibetan, and his French rendering of this may be translated as follows: 'Several thousand elephants resembling Airāvaṇa and Supratiṣṭhita were brought and led in; they supported a canopy worth a hundred, which was raised above the Buddha and the community of monks; several thousand daughters of gods were also brought and led in, and they fanned [the Buddha and the community of monks] with a fan with a jewelled handle.'

22 *bhagavato ratnamayapratimāṃ kārayitvā buddhaharṣaṃ kāritavān*. I follow Speyer's suggestion, in his index of rare forms (1902: 232), that *buddhaharṣa* is the name of a festival. The term does not appear in either BHSD or PED. Feer (1979) translates: 'il fit faire une image de Bhagavat en pierres précieuses, ce qui mit le Buddha dans le ravissement'.

23 Perhaps the torments of hell are referred to here.

24 On how *sāra* as essence is related to the idea of merit-making, see Strong 1983b: 148–60.

25 Presumably this refers to the constant flapping of the ears. My thanks to John Strong for pointing this out to me.

26 Perhaps translating *kālavaiṣamya* as 'quirk of fate' is too liberal. It could also refer to a disturbance in the seasons. The broader meaning is clear, however: the disease is not the king's fault, nor the fault of his citizens, but has arisen because of forces outside the laws of karma.

27 *teṣāṃ sattvānāṃ nidānamāśayānuśayaṃ copalakṣya*. See Edgerton 1953: 296 (under *nidāna*), where he translates this phrase as 'noting the motives, the disposition and inclination of these creatures (who were afflicted with a pestilence; i.e. finding them worthy)'. Feer's rendering — that he observed the cause, seat and effects [of the illness] (1979: 114) — seems a bit forced, since, as Edgerton points out, the term *āśaya-anuśaya* cannot really be applied to the disease. While *āśaya* and *anuśaya* often indicate *bad* dispositions (see Edgerton), elsewhere in the *Avadānaśataka* the compound is used of people ready for a teaching that will lead them to arhatship.

28 *svajīvitamiṣṭaṃ parityajāmi* could also mean 'I abandon my own cherished life' or 'I abandon my life as a sacrifice'.

29 Following Speyer's recommendation (1902: 172n6) that this be read as *rogatā* (= *roga*) + *atīta*.

30 I have tried to preserve the ambiguity in the term *dānasaṃvibhāga*, which could mean simply distribution of gifts, or partaking in gifts, or encouraging others to give gifts.

31 *mātsarya* — see Andy Rotman's discussion and translation of chapter 5 (Rotman 2020).

32 The *antara-kalpa* here presumably refers to the period of destruction between two aeons (*kalpas*). See Edgerton 1953: vol. 2, 38.

33 Or *pretāśrayasadṛśāḥ* could indicate they looked like dead bodies. For the common Buddhist use of *āśraya* as meaning 'body', see Edgerton 1953: vol. 2, 110.

34 There may be a deliberate pun and/or ambiguity here, for *iṣṭa* can mean 'cherished' or 'sacrificed'.

35 This is an interesting and rare case of gender variation between births. Several *jātaka* stories portray Devadatta's attempts to kill the Buddha-to-be, though he rarely succeeds. A story of filicide in the *Jātakatthavaṇṇanā* (542. *Candakumāra-jātaka* or *Khaṇḍahāla-jātaka*) has some resonances with the present tale. In it we find a king persuaded to sacrifice his son in order to gain heaven. The brahmin advisor who schemes to have the prince killed is Devadatta, and the prince himself is the Bodhisattva. The *Culladhammapāla-jātaka* (*Jātakatthavaṇṇanā* 358) also resonates, though here it is an angry king (= Devadatta) who orders his baby son (= the Bodhisattva) to be mutilated and killed, despite the desperate entreaties of his queen. The *Mahādhammapāla-jātaka* (*Jātakatthavaṇṇanā* 447), with its parallel in the *Mahāvastu*, appears unrelated.

36 It is not entirely clear what these *pañcāṅga* are. The term probably refers to the five varieties of music (see Edgerton 1953: vol. 2, *pañcāṅgika*).

37 It is this episode – the gift of eyes to a brahmin – that forms the focus of the Śibi story in the *Jātakatthavaṇṇanā* (499. *Sivi-jātaka*) and Āryaśūra's *Jātakamālā* (2. *Śibi*). Another episode involving the generous King Śibi, in which he sacrifices his flesh to ransom a dove, is also known in Buddhist narrative, as well as in Jain narrative and the *Mahābhārata*.

38 The *dharma* is described as *madhuramadhuraṃ* and *kṣaudraṃ madhvivānedakam*, where *kṣaudra* and *aneḍaka* may be types of honey or simply synonyms for honey, and *madhu* can mean 'sweet' (like *madhura*) or 'honey'. Reproducing such repetition in the translation is problematic.

39 The *indriyāni* may be the six sense faculties (including the mind) or perhaps the five moral faculties (*śraddhā*, *vīrya*, *smṛti*, *samādhi*, *prajñā*). See Edgerton 1953: vol. 2, 114.

40 See Speyer's discussion around the plural use of *dharma* here (1902: 188n9). In order to preserve the plural reading, which seems preferable since we have the plural again later, but also in order to preserve the understanding that it is teachings or revelations of the truth that are being referred to (and not 'phenomena', as is usual for *dharmas* in the plural), I have chosen to translate as '*dharma* teachings'.

41 As in an occurrence noted above, *dharma* is again plural here, which is difficult to render, but clearly intentional.

42 Following Speyer's emendation of *abhilaṣanti* ('are desirous of') to *abhilasanti*. He suggests for the meaning: 'it is only when one feels one's self at ease that the *dharmas* will make their appearance' (1902: 189n8). Feer (1979: 129) translates 'les lois exigent le bien-être', which seems to make best sense of the circumstances; see also his discussion (1979: 129n1).

43 The phrase *kadācit karhicit* seems to indicate not simply 'sometimes' but 'rarely' or 'after a long wait'. For this meaning, see Pāli *kadāci karahaci*.

44 Alternatively, 'let the deity's [*yakṣa*'s] wish be fulfilled', as Feer chooses to translate. However, Śakra has not been referred to as a *deva* since his disguise.

45 Here Speyer (1902: 190) and – following him – Vaidya, inserts * * * indicating a lacuna, though the meaning remains clear.

46 Again, there appears to be a pun here on the word *iṣṭa*, which can mean both 'dear' and 'sacrificed'. Hence, another possible translation is 'reunited with the people you sacrificed'.

47 The word *āhavanīya* in a Vedic and Brahmanical context more specifically refers to the consecrated ritual fire that is worthy of being offered sacrificial oblations. In a Buddhist context, the term has the more general meaning 'worthy of offerings' or 'worthy of honour'.

48 Following Speyer's emendation; see his explanatory note (1902: 195n3).

49 This rather peculiar justification for his name presumably harks back to the advice of Mitra's friend, who suggested raising a son as a daughter in order to ensure the child's longevity.

50 This is my tentative rendering of *okkarika*. It is not clear what sort of tradesman this is, but the Tibetan could be rendered something like

'country merchant'. It is also found spelled *aukarika*. See entries for both in Edgerton 1953: vol. 2. As he argues, an *okkarika* is clearly a member of an urban traders' guild, so perhaps it is a trader in things relating to the countryside, such as farming equipment.

51 Alternatively, *tadanujānāhi* could also, at a stretch, mean 'admit it', hence Feer (1979: 133) translates 'avouele'.

52 See Edgerton 1953: vol. 2, entry for *pauruṣeya* for its meaning of 'servant' or, in this and parallel mentions, a type of crewman. As Edgerton notes, only four types are actually named — *āhāra*, *nāvika*, *kaivarta* and *karṇadhāra* — the roles of which are not clear; my translation is tentative in this regard.

53 In contrast to this version, in the versions of the story in the *Jātakatthavaṇṇanā* (numbers 82, 104, 369 and 439) Maitrakanyaka (or, in Pāli, Mittavindaka) is not the Bodhisattva. Rather, he is a bad man who meets his comeuppance in a hell realm, and is visited there by a god (= Bodhisattva).

54 While a story of a hare sacrificing his life is also known in the *Jātakatthavaṇṇanā* (316. *Sasa-jātaka*) and Āryaśūra's *Jātakamālā* (6. *Śaśa*), in these versions the story is rather different: the Bodhisattva hare offers himself as a meal to a brahmin (Śakra in disguise) as an act of hospitality, and is rewarded by having his form marked on the moon. The AvŚ version has a parallel in Haribhaṭṭa's *Jātakamālā*.

55 The term here is *brahmacariya*, often translated as 'Brahma-faring'. This usually has overtones of celibacy.

56 For a parallel to this exchange between the Buddha and Ānanda, see *Saṃyutta Nikāya* 3.18 and 45.2 (Bodhi 2000: 180–1, 1524–5). It is also repeated in story 40 below.

57 Following Speyer's conjectural reading: *devatānāṃ manaso bhavati prāsādikam* (1902: 214n1). It is possible that the *prāsādika* is being used in the sense of 'engendering faith' but, since it is ordinary people we are talking about here, that seems unlikely.

58 Following Speyer's reconstruction (1902: 217n2).

59 The *dohada*, or pregnancy craving, is a common motif in Indian narrative. The experiences of the mother during pregnancy are intimately related to the character and karmic inheritance of the child she is carrying.

60 The implication would appear to be that *subhāṣita* is here equivalent to *dharma*, hence the title of this story: *Dharmagaveṣī*.

61 On the problematic nature of this sentence, see Speyer 1902: 221n4.

62 A part of the story is missing here, in Speyer's Sanskrit manuscripts and in the Tibetan. See Speyer 1902: 225–6. The missing text must specify, one assumes, that the Buddha was this prince who gave surety for the debt but never paid it, that Anāthapiṇḍada was the friend who lost the game, and that the brahmin was the other man. Indeed, this series of identifications is given in one of Speyer's manuscripts (1902: 226n1) as

well as in Feer's text (1979: 150), although in both cases somewhat later than one might expect.

63 The phrase *nirupadhiśeṣe nirvāṇadhātau parinirvāṇaṃ bhaviṣyati* is tricky to render. In English translations we often talk of someone 'entering *nirvāṇa*', though it might be closer syntactically to speak of someone 'nirvāṇizing', or, here, 'becoming completely nirvāṇized'.

64 As Speyer notes (1902: 228n1), it is difficult to surmise what *ālokasaṃjño* might mean. Vaidya's reading *alokasaṃjño* is no better. I have followed Speyer's suggested emendation to *lokasaṃjñī*.

65 He is a *parivrājaka*, which could also be rendered 'ascetic', though I have not done so here to avoid confusion with *śramaṇa*, which I have translated as 'ascetic' throughout.

66 The story of Subhadra's initiation as the last of the Buddha's personal disciples is familiar from other stories of the Buddha's last days. Compare the *Mahāparinibbāna Sutta* (*Dīgha Nikāya* 16) (Walshe 1995: 267–9). No past-life stories are told in that account. A closer parallel to this AvŚ story, including its embedded past-life stories, is found in Haribhaṭṭa's *Jātakamālā*.

67 Following Speyer's conjecture (1902: 229n2) that *bhavata* should be *bhagavata*, and thus refer to the Buddha rather than to Ānanda. This applies also to the repetition that follows.

68 Vaidya has *buddhānāṃ* in place of Speyer's *vṛddhānāṃ* but this is apparently without basis, and Speyer's reading seems preferable.

69 This is a rather loose translation of *tīrthyāyatanāni*, but the meaning is clear. This is the only occasion on which I have translated as 'sectarian' rather than 'heretic', as Subhadra would presumably not have referred to them in such a disparaging way.

70 These six teachers, associated with non-Buddhist groups, are famous from other sources including the *Sāmaññaphala Sutta* of the *Dīgha Nikāya* (Walshe 1995: 91–109).

71 Speyer suggests (1902: 231n8) that some of the prose is missing here, such that we do not have the full exchange.

72 For the metrical and other problems with these verses, see Speyer 1902: 231–2. Compare the parallel verses in the *Mahāparinibbāna Sutta* (*Dīgha Nikāya* 16).

73 Presumably this is a reference to the stream-enterer, once-returner, non-returner and *arhat*.

74 Here the wordplay on *dharma* as singular 'truth/teaching' and plural 'teachings' or 'constituents of reality' is key to the exchange and I retain the original terms in order to communicate this.

75 The use of *āyuṣman* ('venerable', 'long-lived') here and in the next sentence is odd, since it is usually used in reference to Ānanda. Presumably the text is implying that, after being called forth by the Buddha himself, Subhadra took formal initiation from Ānanda. Quite

why Subhadra is then referred to as *āyuṣman* himself is even harder to explain, though he is of course long-lived.

76 *dharmoparodhikāyāṃ vedanāyāṃ vartamānāyām, chidyamāneṣu dharmeṣu.* In this passage, *dharma* is being used in the sense of elements, bodily and mental. So the Buddha's body is afflicted by pain, not his teaching, and the factors that make up the Buddha are being cut off as he enters *parinirvāṇa.*

77 *mucyamānāsu saṃdhiṣu.* This could refer to his bodily joints, or the bonds tying him to existence.

78 For this translation of *ahāryahāriṇīṃ*, see Edgerton 1953: vol. 2, 85–6.

79 Instead of the *chidyamāneṣu dharmeṣu mucyamānāsu saṃdhiṣu* as found earlier in relation to the Buddha, here we have *marmaṣu* ('mortal parts, vulnerable bits of the body') in place of *dharmeṣu.*

80 This formulaic passage seems to have become distorted and abbreviated, leaving *bāhye* impossible to translate in situ. See Speyer 1902: 237n1.

81 The phrase *pratisaṃlīno babhūva* suggests that he was 'retired' or 'withdrawn', but this is usually understood to be for the purpose of meditation. See Edgerton 1953: vol. 2, *pratisaṃlīna.*

Glossary

This glossary is in English alphabetical order and includes all the major concepts, terms and names contained in the translation. It is indebted to both Andy Rotman's *Divine Stories* Glossary and to Franklin Edgerton's *Buddhist Hybrid Sanskrit Dictionary*. For more discussion of the various types of spirit-deities, see DeCaroli 2004.

aggregates (*skandha*). Five aspects that make up a person: namely, form/body (*rūpa*), feeling (*vedanā*), apperception (*saññā*), conditioning (*saṃskāra*) and consciousness (*vijñāna*).

Airāvaṇa. The celestial elephant mount of Indra/Śakra.

Ajātaśatru. Son of Bimbisāra, and one-time follower of Devadatta. Devadatta is said to have encouraged Ajātaśatru to murder his father in order to seize the throne.

Ajiravatī. A great river that flowed from the Himalayas through Kośala, and Śrāvastī was situated on its banks. It is identified with the present-day Rapti river.

Ānanda. One of the most important disciples of the Buddha, and the Buddha's personal attendant for much of his life. Ānanda is said not to have achieved arhatship until after the Buddha's death. He is known for his devotion to the Buddha and his extraordinary memory for every one of the Buddha's teachings. In the *Avadānaśataka* he is one of the Buddha's most frequent interlocutors.

Anāthapiṇḍada. A wealthy lay supporter of the Buddha, and donor of the Jeta Grove.

Aṅgulimālā. A serial killer who was converted by the Buddha and became a prominent monk and *arhat*.

antigod (*asura*). A class of deity that is depicted in early Indian lore as continually at war with the gods (*devas* or *suras*).

arhat. A 'worthy one', or someone who has achieved awakening. While all awakened beings can be referred to as *arhats*, the term is most often used of awakened disciples (those who have achieved *śrāvakabodhi*).

ascetic (*śramaṇa*). A 'striver' who seeks a religious attainment through a renunciant life. The Buddha and his disciples are often referred to as *śramaṇas* but the term can also apply to non-Buddhist ascetics.

atmospheric deities (*āntarīkṣa*). A type of god or spirit-deity that occupies the space between the earth and the heavens.

bhūta. A type of spirit sometimes translated as 'ghost' as they tend to share the unfortunate characteristics of the hungry ghosts (*pretas*).

Bimbisāra. King of Magadha and patron of the early Buddhist community. His capital city is Rājagṛha.

blessed one (*bhagavān*). An epithet of a *buddha*. It can also be translated as 'lord' or 'exalted one', but 'blessed one' is used consistently in this volume, usually capitalized to indicate reference to Śākyamuni Buddha.

bodhisattva. A being on the way to becoming a *buddha*, usually used to refer to Śākyamuni in his past lives.

Brahmā. An important Indian deity associated with creation and creativity.

Brahmadatta. Commonly named as a past king of the city of Vārāṇasī, he features in dozens of *jātaka* and *avadāna* stories with little narrative detail. For a discussion of how such stock characters might have ended up featuring so often in the literature, see Schopen 2004.

brahmin (*brāhmaṇa*). A priest or religious specialist in early — or 'Brahmanical' — Hindu traditions, and top of the social hierarchy according to the fourfold caste system.

buddha. An 'awakened one': in other words, someone who has achieved liberation from the cycle of rebirth. All awakened beings are *buddhas* yet the term is more usually used as a shorthand for (*anuttarā-*) *samyak sambuddhas*, or '(unsurpassed) full and perfect *buddhas*'. Unlike other types of awakened beings, full *buddhas* realize the truth themselves, found a community of followers and teach the *dharma* to them. 'The Buddha' refers to Śākyamuni, the Buddha of our age.

cakravāka. A type of ruddy duck or goose renowned for the strong attachment between pairs, hence often used in Sanskrit poetry as a symbol of conjugal or enduring love.

calm and insight (*śamatha and vipaśyanā*). The two major types of meditation.

celestial nymph (*apsaras*). A female spirit-deity associated with Śakra's heavens, where they dance to the music of *gandharvas*. They are said to be very beautiful and enticing, and are sometimes sent to seduce humans.

cycle of rebirth (*saṃsāra*). The continual cycle of death and rebirth that affects all but awakened beings. The cycle can include rebirth as a human, animal, hungry ghost, god or hell-being.

defilements (*kleśa*). The bonds that keep everyone in the cycle of rebirth. These are enumerated in a variety of ways, but include such things as passion, ignorance, wrong views and hatred.

Devadatta. The Buddha's cousin and a monk in his community. Devadatta is said to have wanted to take over the leadership of the *saṅgha*, made several attempts on the Buddha's life, and eventually split away with a small number of followers.

Dhanada. Another name for Vaiśravaṇa or Kubera, king of *yakṣas*.

Dhanapālaka. An elephant that was set loose while in rut by Devadatta in one of his attempts to murder the Buddha. The Buddha calmed the elephant through loving-kindness.

dharma. The truth realized by the Buddha, and his teachings, which communicate that truth. In the plural the term refers instead to 'phenomena' or constituents of our experience and has been translated as such, except during stories 9 and 40, in which wordplay on *dharma* and *dharmas* is key to the exchange.

Dhṛtarāṣṭra. King of *gandharvas*.

disciple (*śrāvaka*). A follower of the Buddha: literally, a 'hearer' of the teachings, and one who becomes an *arhat*.

discipline (*vinaya*). Narrowly interpreted as the monastic rules and regulations, but more broadly as training in Buddhist behaviour.

eightfold observance (*aṣṭāṅgasamanvāgata vrata*). Taking on the eight precepts, usually undertaken on an *uposatha* holy day, which is also the 'eighth day'.

eightfold path (*aṣṭāṅgamārga*). The path that leads to awakening: namely, right view, right intention, right speech, right action, right livelihood, right effort, right mindfulness and right concentration.

eighty secondary marks. A list of physical characteristics of a 'great man' in addition to the thirty-two primary marks.

faith (*prasāda*). This term could also be translated a tranquility or purity, and refers to a positivity and clarity of mind usually brought about by an encounter with a *buddha*. A person who engenders faith is known as a *prāsādika* or 'agent of faith'.

fervent aspiration (*praṇidhāna, praṇidhi*). A firm resolution or vow to achieve a particular future state. Often they are aspirations to achieve a form of awakening, but they can also be used for rebirth states and even specific requirements, such as not being reborn from a womb.

five [bad] qualities (*pañcāṅga*). These are the five hindrances (*nīvaraṇa*) to practice: namely, desire, ill-will, physical and mental tiredness, restlessness and doubt.

five realms (*pañcagati*). The realms of rebirth: namely, as a god, a human, an animal, a hungry ghost and a hell-being.

five supernormal knowledges (*pañcābhijñā*). These are possessed by awakened beings, and consist of divine sight, divine hearing, knowledge of the minds of others, recollection of past lives, and supernormal powers.

fivefold wheel of rebirth. The *five realms*, understood as a wheel in constant motion, moving beings forever onwards between the different states.

Fortunate Aeon (*bhadra kalpa*). This is the current aeon, fortunate because it sees five *buddhas* arise, with Śākyamuni as the fourth of these.

four articles of attraction (*catursaṅgrahavastu*). The means by which the Buddha attracts beings to the Buddhist path: namely, through generosity, delightful speech, beneficial conduct and equality; the latter is interpreted either as his empathy for others, or his adoption of the same life that he is preaching to others.

four bases of supernormal power (*caturṛddhipāda*). These four qualities that form the foundation of supernormal powers are desire/zeal (*chanda*), vigour (*vīrya*), intention/mind (*citta*) and investigation (*mīmāṃsā*).

four confidences (*caturvaiśāradya*). Also the four reasons for the fearlessness of a *buddha*. The usual list is: (1) the confidence of being perfectly awakened to all phenomena; (2) the confidence of knowing that all defilements have been destroyed; (3) the confidence of having explained correctly and precisely the conditions that are obstructive to the religious life; and (4) the confidence in the correctness of one's means of salvation for the realization of all success.

four floods (*caturogha*). These are also called the *āsravas* or defilements, and keep a person within the cycle of rebirth. They are usually listed as desire (*kāma*), existence (*bhava*), ignorance (*avidyā*) and views (*dṛṣṭi*).

four noble truths (*caturāryasatyā*). A summary of the Buddha's teaching, presented as his first sermon. The four are: the truth that there is suffering (*duḥkha*), that the suffering has a cause (*samudaya*), that it can end (*nirodha*) and that there is a path to this end (*mārga*).

fourfold army. Elephants, chariots, cavalry and infantry.

fourfold assembly. Monks, nuns, laymen and laywomen.

fruits of stream-entry, once-returning, non-returning and arhatship. Four stages of religious development, culminating in awakening. A stream-enterer (*śrotāpanna*) has made irreversible progress and will attain arhatship within seven births. A once-returner (*sakṛtāgāmin*) will attain arhatship in their next birth, and a non-returner (*anāgāmin*) will have no further rebirth as a human, but attain awakening in one of the highest heavens.

full and perfect *buddha*. See *buddha*.

Gandhamādana Mountain. A mountain in the Himalayas associated with spiritual attainments and wandering ascetics, especially *pratyekabuddhas*.

***gandharva*.** There are two related meanings: (1) A being ready to take rebirth. One must be standing by in order for conception to take place. (2) A type of celestial musician, often an attendant of Śakra.

Gautama. The family name of Śākyamuni Buddha.

god (*deva*). A being resident in one of the heavenly realms. Gods have extremely long lives and additional powers, but are still subject to eventual death and rebirth elsewhere. The gods of the pure abodes are, in Buddhist terms, the best, since this is where people are reborn who are just a tiny way away from becoming an *arhat*.

***gośīrṣa*.** Literally 'ox-head', this is said to be a very precious variety of sandalwood prized in part because of its exotic origins. See McHugh 2012: ch. 9.

Great Indra. This is both another name for Śakra, and the name of a variety of rain that is brought about by that god.

great kings of the four directions. The guardian deities of the four directions: namely, Dhṛtarāṣṭra (king of *gandharvas*), Virūḍhaka (king of *kumbhāṇḍas*), Virūpākṣa (king of *nāgas*) and Kubera/Vaiśravaṇa/Dhanada (king of *yakṣas*).

great snake (*mahoraga*). A serpent-like spirit-deity.

***guhyaka*.** A type of a spirit-deity, similar to *yakṣas*.

heavenly bird (*garuḍa*). A bird-like spirit-deity, enemy of *nāgas*.

heretic (*tīrthika*, less often *pāṣaṇḍika*). In this text, this always refers to followers of non-Buddhist groups, and the disparaging sense of the English term appears appropriate. Nonetheless, it is not an ideal translation, especially for *tīrthika*, which can also be used to refer to Buddhists, and is sometimes then contrasted with other groups referred to as 'other' (*anya-* or *para-*)*tīrthikas*. The alternative 'sectarian' is less communicative and also has unwanted overtones. For a helpful discussion of the problem, see Jones forthcoming.

hungry ghost (*preta*). An unfortunate category of rebirth associated with the karmic results of meanness. Hungry ghosts live on the fringes of our experience and cannot enjoy food. They tend to be dependent on the transfer of merit from human activities in order to progress out of their miserable state.

Indra. Literally 'king', this is also an alternative name for Śakra, king of the gods.

Jambūdvīpa. The southern continent, broadly understood to be India.

Jeta Grove (Jetavana). The site of an important early Buddhist monastery, situated on the outskirts of the city of Śrāvastī. The land was donated by Anāthapiṇḍada.

Kalandakanivāpa. The 'squirrel feeding place'; an area in the Veṇu Grove, the site of the first Buddhist monastery, just outside the city of Rājagṛha.

Kāśi. The region of Vārāṇasī, or people or items related to it.

Kāśyapa. This is a common name and in this text refers either to a *buddha* who arose earlier in the current aeon, or a prominent disciple of the Buddha.

Kauravya. Literally 'belonging to the Kurus' or 'descendent of Kuru', this could refer to any king of the Kurus or place in his realm. The Kuru region in northwest India was once a large and powerful kingdom, closely associated with Vedic religion and central to the epic drama of the *Mahābhārata*.

Kauśika. Another name of Indra/Śakra.

kinnara. A type of spirit-deity usually understood to be half-man and half-animal (most often horse or bird). The literal meaning of *kinnara* is 'what-man', indicating their semi-human appearance. Females, known as *kinnarī*, are usually bewitchingly beautiful.

knowledges, supernormal knowledges and special knowledges (*vidyā*, *abhijñā* and *pratisaṃvid*). The first, *vidyā*, consists of knowledge of past lives, knowledge of passing away and arising of beings, and knowledge of the destruction of the defilements. For the second, see *five supernormal knowledges*. The third, *pratisaṃvid*, consists of knowledge of *dharma*, benefit (*artha*), explanation (*nirukti*) and quick-wittedness/presence of mind (*pratibhāna*).

Kośala. The kingdom just east of Pañcāla and north of Kāśi, at the time of the Buddha presided over by King Prasenajit with his capital city in Śrāvastī.

krośa. The distance a cry can be heard, usually said to be one-quarter of a *yojana*.

Kubera. Chief of the *yakṣas*, also known as Vaiśravaṇa.

kumbhāṇḍa. A type of spirit-deity.

Kuśinagarī. A town in present-day Uttar Pradesh that is the site of the Buddha's *parinirvāṇa*.

lay followers, laymen, laywomen, laypeople. Followers of the Buddha who have not taken ordination as monks and nuns, but remain in normal life, offering food and other support to the monastic community.

Lover of Ahalyā. This is an epithet of Indra/Śakra with Vedic roots, explained by a story found in epic and purāṇic sources involving his seduction of Ahalyā, the wife of powerful sage Gautama, who then cursed Indra.

Magadha. A kingdom in the northeast of India, with its capital city at Rājagṛha.

Mahāmaudgalyāyana. One of the Buddha's two chief disciples, well known for his supernormal powers and ability to visit other realms of rebirth.

Malla. An important kingdom or confederacy east of Kośala, and the area in which the Buddha entered *parinirvāṇa.*

Mānastabdha. A proud brahmin who was converted by the Buddha and became an *arhat.*

Māra. A god or demon that represents death and fights to keep his lordship over beings who are trapped in the cycle of rebirth, assisted by an army.

Markaṭahrada. Literally 'monkey pool', this is the site of a hall near Vaiśālī that is frequented by the Buddha and his monks.

Maruts. Wind gods, attendants of Indra/Śakra.

Maudgalyāyana. See *Mahāmaudgalyāyana.*

merit (*puṇya*). The result of a good deed. It can also be used to describe the deed itself, as 'meritorious' or 'merit-making'. Sometimes *puṇya* appears in the plural but is still best translated as 'merit', which functions as an uncountable noun.

Mount Meru. The mountain at the centre of the universe, often used in metaphors as the epitome of what is unmoveable.

Nāḍakanthā. A village not far from Rājagṛha.

nāga. A snake or serpent-deity. These are associated with underwater palaces and the guardianship of treasure, but they can also appear above ground and take on human form.

Nanda. Half-brother to the Buddha; according to tradition, he ordained a little accidentally, and struggled to overcome his overwhelming attachment to his wife, although he did in the end become an *arhat* with the Buddha's help.

Nandana Grove. Śakra's heavenly gardens, populated by gods, *gandharvas* and *apsarases.*

Nārāyaṇa. A deity, usually understood to be the same deity as that better known as Viṣṇu, prominent within Hindu traditions.

nine successive attainments (*navānupūrvavihāra*). These progressive meditative stages consist of the four *dhyānas* or meditative absorptions, the four formless meditations, and finally cessation of feeling and perception.

nirvāṇa. Release from the cycle of rebirth, or the 'going out' of the causes of rebirth. There are two stages to the attainment: the first stage, '*nirvāṇa* with remainder' is attained during life. After that time, the person is awakened and will not be reborn, but they continue to live. Then at death they attain '*nirvāṇa* without remainder', also known as 'complete *nirvāṇa*' (*parinirvāṇa*).

noble treasures (*āryadhana*). In the Pāli tradition these are seven in number: faith, good conduct, shame, fear of evil, learning, liberality and wisdom.

Pañcāla. A powerful kingdom in the upper Gangetic plain, in present-day Uttar Pradesh.

Pañcaśikha. A famous *gandharva* or celestial musician, skilled in the lute, and said to be a supporter of the Buddha.

***parinirvāṇa*.** See *nirvāṇa*.

***piśāca*.** A type of spirit-deity that is usually violent and destructive.

Prasenajit. King of Kośala, with his capital city of Śrāvastī, and a key patron of the Buddha.

***pratyekabodhi*.** The awakening of a *pratyekabuddha*.

***pratyekabuddha*.** A 'solitary *buddha*' or 'independent *buddha*', who achieves awakening without access to a *buddha*'s teachings or monastic path, but who does not go on to found a community of his own. *Pratyekabuddhas* can only arise in times when Buddhism is absent from the world.

precepts (*śikṣāpadāni*). Five precepts are undertaken by a layperson: not to kill, steal, commit sexual impropriety, lie, or take intoxicants. Additional precepts may be undertaken on holy days, and when ordaining as a novice. Full monastics have hundreds of training rules to abide by.

Pūraṇa Kāśyapa. A contemporary of the Buddha and a rival teacher. He is said to have denied the workings of karma and hence taught that there was no point in doing good deeds. [For Purāṇa, an officer of King Prasenajit, see *Ṛṣidatta and Purāṇa*.]

quinquennial festival (*pañcavarṣika*). A large festival, lasting five years, and involving extensive gift-giving to the *saṅgha* by a monarch. See Strong 1983b: 91–6, Strong 1990 and Deeg 1995.

Rājagṛha. The capital city of Magadha and one of the great cities of north India during the time of the Buddha, when it was ruled by Bimbisāra.

***rākṣasa*.** A type of spirit-deity that is usually violent and destructive.

Revata. A senior monk in the Buddha's community.

***rohita* fish.** A 'red' fish, possibly what is now called rohu, a type of carp commonly eaten in northern India, though in the text it has more magical and elusive qualities.

root of virtue (*kuśalamūla*). An action that will bear good fruits in a future time. In the *Avadānaśataka* this is a necessary criterion for being predicted to future awakening, and usually takes the form of a faithful gift or act of service.

Ṛṣidatta and Purāṇa. These two brothers were officers of King Prasenajit in Śrāvastī, and prominent lay followers of the Buddha.

Ṛṣipatana. The 'landing spot of the sages', and site of the deer-park in which all *buddhas* give their first sermon. It is not far from the city of Vārāṇasī.

Śakra. Also known as Indra; king of the gods, and lord of the Heaven of the Thirty-three, which is where the thirty-three gods of the Vedic pantheon reside. Śakra interacts frequently with humans, being associated with rain and fertility, as well as with testing the virtue of human beings including the Bodhisattva.

saṅgha. Community, narrowly interpreted as the monastic community of monks and nuns, more broadly the community of Buddhist supporters, including male and female lay followers.

Śāradvatīputra. One of the two chief disciples of the Buddha, along with (Mahā-)Maudgalyāyana.

śāstra. A treatise or authoritative text, often those associated with Hindu traditions, covering everything from religion to love to warfare.

sense bases (*āyatana*). The six senses (eye, ear, nose, tongue, body, mind) and their objects (the visible, sound, smell, taste, tactile objects, mental objects).

seven factors of awakening (*saptabodhyaṅga*). These are the qualities that lead one to awakening: namely, mindfulness (*smṛti*), investigation of the *dharma* (*dharmapravicaya*), vigour (*vīrya*), joy (*prīti*), tranquillity (*praśrabdhi*), meditative concentration (*samādhi*) and equanimity (*upekṣa*).

Śiva. A god, associated with powerful asceticism, who became very prominent in Hindu traditions.

six perfections (*ṣaṭpāramitā*). The virtues required for the achievement of full buddhahood: namely, generosity, good conduct, forbearance, vigour, meditation and wisdom.

six qualities (*ṣaḍaṅga*). Retaining equanimity in one's response to the six senses (sight, sound, smell, taste, touch and mind/thought).

spirit-deities. A term covering all forms of semi-divine beings, including *gandharvas*, *nāgas*, *yakṣas* and so on. For further discussion and the problems of typology, see DeCaroli 2004.

Śrāvastī. Capital city of Kośala, and one of the great cities of north India during the time of the Buddha, when it was ruled by King Prasenajit. It was also the home town of Anāthapiṇḍada and the site of the Jeta Grove.

stūpa. A reliquary or monument in honour of an awakened being, usually a *buddha*.

suparṇa. Another term for *garuḍa*, a divine bird.

sūtra. A discourse or teaching of the Buddha; one of the three categories of teachings, along with the *vinaya* and *abhidharma*, to make up the Buddhist scriptures.

***tathāgata*.** An epithet of a *buddha*, indicating that he has 'gone-thus' or 'become-thus': in other words, that he has reached an ineffable state.

ten powers (*daśabala*). Powers through which the Buddha is able to act for the benefit of others, mostly forms of knowledge such as knowing his past lives, the inclinations of beings, the effects of karma, and what is possible and impossible.

thirty-seven factors of awakening (*saptatriṃśad bodhipakṣyadharmā*). These consist of: the four foundations of mindfulness; the four exertions; the four bases of supernormal power; the five moral faculties; their five corresponding powers; the seven factors of awakening; and the eightfold path.

thirty-two marks of a great man. Physical characteristics that distinguish a 'great man' (*mahāpuruṣa*) from ordinary humans. A great man will become either a *buddha* or a wheel-turning king.

three special applications of mindfulness (*trīṇyāveṇikāni smṛtyupasthānāni*). Three qualities of the mind of a *buddha*, who maintains equanimity when his audience is (1) attentive, (2) inattentive and (3) a mixture of both.

threefold self-control (*tridamatha*). Restraint in body, speech and mind.

triple world (*tridhātu*) **or three worlds** (*triloka*). The realm of desire (*kāma-dhātu*), which includes hells, hungry ghosts, humans and animals, as well as the six lowest heavens; the realm of pure form (*rūpa-dhātu*), which includes the higher heavens; and the formless realm (*arūpa-dhātu*), which is a series of abstract realms that map onto the formless meditations.

***udumbara* tree.** Ficus glomerata or Ficus racemosa. The flowers cannot be seen as they are within the fruit. A legend therefore emerged that the tree only flowers extremely rarely, hence the tree is used as a simile for rarity and precious opportunity.

unsurpassed perfect and full awakening. See *buddha*.

Upendra. Literally the younger brother of Indra, this is used in Hindu texts to refer to Kṛṣṇa or Viṣṇu. In the *Avadānaśataka*, Upendra is always part of a compound with Indra, and is in the plural. While the presence of a plural to indicate a dual compound is not unusual in Buddhist Sanskrit, the term it could also indicate Indra's younger brothers plural, the gods in general.

Urubilva-Kāśyapa. A matted-haired ascetic who believed he had become an *arhat* and had a group of followers. The Buddha converted him and his followers to the Buddhist path. He then did achieve the state of an *arhat*.

***uṣṇīṣa*.** A protuberance on the top of a *buddha*'s head which makes it appear turban-like. It is the last of the thirty-two marks of a great man.

Uttara. This is a fairly common name but here refers to person Śākyamuni was born as in the past when he was predicted to future buddhahood by Kāśyapa Buddha.

Vaijayanta Palace. Śakra's own palace in the Heaven of the Thirty-three (Trāyastriṃśa).

Vaiśālī. A large and prosperous city in present-day Bihar.

Vaiśravaṇa. Also known as Kubera; lord of the *yakṣas* and hence representative of great wealth. One of the great kings of the four directions.

Vārāṇasī. Also known as Benares and Kāśī, this major city lies on the banks of the River Ganges in Uttar Pradesh, close to the site of the Buddha's first sermon.

Varuṇa. A deity known from Vedic times, where he is god of sovereignty; later he is increasingly associated with the oceans and is guardian deity of the western direction.

Vāsava. An epithet of Śakra/Indra, indicating his lordship over the Vasu gods.

Vedas. Foundational scriptures for Vedic, Brahmanical and later Hindu traditions, consisting of ritual texts and hymns to deities.

Vedic expositions (*vedāṅgas*). Usually said to be six in number, these are classes of works that aid exposition of the *Vedas*, such as metrics and linguistics.

Vemacitri. Chief of the antigods (*asuras*).

Veṇu Grove (Veṇuvana). Site of the first Buddhist monastery, just outside the city of Rājagṛha. It was donated by King Bimbisāra.

victor (*jina*). An epithet of a *buddha*, for he has conquered the realm of rebirth.

Vipaśyin. A *buddha* of the past, named in some of the earliest lists of past *buddhas*. He is earlier than Kāśyapa.

virtuous root. See *root of virtue*.

Virūḍa. King of the *kumbhāṇḍas*, and one of the great kings of the four directions.

Virūpākṣa. King of the *nāgas*, and one of the great kings of the four directions.

Viśākhā the mother of Mṛgāra. A prominent female lay follower of the Buddha, resident in Śrāvastī.

Viśvakarman. A divine architect, responsible for the design of everything from heavenly palaces to celestial nymphs to hermitages for the Bodhisattva.

well-farer (*sugata*). An epithet of a *buddha*, perhaps parallel to *tathāgata* ('thus-gone' or 'thus-like') and hence indicating that a *buddha* is 'well-gone', or else that he has 'gone to bliss'.

wheel-turning king (*cakravartin*). An emperor who rules the four corners of the earth without the need for force. An 'armed wheel-turning king' (*bala-cakravartin*) is slightly inferior since he requires an army.

worldly thought (*laukika citta*). A thought that is readable by the gods, usually referring to a commanding thought from the Buddha.

yakṣa. A spirit-deity or minor god, usually resident in a natural feature such as a tree, pool or forest. They can be supportive or threatening, and often function as guardians of treasure.

Yaśodharā. The Buddha's wife; later she became a nun and achieved awakening.

yojana. A unit of distance, defined as the distance one can travel on a single yoke of an ox.

Bibliography

Anālayo, Bhikkhu. 2010. 'Paccekabuddhas in the *Isigili-sutta* and its *Ekottarika-āgama* Parallel'. *Canadian Journal of Buddhist Studies* 6: 5–36.

Appleton, Naomi. 2010. *Jātaka Stories in Theravāda Buddhism: Narrating the Bodhisatta Path.* Farnham, UK: Ashgate.

Appleton, Naomi. 2011. 'In the Footsteps of the Buddha? Women and the Bodhisatta Path in Theravāda Buddhism'. *Journal of Feminist Studies in Religion*, 27/1: 33–51.

Appleton, Naomi. 2013. 'The Second Decade of the *Avadānaśataka*'. *Asian Literature and Translation* 1/7: 1–36.

Appleton, Naomi. 2014. 'The Fourth Decade of the *Avadānaśataka*'. *Asian Literature and Translation* 2/5: 1–35.

Appleton, Naomi. 2015. 'The "Jātakāvadānas" of the *Avadānaśataka*: An Exploration of Indian Buddhist Narrative Genres'. *Journal of the International Association for Buddhist Studies* 38: 9–31.

Appleton, Naomi. 2017. *Shared Characters in Jain, Buddhist and Hindu Narrative: Gods, Kings and Other Heroes.* Abingdon, Oxon and New York: Routledge.

Appleton, Naomi. 2019a. '*Jātaka* Stories and *Paccekabuddhas* in Early Buddhism'. In Naomi Appleton and Peter Harvey (eds.), *Buddhist Path, Buddhist Teachings: Studies in Memory of L.S. Cousins*, 305–18. Sheffield: Equinox. Also published in *Buddhist Studies Review* 2018.

Appleton, Naomi. 2019b. 'Dialogues with Solitary Buddhas'. In Brian Black and Chakravarthi Ram-Prasad (eds.), *In Dialogue with Classical Indian Traditions: Encounter, Transformation and Interpretation*, 36–50. Abingdon, Oxon and New York: Routledge.

Bodhi, Bhikkhu (trans.). 2000. *The Connected Discourses of the Buddha: A Translation of the Saṃyutta Nikāya.* Boston, MA: Wisdom.

Bodhi, Bhikkhu (trans.). 2017. *The Suttanipāta: An Ancient Collection of the Buddha's Discourses, Together with its Commentaries.* Boston, MA: Wisdom.

Clarke, Shayne. 2014. *Family Matters in Indian Buddhist Monasticisms.* Honolulu: University of Hawai'i Press.

Collett, Alice. 2004. *Buddhist Narrative Literature in Context: A Study of Stories from the Avadānaśataka and Vicitrakarṇikāvadāna Including Editions and Translations.* PhD thesis, Cardiff University.

Collett, Alice. 2006. 'List-Based Formulae in the *Avadānaśataka*'. *Buddhist Studies Review* 23/2: 155–85.

Collett, Alice. 2009. 'Somā the Learned Brahmin'. *Religions of South Asia* 3/1: 93–109.
Cone, Margaret. 2001–10. *A Dictionary of Pāli*. Oxford/Bristol: Pali Text Society.
Covill, Linda (trans.). 2007. *Handsome Nanda by Ashvaghosha*. New York: New York University Press & JCC Foundation.
Cowell, E.B. (ed.; several translators). 1895–1907. *The Jātaka, or Stories of the Buddha's Former Births*. 6 vols. Cambridge University Press.
Cutler Mellick, Sally. 1997. 'Still Suffering after All These Aeons: The Continuing Effect of the Buddha's Bad Karma'. In Peter Connolly and Sue Hamilton (eds.), *Indian Insights: Buddhism, Brahmanism and Bhakti*, 63–82. London: Luzac Oriental.
DeCaroli, Robert. 2004. *Haunting the Buddha: Indian Popular Religions and the Formation of Buddhism*. Oxford & New York: Oxford University Press.
Deeg, Max. 1995. 'Origins and Development of the Buddhist Pañcavārṣika'. *Nagoya Studies in Indian Culture and Buddhism*, 16: 67–90.
Demoto, Mitsuyo. 2006. 'Fragments of the *Avadānaśataka*'. In Jens Braarvig (ed.), *Buddhist Manuscripts, Vol. III*, 207–44. Oslo: Hermes Publishing.
Dhammajoti, Bhikkhu K.L. 2009. *Sarvāstivāda Abhidharma*. University of Hong Kong, Centre for Buddhist Studies.
Edgerton, Franklin. 1953. *Buddhist Hybrid Sanskrit Grammar and Dictionary*. 2 vols. New Haven: Yale University Press.
Endo, Toshiichi. 1997. *Buddha in Theravada Buddhism: A Study of the Concept of Buddha in the Pali Commentaries*. Dehiwela, Sri Lanka: Buddhist Cultural Centre.
Fa Chow. 1945. 'Chuan Tsi Pai Yuan King and the Avadānaśataka'. *Visva-Bharati Annals* 1: 33–55.
Fausbøll, V. (ed.). 1877–96. *The Jātaka Together with its Commentary Being Tales of the Anterior Births of Gotama Buddha*. 6 vols. London: Trübner & Co.
Feer, Léon (trans.). 1979. *Avadâna-Çataka: Cent legends bouddhiques*. Amsterdam: APA-Oriental Press. Originally Annales du Musée Guimet 18. Paris: E. Leroux, 1879.
Fifield, Justin. 2008. *Faith, Miracles and Conversion in the* Avadānaśataka: *A Translation and Analysis of the First Decade of Stories*. MA Thesis, University of Texas at Austin.
Fiordalis, David V. 2008. *Miracles and Superhuman Powers in South Asian Buddhist Literature*. Doctoral dissertation, University of Michigan.
Fiordalis, David V. 2010 [2011]. 'Miracles in Indian Buddhist Narratives and Doctrine'. *Journal of the International Association for Buddhist Studies* 33/1–2: 381–408.
Fiordalis, David V. 2019. 'The *Avadānaśataka* and the *Kalpadrumāvadānamālā*: What should we be doing now?' *Critical Review for Buddhist Studies* 25.
Fiordalis, David V. forthcoming. 'Buddhas and Body Language: The Narrative Trope of the Buddha's Smile'. In Natalie Gummer (ed.), *The Language of the Sūtras*. Berkeley, CA: Mangalam Research Center.
Formigatti, Camillo. A. 2016. 'Walking the Deckle Edge: Scribe or Author? Jayamuni and the Creation of the Nepalese *Avadānamālā* Literature'. *Buddhist Studies Review* 33/1–2: 101–40.
Granoff, Phyllis. 2010. 'Maitreya and the *Yūpa*: Some Gandharan Reliefs'. *Bulletin of the Asia Institute*, 24: 115–28.
Harrison, Paul. (ed.). 2018. *Setting Out on the Great Way: Essays on Early Mahāyāna Buddhism*. Sheffield: Equinox.
Harvey, Peter. 2007. 'Pratyeka-Buddhas'. In Damien Keown and Charles S. Prebish (eds.), *Encyclopedia of Buddhism*, 600–2. Abingdon: Routledge.

Horner, I.B. (trans.). 1975. *The Minor Anthologies of the Pali Canon. Part III: Chronicle of Buddhas (Buddhavaṃsa) and Basket of Conduct (Cariyāpiṭaka)*. Oxford: Pali Text Society.

Jayawickrama, N.A. (ed.). 1974. *Buddhavaṃsa and Cariyāpiṭaka*. London: Pali Text Society.

Jones, J.J. (trans.). 1949–56. *The Mahāvastu*. 3 vols. London: Luzac & Co.

Jones, C.V. forthcoming. 'Translating Tīrthikas: Enduring "Heresies" in Buddhist Translation'. In Alice Collett (ed.), *Translating Buddhism: Historical and Contextual Perspectives*. Albany NY: State University of New York Press.

Katz, Nathan. 1982. *Buddhist Images of Human Perfection: The Arahant of the Sutta Piṭaka Compared with the Bodhisattva and Mahāsiddha*. Delhi: Motilal Banarsidass.

Khoroche, Peter (trans.). 1989. *Once the Buddha Was a Monkey: Ārya Śūra's Jātakamālā*. Chicago and London: University of Chicago Press.

Khoroche, Peter. (trans.). 2017. *Once a Peacock, Once an Actress: Twenty-four Lives of the Bodhisattva from Haribhaṭṭa's Jātakamālā*. Chicago and London: University of Chicago Press.

Kloppenborg, Ria. 1974. *The Paccekabuddha: A Buddhist Ascetic*. Leiden: E.J. Brill.

Kong, Choy Fah. 2012. *Saccakiriyā: The Belief in the Power of True Speech in Theravada Buddhist Tradition*. Singapore: Published by the author.

La Vallée Poussin, Louis de. 1908–27. 'The Pratyekabuddha'. In *Encyclopedia of Religion and Ethics*, 10: 152–4.

Lenz, Timothy. 2010. *Gandhāran Avadānas: British Library Kharoṣṭhī Fragments 1-3 and 21 and Supplementary Fragments A-C*. Seattle: University of Washington Press.

Lilley, Mary E. (ed.). 1925–27. *The Apadāna of the Khuddaka Nikāya*. 2 vols. London: Pali Text Society.

McHugh, James. 2012. *Sandalwood and Carrion: Smell in Indian Religion and Culture*. Oxford and New York: Oxford University Press.

Morris, R. (ed.). 1882. *The Buddhavaṃsa and the Cariyāpiṭaka*. London: Pali Text Society.

Muldoon-Hules, Karen. 2009. 'Of Milk and Motherhood: The Kacaṅgalā Avadāna Read in a Brahmanical Light'. *Religions of South Asia* 3/1: 111–24.

Muldoon-Hules, Karen. 2013. 'The *Avadānaśataka*: The Role of Brahmanical Marriage in a Buddhist Text'. In Alice Collett (ed.), *Women in Early Indian Buddhism: Comparative Textual Studies*. Oxford and New York: Oxford University Press.

Muldoon-Hules, Karen. 2017. *Brides of the Buddha: Nuns' Stories from the Avadānaśataka*. Lanham, MD: Lexington.

Nattier, Jan. 2004. 'Buddha(s)'. In Robert E. Buswell (ed.), *The Encyclopedia of Buddhism*, 71–4. New York: Macmillan Reference.

Norman, K.R. 1983. 'The Pratyeka-Buddha in Buddhism and Jainism'. In Philip Denwood and Alexander Piatigorsky (eds.), *Buddhist Studies: Ancient and Modern*, 92–106. London and Dublin: Curzon.

Ohnuma, Reiko. 2007. *Head, Eyes, Flesh, and Blood: Giving Away the Body in Indian Buddhist Literature*. New York: Columbia University Press.

Panglung, Jampa Losang. 1981. *Die Erzählstoffe des Mūlasarvāstivāda-Vinaya: Analysiert auf Grund der tibetischen Übersetzung*. Tokyo: Reiyukai Library.

Ray, Reginald A. 1994. *Buddhist Saints in India: A Study in Buddhist Values and Orientations*. New York and Oxford: Oxford University Press.

Reynolds, Frank E. 1997. 'Rebirth Traditions and the Lineages of Gotama: A Study in Theravāda Buddhology'. In Juliane Schober (ed.), *Sacred Biography in the Buddhist Traditions of South and Southeast Asia*, 19–39. Honolulu: University of Hawai'i Press.

Rotman, Andy (trans.). 2008. *Divine Stories: Divyāvadāna Part 1*. Boston, MA: Wisdom Publications.

Rotman, Andy. 2009. *Thus Have I Seen: Visualizing Faith in Early Indian Buddhism*. Oxford and New York: Oxford University Press.

Rotman, Andy (trans.). 2017. *Divine Stories: Divyāvadāna Part 2*. Boston, MA: Wisdom Publications.

Rotman, Andy. 2020. *In the Realm of the Hungry Ghosts: Avadānaśataka Stories 41-50*. Boston, MA: Wisdom Publications.

Salomon, Richard. 2018. *The Buddhist Literature of Ancient Gandhāra: An Introduction with Selected Translations*. Somerville, MA: Wisdom Publications.

Schopen, Gregory. 2004. 'If You Can't Remember, How to Make It Up: Some Monastic Rules for Redacting Canonical Texts'. In *Buddhist Monks and Business Matters: Still More Papers on Monastic Buddhism in India*, 395–407. Honolulu: University of Hawai'i Press.

Senart, É. (ed.). 1882–97. *Le Mahâvastu*. 3 vols. Paris: Imprimerie Nationale.

Smith, Helmer (ed.). 1916–18. *Paramattha-jotikā*. 2 vols. London: Pali Text Society.

Speyer, J.S. (ed.). 1958 [1902–1909]. *Avadānaçataka: A Century of Edifying Tales Belonging to the Hīnayāna*. The Hague: Mouton & Co.

Strong, John S. 1979. 'The Transforming Gift: An Analysis of Devotional Acts of Offering in Buddhist *Avadāna* Literature'. *History of Religions* 18/3: 221–37.

Strong, John S. 1983a. 'Buddhist Avadānas and Jātakas: The Question of Genre'. Paper presented at the American Academy of Religion meeting, Dallas.

Strong, John S. 1983b. *The Legend of King Aśoka: A Study and Translation of the Aśokāvadāna*. Princeton, NJ: Princeton University Press, pp. 107–23.

Strong, John S. 1990. 'Rich Man, Poor Man, Bhikkhu, King: The Quinquennial Festival and the Nature of Dāna'. In Russell F. Sizemore and Donald K. Swearer (eds.), *Ethics, Wealth, and Salvation: A Study in Buddhist Social Ethics*. Columbia, SC: University of South Carolina Press.

Strong, John S. 1992. *The Legend and Cult of Upagupta: Sanskrit Buddhism in North India and Southeast Asia*. Princeton, NJ: Princeton University Press.

Strong, John S. 2011. 'The Buddha as Ender and Transformer of Lineages'. *Religions of South Asia* 5/1–2: 171–88.

Strong, John S. 2012. 'Explicating the Buddha's Final Illness in the Context of His Other Ailments: The Making and Unmaking of Some *Jātaka* Tales'. *Buddhist Studies Review* 29/1: 17–33.

Tournier, Vincent. 2017. *La formation du Mahāvastu et la mise en place des conceptions relatives à la carrière du bodhisattva*. Paris: École française d'Extrême-Orient.

Vaidya, P.L. (ed.). 1958. *Avadāna-Śataka*. Darbhanga: Mithila Institute. Also available on the Göttingen Register of Electronic Texts in Indian Languages: http://gretil.sub.uni-goettingen.de/gretil/1_sanskr/4_rellit/buddh/avsata_u.htm

Walshe, Maurice (trans.). 1995. *The Long Discourses of the Buddha: A Translation of the Dīgha Nikāya*. Boston, MA: Wisdom.

Walters, Jonathan S. 1990. 'The Buddha's Bad Karma: A Problem in the History of Theravāda Buddhism'. *Numen* 37: 70–95.

Walters, Jonathan S. (trans.). 2018. *Legends of the Buddhist Saints: Apadānapāli*: http://apadanatranslation.org

Willemen, Charles, Bart Dessein and Collett Cox. 1998. *Sarvāstivāda Buddhist Scholasticism*. Handbuch der Orientalistik: Zweite Abteilung Indien 11. Leiden: Brill.

Wiltshire, Martin G. 1990. *Ascetic Figures before and in Early Buddhism: The Emergence of Gautama as the Buddha*. Berlin and New York: Mouton de Gruyter.

Index

Abhayaprada (future *buddha*) 13, 96
Abhidharma 5
Acala (future *buddha*) 13, 93
aggregates (*skandhas*) 106, 110, 115, 120, 127, 135, 141, 155, 168, 206, 213, 223
Airāvaṇa (celestial elephant) 138, 217n1, 223
Ajātaśatru (king) 18, 94–6, 112, 117–19, 223
Ajiravatī (river) 97–8, 223
Ajita Keśakambala (heretical teacher) 209
Ānanda (disciple) 10, 30, 36, 42, 61n62, 67, 70–1, 73, 79, 81, 85–6, 88, 89–90, 93, 96, 117, 120, 126–7, 131, 140, 149, 152, 157–8, 159, 161, 163, 164–5, 166, 183, 197, 207–10, 215, 223
Anāthapiṇḍada (lay supporter) 16, 23, 24, 28, 87, 164, 198–200, 204–6, 223
Anāthapiṇḍada's park *see* Jeta Grove
Aṅgulimālā (disciple) 2–3, 160, 223
antigods (*asuras*) 51, 124, 135, 199, 233
see also formulaic passages: spirit deities revere the Buddha
Apadāna 52, 61n62
arhatship 2–4, 6–7, 29–30, 49–53, 56n12, 89, 92–3, 98–9, 101, 105, 110, 123–4, 131, 134, 193–4, 200, 207, 211, 214, 224
see also formulaic passages: achievement of arhatship; four fruits
ascetic Gautama *see* Śākyamuni Buddha
ascetic practices 150
ascetics (*śramaṇa*) 16, 74–5, 154, 161, 187, 210, 224
see also heretics (*tīrthika*); mendicants (*parivrājaka*)
Aśoka (third-century BCE Indian emperor) 45, 48, 50
Aśoka (nephew of Kāśyapa Buddha) 46, 50, 213–14
aspirations *see* fervent aspirations
asuras *see* antigods
Atibalavīryaparākrama (future *buddha*) 12, 79
avadānamālā texts 48
Avadānaśataka, history and structure of 4–9, 39–41, 45–51

Bhāgīratha (past *buddha*) 57n25, 99–100
Bimbisāra (king) 17, 19, 67, 133–6, 141, 224
Bodhisattva/*bodhisattva* 4, 20, 21–9, 38, 40, 46–7, 53, 170, 196, 203–4, 224
bodily sacrifice 25, 26, 40, 41, 169–70, 176, 178–9, 182, 195–6, 201–4, 212
Brahmā (god) 51, 75, 134, 144, 147, 153, 183–4, 185, 205, 224
Brahmā (past *buddha*) 102–3
Brahmā heavens 69, 125, 139
Brahmadatta (king) 144, 153, 172–4, 175–6, 201, 206, 224

brahmins (*brāhmaṇas*) 7, 16, 20, 66–71, 74–5, 83, 92, 108–10, 113–15, 132, 154, 161, 173, 175, 179, 187, 204–5, 210, 224
Buddha/*buddhas*
epithets of *see* formulaic passages: epithets of a *buddha*
multiple *buddhas* 4, 6, 10–21, 42–5, 49–51, 52–3, 57n25
physical appearance of *see* formulaic passages: physical form of a *buddha*
qualities of *see* formulaic passages: qualities of *buddhas* who survey the world
smile of 10, 30, 32–3, 34, 40, 41–5, 46–8
see also formulaic passages: Buddha's smile
see also Śākyamuni Buddha
buddhahood 4, 6, 8, 11, 26–7, 28, 46–7, 50, 52–3
see also formulaic passages: aspiration to buddhahood, prediction of future buddhahood; three paths to awakening
Buddhavaṃsa 20, 21

Cakrāntara (future *pratyekabuddha*) 152
cakravartin *see* wheel-turning king
Candana (past *buddha*) 17, 57n25, 106–7
Candana (past *pratyekabuddha*) 32, 143–6
Candra (past *buddha*) 57n25, 111–2
celestial musicians *see gandharvas*
celestial nymphs (*apsarases*) 76, 186, 188–90, 224
conception, three criteria for 75, 144, 185
cycle of rebirth (*saṃsāra*) 2, 4, 6–7, 30, 42, 45–6, 53, 69, 93, 100, 103, 112, 114, 116, 120, 123, 125, 131, 132, 136, 139, 142, 147–8, 156, 162, 170, 176, 193–4, 197, 211, 212, 215, 225

Daśaśiras (past *pratyekabuddha*) 152–6
Devadatta (schismatic monk) 22, 27, 40, 112, 117–18, 174–6, 218n35, 225
Dhanada 51, 134, 225
see also Vaiśravaṇa
dharma(s) (truth, teaching[s])
achievement of *buddha* 53, 80, 88
Buddha gives a *dharma* teaching 78, 89, 91–2, 97–8, 101, 105, 110, 114, 119, 157, 159, 160, 164, 183–4, 193, 200, 214
constituents of reality 5, 39, 208–10
and discipline 154, 210
see also formulaic passages: Buddha's smile
miraculous power of 20, 34, 38, 40, 59n41
qualities of 91, 180
rarity and preciousness of 25–7, 40, 181–3, 197–204
see also formulaic passages: qualities of good man; three jewels or refuges
Dharmagaveṣī *see* Subhāṣitagaveṣī
Dharmapāla (prince) 174–6
Dharmaśuddhi (king) 120
Dhṛtarāṣṭra (king of *gandharvas*) 51, 134, 225
Dīgha Nikāya 53, 221nn66,70,72
discipline (*vinaya*) 67, 69, 125, 139, 148, 154, 210, 225
Divyāvadāna 5, 52, 59n42, 60n54, 61n64, 216nn5,12
Durmatī (queen) 175–6

eightfold path 210
see also formulaic passages: qualities of *buddhas* who survey the world

faith (*prasāda, śrāddha*) 11, 17, 31, 35, 36, 38, 41, 44, 51, 56n13, 67–8, 72, 76, 78, 80–1, 85, 86, 91–3, 95, 99, 101–2, 107, 110–12, 113–16, 118–19, 128, 134, 136, 137, 142, 145, 147, 152, 157,

159, 160, 163, 166, 170, 182, 192, 193, 198, 211, 214, 225
see also formulaic passages: Buddha's smile, prediction of future buddhahood, prediction of future *pratyekabodhi*
fervent aspirations 10, 11, 30, 34, 39, 68, 72–3, 79, 81, 85, 87, 89, 93, 96, 99–100, 102, 132, 138, 164, 212, 225
see also formulaic passages: aspiration to buddhahood
formulaic passages
achievement of arhatship 92–3, 123–4, 131, 193–4
aspiration to buddhahood 68, 73, 81, 85, 87, 89, 93, 96, 138
Buddha's smile 68–71, 73, 79, 81, 85, 87, 89, 93, 96, 124–7, 138–41, 147–9, 152, 157, 159, 161, 163, 164, 166
deeds have inevitable consequences 99, 101–2, 106, 110, 115, 119–20, 127, 131, 135, 141, 155, 168, 205–6, 213
epithets of a *buddha* 45, 99, 102, 106, 111, 115, 120, 128, 132, 135, 141, 155, 213
physical form of a *buddha* 44, 68, 78, 87, 130, 132, 146, 152, 155, 162, 166, 193, 204–5
prediction of future buddhahood 71, 73, 77, 79, 81, 86, 88, 90, 93, 96, 140–1
prediction of future *pratyekabodhi* 127, 149, 152, 158, 159, 161–2, 163, 165, 166
qualities of *buddhas* who survey the world 77–8, 83–4, 104–5, 108–9, 113–14, 122–3, 129–30, 150–1
qualities of good man 67, 80, 154, 157, 158, 168, 172, 175, 178, 201
spirit deities revere the Buddha 66, 72, 74, 79, 82, 86, 88, 90, 94, 97, 100, 103, 108, 112, 117, 121, 129, 133, 137, 143, 146, 150, 152, 156, 158, 160, 162, 163, 165, 167, 171, 174, 177, 180, 183, 192, 197, 204, 207
Fortunate Aeon (*bhadra kalpa*) 213, 226
four fruits (stream-entry, once-returning, non-returning, arhatship) 98, 101, 105, 110, 221n73, 226
see also fruit of stream-entry
four noble truths 98, 105, 110, 114, 119, 160, 161, 226
friendship, importance of 196–7, 214–15
fruit of stream-entry 2, 115, 161
see also four fruits
full and perfect buddha *see* Buddha/ *buddhas*

Gandhamādana Mountain 6, 85, 227
Gandhamādana (future *pratyekabuddha*) 162–3
gandharvas
celestial musicians 51, 123, 134, 138, 199, 227
necessary for pregnancy *see* conception, three criteria for
garuḍas *see* heavenly birds
Gautama *see* Śākyamuni Buddha
generosity/gift-giving 10–11, 14–15, 17, 25–6, 28, 29, 30, 31, 34, 36–7, 38–40, 56n13, 75, 83, 171–4, 179, 186, 192, 212
see also formulaic passages: aspiration to buddhahood, prediction of future buddhahood, prediction of future *pratyekabodhi,* qualities of good man
gods (*devas*) 7, 15, 20, 26, 29, 35, 42, 44, 51, 67, 68, 73, 75, 76, 80, 81, 83, 91, 92, 101, 107, 114, 119, 124, 134, 135, 144, 145, 153, 161, 164, 170, 183–4, 185, 191, 196, 198, 199, 205, 227
see also formulaic passages: Buddha's smile, epithets of a *buddha*, spirit deities revere the Buddha

gośīrṣa sandalwood 101–2, 135, 227
Great Indra rain 105–7, 173, 196, 227
great kings of the four directions 101, 227
great snakes (*mahoragas*) 124, 135, 199, 227
 see also formulaic passages: spirit deities revere the Buddha
guhyaka 181–2, 202–3, 227
 see also yakṣas

heavenly birds (*garuḍas, suparṇas*) 51, 124, 134, 135, 199, 227
 see also formulaic passages: spirit deities revere the Buddha
heavens 4, 7, 161, 184, 191, 198
 see also Brahmā heavens; formulaic passages: Buddha's smile, prediction of *pratyekabodhi*, qualities of *buddhas* who survey the world
hells 161
 see also formulaic passages: Buddha's smile
heretics (*tīrthika*) 7, 16, 67, 78, 83, 86–7, 91–3, 115, 137, 209, 221n69, 227
 see also ascetics (*śramaṇa*); mendicants (*parivrājaka*)
hungry ghosts (*preta*) 4, 7, 29, 42, 45, 172, 199, 227
 see also formulaic passages: Buddha's smile

Indra *see* Śakra
Indradamana (past *buddha*) 57n25, 115–6
Indradhvaja (past *buddha*) 57n25, 132

Jambūdvīpa 192, 202, 204, 228
jātaka genre 21–9, 36, 48, 58nn26,29,31, 61n62, 216n4, 218n35
Jātakamālā of Āryaśūra 21, 58n26, 219n37, 220n54
Jātakamālā of Haribhaṭṭa 21, 58n26, 220n54, 221n66
Jātakatthavaṇṇanā 21, 58n26, 61n62, 218n35, 219n37, 220nn53,54
Jeta Grove
 featuring in story 80, 91, 94–5, 105, 121–2, 193, 198–201
 formulaic setting for story 74, 80, 82, 86, 88, 90, 94, 103, 121, 129, 146, 156, 158, 164, 165, 167, 171, 177, 180, 183, 192, 198, 204

Kakuda Kātyāyana (heretical teacher) 209
Kalandakanivāpa *see* Veṇu Grove
Kanakamuni (past *buddha*) 49
karma 6, 8–9, 25, 28–9, 30–1, 46, 49–50, 83, 129, 146, 155, 189–91, 216n3, 217n13, 218n26
 see also formulaic passages: deeds have inevitable consequences; merit
Kāśi (kingdom) 89, 95, 133–6
Kāśyapa (past *buddha*) 46, 49–50, 62n66, 146, 213–4
Kāśyapa (disciple of Śākyamuni Buddha) 198
 see also Urubilva-Kāśyapa
Kāśyapa (heretical teacher) *see* Pūraṇa Kāśyapa
Kauravya (city) 100–1
Kauśika *see* Śakra
kinnaras 124, 135, 199, 228
 see also formulaic passages: spirit deities revere the Buddha
Kośala (kingdom) *see* Prasenajit the Kośalan king
Krakucchanda (past *buddha*) 49
Kṣemaṃkara (past *buddha*) 57n25, 135–6
Kubera 75, 103, 108, 144, 153, 185, 228
 see also Vaiśravaṇa
kumbhāṇḍas 51, 101, 134, 228
Kuśinagarī (city) 207–8, 211–13, 228

Magadha (kingdom) 133–5, 141, 143, 153, 160, 229

Mahāmaudgalyāyana (disciple) 17, 137–8, 198, 229
Mahāvastu 20, 52, 57n25, 58n27, 218n35
Mahāyāna 4, 5, 52–3
Maitrakanyaka (merchant) 183–92
Mallas (people of Malla kingdom) 207, 211–13, 229
Mānastabdha (disciple) 2, 160, 229
Māra (adversary of Buddha) 199, 229
Markaṭahrada (place near Vaiśālī) 72, 229
marks of a great man
  on *buddha*
    see formulaic passages: physical form of a *buddha*
  on *pratyekabuddha* 144–5, 154
Maruts (gods) 100–1, 229
Māskarī Gośālīputra (heretical teacher) 209
Maudgalyāyana *see* Mahāmaudgalyāyana
mendicants (*parivrājaka*) 207–11, 221n65
  see also ascetics (*śramaṇa*); heretics (*tīrthika*)
merit (*puṇya*) 28–9, 30–1, 47, 49, 118, 161, 174, 177–9, 186, 189–90, 198, 203, 229
  field of 25, 31, 34, 46, 50, 118, 163, 164, 199
  see also karma; roots of virtue
miracles 11, 14–17, 31, 34, 37–41, 59n41, 68, 73, 80, 81, 87, 91, 112–17, 154, 160, 163, 164, 203
Mitra (merchant) 185–7
Mount Meru 182, 229
Mūlasarvāstivāda 5, 55nn5,8

Nāḍakanthā (village) 108–10, 229
nāgas 51, 101, 124, 134, 229
  see also formulaic passages: spirit deities revere the Buddha
Nanda (lazy boy) 76
Nanda (disciple) 2–3, 55n2, 160, 198, 229
Nandana Grove 76, 138, 186, 229
Nārāyaṇa (god) 16, 87, 150–2, 229
Nirgrantha Jñātaputra (heretical teacher) 209
Nirmala (future *pratyekabuddha*) 165
nirvāṇa 3, 8, 10, 50, 107, 114, 136, 142, 161, 170, 193, 207–15, 229
  see also formulaic passages: aspiration to buddhahood
noble treasures (*āryadhana*) *see* formulaic passages: qualities of *buddhas* who survey the world

Padmaka (king) 167–71
Padmottama (future *buddha*) 12, 88
Padmottara (future *pratyekabuddha*) 36, 149
Pañcāla (kingdom) 88–90, 230
Pañcaśikha (*gandharva*) 19, 123, 138, 230
parinirvāṇa see nirvāṇa
perfections *see* six perfections
Prabodhana (past *buddha*) 57n25, 128, 217n19
praṇidhāna, *praṇidhi see* fervent aspirations
prasāda see faith
Prasenajit the Kośalan king 88–9, 94–5, 121–2, 131, 205
pratyekabodhi, *pratyekabuddhas* 2–4, 6, 8, 29–37, 38, 40, 41, 42, 46–51, 52–3, 55n3, 59nn38,42, 61n62, 127, 143–66, 230
  see also formulaic passages: prediction of future *pratyekabodhi*
precepts 92, 230
predictions 11, 15, 20, 29, 30–1, 34–5, 37, 39–40, 41–2, 46–7, 50, 53
  see also formulaic passages: prediction of future buddhahood, prediction of future *pratyekabodhi*
Purāṇa (officer of Prasenajit) 205
Pūraṇa Kāśyapa (heretical teacher) 15, 16, 76, 90–1, 209, 230
Pūrṇa (past *buddha*) 57n25, 141–2

Pūrṇa/Saṃpūrṇa (brahmin householder) 57n15, 66–71
Pūrṇabhadra (future *buddha*) 12, 71

quinquennial festival 17, 117–21, 230

Rājagṛha (city)
featuring in story 67, 114, 118–9, 133, 150–2, 162–3
formulaic setting for story *see* Veṇu Grove
Ratnamati (future *buddha*) 12, 73
Ratnaśaila (past *buddha*) 57n25, 120
Ratnottama (future *buddha*) 12, 81
rebirth *see* cycle of rebirth
Revata (disciple) 198, 230
rohita fish 169–70, 230
roots of virtue (*kuśalamūla*) 10–11, 30, 36, 49, 52, 71, 100, 114, 145, 151, 156, 164, 198, 230
see also formulaic passages: aspiration to buddhahood, deeds have inevitable consequences, prediction of future buddhahood, prediction of future *pratyekabodhi*, qualities of *buddhas* who survey the world
Ṛṣidatta (officer of Prasenajit) 205
Ṛṣipatana (location of deer park) 89, 213, 231

Śakra (king of the gods) 17, 20, 26–7, 51, 57n22, 75, 85, 100–1, 105–7, 113–14, 118–19, 134, 137–8, 142, 144, 153, 173, 179, 181–2, 185, 196, 202–3, 205, 231
see also Great Indra rain
Śākyamuni Buddha (most recent *buddha*) 3, 4, 6, 8–9, 10–11, 16–17, 20–1, 26, 31, 35, 39–47, 49–53, 214
see also Buddha/*buddhas*
Śākyamuni (future *buddha*) 12, 86
saṃsāra *see* cycle of rebirth
Saṃsārottaraṇa (future *pratyekabuddha*) 161–2
saṅgha 67, 92, 96, 99, 101, 105, 110, 112, 231
Sañjayī Vairūṭīputra (heretical teacher) 209
Śāradvatīputra (disciple) 198, 231
Sarvāstivāda 5, 39, 55nn5–7
śāstras (treatises) 76, 83, 231
Śibi (king) 177–9
Siṃha (general) 72–3
Śītaprabha (future *pratyekabuddha*) 159
Śiva (god) 75, 103, 108, 144, 153, 185, 231
six perfections (*ṣaṭpāramitā*) 11, 25–6, 28, 37, 58n30, 231
see also formulaic passages: prediction of future buddhahood, qualities of *buddhas* who survey the world
smile of a *buddha* *see* Buddha: smile of; formulaic passages: Buddha's smile
śrāvakabodhi *see* arhatship
Śrāvastī (city)
featuring in story 74, 79, 80, 82, 87, 90, 94, 103–5, 121–4, 129–30, 146–7, 156, 158, 164, 165–6, 177, 192, 204–5, 231
formulaic setting for story *see* Jeta Grove
stūpas 49, 107, 136, 143, 146, 153–4, 231
Subhadra (disciple) 207–15
Subhāṣitagaveṣī (king) 201–4
Sūkṣmatva (future *pratyekabuddha*) 158
Sundaraka (prince) 181–3
Sundarikā (queen) 181–3
Supriya (musician) 121–4
Surūpa (king) 180–3
sūtras (discourses) 20, 86, 91–2, 171–2, 183–4, 231

thirty-two marks of a great man *see* marks of a great man
three jewels or refuges 67, 92, 96, 99, 101, 105, 110, 112
three paths to awakening 2–4, 8, 52–3
truth, power of 15–16, 38, 57n18, 91, 169, 196

udumbara tree 117, 209, 232
unsurpassed perfect and full awakening *see* buddhahood
Upendra (god) 124, 131, 194, 232
Urubilva-Kāśyapa (disciple) 2, 160
uṣṇīṣa 10, 42, 70, 140, 232
Uttara (Bodhisattva in time of Kāśyapa Buddha) 214, 233

Vaḍika (boy) 82–6
Vaijayanta Palace 118, 233
Vaiśālī (city) 72, 233
Vaiśravaṇa
  king of *yakṣas* 205, 233
  wealthy man compared to 67, 74, 82, 94, 137, 158, 185, 192, 205, 225, 233
  see also Dhanada; Kubera
Vārāṇasī (city) 89, 144, 153, 168, 173, 175, 180, 185, 188, 201, 206, 213, 233
Varuṇa (divine king) 75, 103, 108, 144, 153, 185, 233
Vāsava *see* Śakra
Vedas 113, 132, 233
Vedic expositions (*vedāṅgas*) 132, 233
Vemacitri (king of antigods) 51, 134, 233
Veṇu Grove 66, 108, 112, 117, 133, 137, 150, 162, 174
Vijaya (future *buddha*) 13, 90
vinaya *see* discipline
Vipaśyin (past *buddha*) 30–1, 34, 42, 49, 155–6, 233
virtuous root *see* roots of virtue
Virūḍa (king of *kumbhāṇḍas*) 51, 134, 233
Virūpākṣa (king of *nāgas*) 51, 134, 233
Viśākhā (laywoman) 205
Viśvakarman (divine architect) 101, 233
vows *see* fervent aspirations
Vulgusvarā (future *pratyekabuddhas*) 166

wheel-turning king (*cakravartin*) 42, 51, 60n54, 70, 74, 126, 134, 139, 144, 148, 185, 233
worldly thought (*laukika citta*) 17, 26, 85, 101, 105, 123, 234

yakṣas 26, 51, 101, 124, 134, 181–2, 199, 202–3, 234
  see also formulaic passages: spirit deities revere the Buddha
Yaśodharā (wife of Śākyamuni) 183, 234
Yaśomatī (General Siṃha's daughter) 72–4

CPSIA information can be obtained
at www.ICGtesting.com
Printed in the USA
JSHW030217200121
10964JS00001B/8

9 781781 798973